Also available at all good book stores

9781785316470

9781785313929

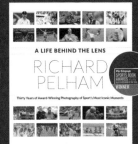

9781785315466

9781785317576

9781785317927

9781785317613

9781785318825

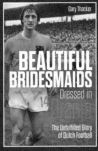

9781785318467

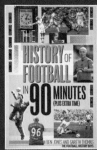

9781785318399

A History of Football
in 100 Objects

A History of Football in 100 Objects

THE ALTERNATIVE FOOTBALL MUSEUM

ANDY BOLLEN

First published by Pitch Publishing, 2021

Pitch Publishing
A2 Yeoman Gate
Yeoman Way
Worthing
Sussex
BN13 3QZ
www.pitchpublishing.co.uk
info@pitchpublishing.co.uk

ISBN 978 1 80150 058 6

Typesetting and origination by Pitch Publishing
Printed and bound in India by Replika Press Pvt. Ltd.

Contents

THE FLAWED, THE CRAZY AND THE CHEATS

HUMBLE ORIGINS OF GIANTS
AND UNUSUAL CLUBS

Acknowledgements

Thanks to my wife Sharron for her editing and support. I'd like to thank Paul and Jane at Pitch Publishing and from the production side, Gareth Davies, Graham Hales, Duncan Olner and Dean Rockett. During the writing of this book we lost both Diego Maradona and Kevin McCarra – a wonderful journalist who would be miffed to be included in a sentence beside Diego. Thanks to them and finally, thanks to you and football fans everywhere. Ax

With thanks to:
Forbes Magazine
Lowe, Sid: *Fear and Loathing in La Liga: Barcelona v Real Madrid.* (Yellow Jersey, 2014)
Nutmeg magazine
Bundesliga.com
The Guardian

Food and Drink

Football, food and drink have always been inextricably linked, from pie and Bovril to the prawn sandwich.

Object: Oyster
Subject: Pichichi

Since the 1950s, the Spanish sports newspaper *Marca* has awarded the Trofeo Pichichi to the top goalscorer in La Liga. Anyone with an elementary knowledge of the Spanish game will have heard of the Pichichi (roughly translated as 'little duck'); however, few will know the origins of the coveted trophy. The award was named after the Athletic Bilbao striker Rafael 'Pichichi' Moreno Aranzadi. The trophy itself would be more accurate had it been an Oscar, such was the drama connected to Aranzadi's life.

'Pichichi', so-called because of his slight frame and build, was only 5ft 1in. He wasn't your usual footballer. When he signed in 1911, football was still in its infancy in Spain and La Liga wouldn't be formed until 1929. His father was a lawyer and the mayor of Bilbao; his family were well known, high profile and successful. His uncle, Miguel de Unamuno, was a celebrated Spanish novelist, poet, playwright and philosopher. His family baulked at his love of football. It was so common, this pastime which consumed his every thought and deed. Why was he so mad about football?

The player's well-to-do and highly educated family tried their best to keep him away from the game. At school, teachers struggled, his family tried to calm him but he was described as headstrong, mischievous, and a troublemaker. Eventually, he reluctantly attended university to study law but failed every exam in his first year, dropped out and focused on his football, something he excelled at. When the game was brutal, he was brave; a skilful inside-left who was a prolific scorer.

Pichichi became a bona fide star with Athletic Bilbao. Despite his height, he was especially efficient with headers and wore a white bandana which he claimed protected him from the hard edges of the stitching on the ball. He scored the first goal in Athletic Bilbao's newly built stadium, San Mamés, and would win four Copa del Rey trophies, scoring 200 times in 170 games, winning five Campeonato Regional Vizcaíno titles. His prowess caught the eye of many clubs, including top English sides, but he would never leave his beloved Bilbao.

He represented the first Spanish national side at the 1920 Olympics, playing five times before he eventually retired aged 29. Pichichi loved and enjoyed the fame and it would be fair to say his celebrity status may have gone to his head and affected his game. With the same unavoidable inevitability of tide and time, he chose football's well-trodden path; teammates and fans started to resent his fame, noticing he wasn't playing for the team but himself. When it started to go wrong on the park, they were quick to blame Pichichi. They wanted him out – and he obliged.

Pichichi quit playing but decided to stay involved in the game by becoming a referee. He quickly realised being a referee was not like the real thing, playing the game he loved, with that thrill and excitement of playing and entertaining.

Spain was shocked when Rafael 'Pichichi' Moreno Aranzadi died in March 1922, a couple of months short of his 30th birthday. The cause of death was reported as typhoid fever, caught from eating contaminated oysters. His family, however, blamed it on his lifestyle and his involvement in this vulgar game. His death was met with a huge outpouring of grief, mainly from the same fans who had previously booed him out of the club.

In 1926, Athletic Bilbao, as a mark of respect, commissioned a bust of Pichichi for San Mamés, and to this day each opposition captain who plays at the club is invited to lay flowers beside the legendary striker. When Athletic moved to their brand-new stadium in 2013, the bust was placed by the entrance of the players' tunnel, where the tradition is still maintained.

Marca's award ensures Pichichi's legend lives on with every great scorer, from Alfredo Di Stéfano to Lionel Messi, thinking of the player when they lift the trophy and no doubt having a neurotic fear of ordering oysters in a restaurant.

Object: Dog Biscuits
Subject: Pickles and the Jules Rimet Trophy

I know from personal experience that Border Collies are intelligent dogs. Our Shane (circa 1974–89) could buy and sell you for a bone from Mum's soup, and, for a few chews, arrange a deal to eat your homework when required.

Pickles the Border Collie came to prominence in March 1966 when he found the Jules Rimet Trophy. The trophy is named after the football administrator and third president of FIFA, who initiated the first World Cup in 1930. The Jules Rimet Trophy was stolen in the early hours of a Sunday morning when on special display at a stamp collectors' exhibition in London's Westminster Hall. The FA moved swiftly to secretly commission a silversmith called George Bird to make a replica World Cup trophy, which, thanks to Pickles, was not required. This would later be used by the England team at official functions until 1970. The original was handed on for the Mexico World Cup and Bird was returned the replica which he allegedly kept in a shoe box under his bed until his death.

Intrepid cops from the Flying Squad were soon on the case. The then-FA chairman had received a ransom note from some nark called Jackson, demanding £15,000. Detectives morphed into full Sweeney mode and showed up in Battersea Park with a suitcase weighed down with newspapers covered with fake bank notes. Jackson wasn't actually Jackson but a former soldier named Edward Betchley, who was nicked and jailed.

Even though Bletchley was arrested, they still didn't have the Jules Rimet Trophy. Then, as if by magic, on Sunday, 27 March, England's second most famous Border Collie – after the late *Blue Peter* presenter John Noakes's Shep – stepped into the international limelight. The dog's owner, Dave Corbett from Norwood, south London, got the glory but it was Pickles who saved the day. The dog sniffed around his neighbour's car and refused to come when called. Dave approached to put the lead on but saw Pickles was distracted. He would later tell the world's media, 'As I was putting the lead on I noticed this package lying there, wrapped just in newspaper but very tightly bound with string.' I'm not sure about you but tightly bound with string, and a dog sniffing – Pickles would have been disappointed to find the World Cup, he'd be hoping for six juicy steaks. Dave continued, 'I tore a bit off the bottom and there was a blank shield, then there were the words Brazil, West Germany and Uruguay printed. I tore off the other end and it was a lady holding a very shallow dish above her head. I'd seen the pictures of the World Cup in the papers and on TV so my heart started thumping.'

When Corbett entered his local police station to hand in the trophy, the police were busy having a cup of tea and remained indifferent to the importance of the discovery. After they had a look, a detective appeared and took Corbett to Scotland Yard for questioning. Corbett was, at least at that point, now a suspect. After an hour he was driven home, to find his street swamped with the press and photographers.

Fame beckoned for Pickles and his owner. Dave would eventually receive £6,000 as a reward. To put this into some kind of context, the World Cup winners each received £1,360. Dave bought a place in Surrey with the reward stash and would appear in court as a witness for the prosecution. Betchley would be jailed.

Such was their new-found fame that Pickles and Dave were invited to the celebratory dinner held after the final, ahead of the wives. Bobby Moore even took Pickles out on to the balcony and held him up to a rousing reaction. The dog received an award from the National Canine Defence League – now the Dogs Trust – in a Kensington hotel. Along with the silver medal, there was a silver platter – containing £53 from a whip-round from hotel staff – a rubber bone and a year's supply of free dog food. The pressure got to poor Pickles, who died a year later. He's buried at the bottom of Dave's garden.

The trophy was given to Brazil after their third win in Mexico but was stolen from the Brazilian Football Confederation in 1983. FIFA bought the replica Jules Rimet Trophy made by Bird in 1997 at auction for £245,000 and it was eventually loaned and then gifted to the National Football Museum in Manchester.

Fanorak Fact: Pickles starred in the Galton and Simpson movie *The Spy with the Cold Nose*.

Object: Pie
Subject: William 'Fatty' Foulke

William Henry Foulke, better known as 'Fatty' Foulke, was a goalkeeper, born in Dawley, Shropshire, in 1874. He was, quite literally, an all-rounder; a remarkable sportsman, footballer and cricketer. Across his career, in widely varying reports, he weighed anything between 20 to 25 stones and stood between 6ft 2in and 6ft 9in (he looked taller in team photographs beside men whose average height then was 5ft 5in).

Foulke impressed from the start, playing for his work's side, Blackwell Colliery, and in 1894, signed for Sheffield United, for £20. He would go on to play more than 350 times for Sheffield United, helping them win the Football League title in 1897/98, missing only one game. The side won the FA Cup in 1898/99, beating Derby County 4-1 at Crystal Palace. In the 1899/1900 season Sheffield United were runners-up to a brilliant Aston Villa side in the league. In 1901 they were beaten in the FA Cup Final by Spurs after a replay, in what was the first FA Cup Final covered by Pathé News.

In the 1902 final, against Southampton, it was Foulke who would star again. The game went to a replay after the referee allowed a contentious goal. After the match, Foulke spotted the referee Tom Kirkham and confronted him. It must have been a sight to behold as the FA secretary tried to hold back a naked stopper who wanted to kill the referee, now trying to hide in a broom cupboard. In the replay, Foulke made a massive clearance that resulted in Sheffield United scoring. Although Southampton eventually equalised, Foulke played a blinder in helping United get it over the line with a winning goal from William Barnes, with ten minutes remaining. C.B. Fry appeared for Southampton.

Foulke also played cricket, and while turning out for Blackwell Colliery in the Derbyshire League, captivated with his performances. His goalkeeping skills meant he was fast and alert, making him a fine slip catcher as well as a powerful bowler. Foulke's performances saw him selected to play for Derbyshire against Essex in the County Championship. He scored 53 runs but badly injured his fingers (splitting two of them) while fielding and came off. When fit, he came back for another three matches but despite loving cricket, he soon realised it impacted on his football. He remains in the record books as cricket's heaviest ever first-class player.

In 1905, he was signed by a newly formed club called Chelsea who paid a transfer fee of £50 (the average working wage then was £1 a week). He was, effectively, Chelsea's first goalkeeper and was signed by canny directors who knew the sheer presence, size and shape of Foulke would intrigue fans and have the crowds packed in.

In this period, he was probably one of the most popular footballers around. Spectators came to see him playing but also to marvel at his size, like some kind of fat giant or circus freak, while up against smaller, slimmer men. Physically, he looked like a taller version of Oliver Hardy; heavier yet more muscular. Also, like Hardy, he was surprisingly quick and agile on his feet. One newspaper commented on a game in 1895, 'In Foulke, Sheffield United have a goalkeeper who will take a lot of beating. He is one of those lengthy individuals who can take a seat on the crossbar whenever he chooses and shows little of the awkwardness usually characteristic of big men.'

In a season at Chelsea, he saved ten penalties. He then moved to Bradford, again for £50. By this time, his weight was close to 25 stones. He would play for England once. This could have been more but such was the keeper's ferocious temper, selectors were reluctant to reward him with a cap. The FA also frowned upon Foulke's party piece for the fans. He liked to use his weight to lower the crossbar, which was seen as a terrible display of bad sportsmanship, and conspired to limit his international career.

After football, he owned a pub and shop in Sheffield and was arrested by police when involved in illegal betting and fined £25. This was before registered gambling. He died in May 1919, aged 42, of cirrhosis of the liver.

Object: Garlic

Subject: Witches of Deportivo La Coruña

Galicia, in the north-west of Spain, is best known for its capital, Santiago de Compostela. Here, pilgrims from across the world come to visit the final resting place of St James. Even Jed Bartlett from *The West Wing* took time out to make an emotional film about the walk, called *The Way*. Millions have hiked the 78km route, a myriad of roads and paths which make up the Caminos de Santiago, to visit the apostle's tomb. St James was beheaded by King Herod and, according to Spanish tradition, his remains were taken to Santiago de Compostela and rest in the great cathedral there.

The region is famed for its wonderful seafood and stunning natural beaches but is also steeped in myth and legend, and best known for its witches. The locals are exceptionally superstitious. The biggest football club in the region is Deportivo La Coruña, and before any home games at Deportivo's Riazor, the fans throw garlic across the pitch, all in the name of superstition and to ward off evil spirits. Elsewhere in the world, garlic is handy for scaring vampires but in Galicia, is used to chase off witches. This practice goes back, like most of these customs generally do, to the Roman Empire and a mix of the Celtic heritage.

From 1991 until 2010 the side remained unbeaten by Real Madrid. Deportivo were Madrid's bogey team. This, of course, was attributed to the copious amount of garlic spread across the pitch. Instead of the magic of the garlic warding off the Madrid giants perhaps it was the ingrained dislike for the treatment of their forefathers by General Franco that fired them up when playing *Los Blancos*.

Franco wanted a unified nation, with no regional differences; everyone in Spain had to speak the same language. He removed and outlawed Gallego (the language of Galicia) from schools. Like the Catalans and Basques, this made the Galicians even more protective of their culture and heritage and more resentful toward Franco. Gallego is an officially recognised language, Romanesque in origin, with a twist of Spanish and Portuguese and spoken by 2.4 million people.

The garlic is believed to bring luck and scare off evil spirits, especially the *meigas,* or witches. If they had thought it through, they could have flipped the whole scenario on its head and embraced the witches. Teams always need a new broom, someone who can leave opponents spellbound and better still, change the line-up and adopt a sweeper.

As of May 2021, Deportivo La Coruña are playing in Segunda División B – Group 1, the third tier of Spanish football. They were relegated from La Liga at the end of 2017/18 and haven't looked like they're handling it too well. Perhaps they need to introduce something else to bring them some luck, like a copious amount of goals.

Object: Pizza
Subject: Pizzagate

Football and the obsessive media around it are always keen to elevate a story to a 'gate'. It requires sufficient shock value for elevation to a 'gate', but once it is, you know the story has arrived. This slice of pizza is in the museum as a reminder of the item controversially lobbed at a knight of the realm, Sir Alex Ferguson, at Old Trafford, in the aftermath of another rowdy and at times farcical match against Arsenal.

The rivalry between Manchester United and Arsenal was real. These games provided drama and entertainment, mostly for the wrong reasons. From Patrick Vieira and Roy Keane having a go in the tunnel to Martin Keown vs Ruud van Nistelrooy to the Battle of the Buffet: Pizzagate.

For background and context, there was a time when people would organise an afternoon in the pub to see Manchester United square up to Arsenal. If they were playing on a Sunday afternoon, it was always one of those fixtures that could easily ignite and spill over and, on some occasions, an entertaining game of football sometimes broke out. Between 1995 and 2004, both were going at each other hammer and tongs. Manchester United (six) and Arsenal (three) had won nine successive Premier League titles between them. Games were played with a nasty, vicious edge.

Until Arsène Wenger came to English football, most managers cowered away from Alex Ferguson and his mind games but not the Frenchman. He fearlessly used the media to take on Ferguson and it was box office. In his first full season, 1997/98, Wenger's Arsenal picked up a massive result at Old Trafford on the way to the title, with Marc Overmars scoring the winning goal. By 2004 tensions were high in the build-up to the Pizzagate game because of the corresponding fixture in the previous season. Arsenal players bullied and jumped over and around Ruud van Nistelrooy after he missed a last-minute penalty. Ferguson and his side were pumped up because of that over-aggressive reaction.

There was another strand to the story. Arsenal had gone 49 games without defeat and were lording it up as the Old Trafford fixture approached, deliberately and quite rightly, trying to get inside the heads of the United players. Of course, United were determined to stop them making it 50 games unbeaten on their turf.

Building up, Ferguson and Wenger behaved more like heavyweight boxing promoters talking up a big fight than football coaches. Ferguson reminded everyone about Arsenal's behaviour on his striker the season before, 'They got away with murder. What the Arsenal players did was the worst I have witnessed in sport.' A bit of hyperbole from someone who had watched Eric Cantona kung fu kick a Crystal Palace fan at Selhurst Park (ironically, he applied Wenger's regular 'I didn't see it' card at Selhurst Park; strange for a manager who rarely misses anything). Wenger resorted to Resistance mode, with reference made to a firing squad, 'Maybe it would be better if you have us put up against a wall and shot us all,' before adding, 'I hope that he will calm down.'

So, on 24 October 2004, the contest unfolded. United won 2-0 and Arsenal didn't take it too well. The game was tough, a hard, blood and snotters physical encounter and again had no end of controversy. The Neville brothers were booked; Thierry Henry, Robert Pires and the late José Antonio Reyes were targeted, brutally at times. Arsenal's creative players were kicked out of the game and the Gunners, in turn, did the same to quieten Cristiano Ronaldo, kicking him off the park.

The referee, Mike Riley, missed van Nistelrooy dangerously rake his studs down Ashley Cole's ankle and was later pilloried for refusing to act on Rio Ferdinand taking out Freddie Ljungberg. Riley awarded a soft penalty when Sol Campbell brought down Wayne Rooney, and van Nistelrooy scored from the spot. Rooney added the second.

Afterwards, in the tunnel, players began clashing. Wenger was yelling abuse and hurling insults; part university professor, part basketball player, part football hooligan. Arsenal started using their lovely buffet as ammunition, and chicken, sandwiches and soup were thrown. Inevitably a bit of pizza landed on Ferguson and he was 'apoplectic', a word he struggled to pronounce such was his fury and rage. The headline in *The Sun* was 'WAR AND PIZZA!!'

According to Cole's erudite and highbrow autobiography, Sir Alex didn't take it too well. It was less a scene of top sporting professionals and more like chaos in the canteen of *Grange Hill*. As the years passed, the true identity of the Arsenal player who fired the lone pizza from the grassy knoll was finally revealed. While doing some co-commentary for BBC Five Live, Martin Keown let the cat out of the bag, identifying the hitman as the Spaniard, Cesc Fàbregas.

Unsurprisingly, the accuracy of the red top reportage and despatches from the front line of the Battle of Old Trafford, or the Battle of the Buffet, remained vague and inaccurate. Surely something had to flip? What caused the fracas? Someone or something had to light the touchpaper? Well, some interesting reports point to Wenger having an altercation in the tunnel with van Nistelrooy. That would make sense. If the Arsenal players see their boss in the middle of it, they will think they can hammer in too.

Wenger had a pop at the referee in the post-match interviews, basically calling Riley a United fan, 'Riley decided the game like we know he can do at Old Trafford. We were robbed. There was no contact at all for the penalty, even Rooney said so. We can only master our own performance and not the referee's performance.' Wenger also had a go at van Nistelrooy.

Sir Alex was in a state of shock, later admitting, 'The next thing I knew I had pizza all over me. We put food into the away dressing room after every game. Pizza, chicken. Most clubs do it. Arsenal's food was the best. They say it was Cesc Fàbregas who threw the pizza at me but to this day, I have no idea who the culprit was.'

Van Nistelrooy was banned for three games for his tackle on Cole and Wenger fined £15,000 for calling the Dutch striker a cheat. That year, it was José Mourinho's Chelsea who won the title. In the FA Cup Final, Arsenal beat United in a penalty shoot-out. Meanwhile, the fans couldn't wait for the next instalment.

Object: Shrimp
Subject: Transfer of Kenneth Kristensen

I have always been intrigued and interested in the quirkier side of football but this particular story, emanating from the lower reaches of the Norwegian leagues, takes the biscuit – or the shrimp.

They say a natural-born striker can score at any level. It doesn't matter what level you're playing at, *if you know where the goals are*, you're a prized asset. If you perform well for your team, someone bigger and better will come along and sign you. Norwegian striker Kenneth Kristensen was no different and having scored 14 goals for his club, Vindbjart, he was catching the eye. But their rivals, who were around the same level, called Flekkerøy Idrettslag, hereby known as Fløey, were seriously interested. This is not the EPL or La Liga with truckloads of cash swirling around. They did not have the money to pay for the player. This transaction occurred further down the leagues and, more specifically with this deal, quite literally, further down the food chain.

So, let's clarify and explain what was going on. In 2001/02, the striker from Vindbjart, of the Norwegian second division (the third tier of Norwegian football), Kenneth Kristensen, was sold to Fløey for his bodyweight in fresh shrimp. Yes, that's right, shrimp.

At first you would assume there was something fishy about it but no, the player had been on holiday and spent time there. They are based on an island port off the south coast of Norway, in Kristiansand, 187 miles south of Oslo. When the player told his chairman Vidar Ulstein he wanted to move there, Ulstein wasn't happy but remained pragmatic.

So his logic was fine, if he loves it there so much, let's sell him to them if they are interested.

Fløey, though, weren't too flash with cash and were struggling, so Vindbjart said they could pay in shrimp. 'Kenneth was very eager to play for Floey,' Ulstein underlined, 'and we didn't want to be difficult. But he was under contract for us, so of course we had to demand some kind of compensation.'

A deal was arranged and the unusual form of payment agreed upon. After all, Flekkeroy's most abundant commodity was seafood. Their chairman, Rolf Guttormsen, said, 'I had no idea if it was a joke or deadly serious. The Vindbjart chairman said that it was a bit of both, but they wanted the shrimp. No problem, we have enough shrimp.' The transfer was done with all the showbiz style and pizazz of a heavyweight world title weigh-in, with cameras, press and scales.

What would the deal have been if Barcelona, Real Madrid or Manchester United were interested? Would the transfer be paid in the player's body weight in lobster, oysters or caviar? Maybe the prawn sandwich brigade in the posh seats would have approved? A story in football like this and not one eagle-eyed editor worth their salt thought of the headline 'Kenneth Crustacean'.

Object: Sausage Meat
Subject: Wacky World of the Romanian Transfer Window

It is a safe assumption that Sky Sports News would not have covered the transfer activity of the Romanian Second Division club UT Arad. If they had, they would have to explain to viewers that in 2006 they sold Marius Cioara to fourth division club Regal Horia for 15kg of sausage meat. What was the agent's cut on this transfer? Not a sausage.

Initially the transfer was greeted and welcomed in a charming, funny way. This, after all, was a time of over-inflated transfer fees and billionaire owners willing to shell out on unheard-of players for ridiculous amounts of money. Clubs appeared unaware they could be risking their existence with their cavalier behaviour. This was a refreshing if unusual transfer but even at this level, transfer fee arrangements in deals like this can be fraught and full of danger.

The deal with Regal Horia was no different. After the story was leaked by the Romanian media, the player did not play a game for them. He quit after they had paid out on sausage meat. 'We are upset because we lost twice – firstly because we lost a good player and secondly because we lost our team's food for a whole week,' explained an irate Regal Horia official.

The whole transfer sounds like Sid James was the agent in a plotline from *Hancock's Half Hour*. It transpired that despite the slightly cheap deal going through, after Regal Horia had signed Cioara, he decided, due to the abuse he was receiving and various jokes about 'links', having to 'beef' up and sausage-related insults, he was done with the game and quit. He had a complete change of career, moved to Spain, and, with no sense of irony, decided to become a farmer.

Perhaps there's a tradition of Romanian meat-related transfers. Ion Radu, a midfielder for CSM Jiul Petroşani, was also transferred as if he was prize beef in a cattle market. To sign him, Romanian fourth division side SCM Râmnicu Vâlce offered two tonnes of beef and pork. The club's president tried to explain that the meat would be sold and the money raised would go to help pay the players' salaries. The mind boggles.

Confirmation that Romanian football is still run like it's the 1950s came in 2007 when clubs were interested in Minerul Lupeni's goalkeeper, Christian Bălgrădean, and we had another bizarre transfer story. The Minerul chairman, Cornel Rasmerita, told representatives he wanted enough for a gas pipe for Lupeni, the town he served as mayor, and to ensure the deal proceeded, the transfer would be a free – if the buyers paid €163,000 for the gas supply line. Rasmerita said, 'I know our keeper is wanted by a number of top clubs, and I'm willing to let him go if the owner makes an investment in the gas pipe that my town needs so much.' It was an investment, not a transfer, but the town got their pipeline.

Fashion

Fashion has played a huge part, pervading throughout our game, in every era, in each decade; often cool and iconic, just as often shocking and chronic.

Object: Fedora
Subject: Malcolm Allison's Lucky Hat

Football is notorious for pigeonholing people. Players gain a bad reputation and the label sticks. No matter the achievement, the game enjoys paring everything down to a specific character flaw. Maradona; the hand of God and coke cheat. Pelé – advertised Viagra. George Best – an alcoholic master-shagger. These descriptions may have an element of truth, yet over time they erode at the careers of those involved.

In Malcolm Allison's case, most of the pigeonholing of the coach, most widely associated with Manchester City and Crystal Palace, was self-inflicted. He was the flamboyant, fedora-wearing impresario playboy, who behaved like P.T. Barnum with a touch of Hugh Hefner. He is viewed as a figure famed for generating publicity. Allison could have been managing and promoting a rock group or running a record label. Yet the skills and attributes that made him a sought-after coach were overshadowed by his fedora, fat cigars, and womanising.

All of this detracted from what those within the game knew: Malcolm Allison was an innovative coach, ahead of his time, whose teams were super fit, well drilled, and tactically organised. Team fitness and shape were paramount. To improve suppleness and stretching, his teams would train with ballet dancers. Not only was it great for underused muscles but it helped recovery – not to mention a great photo opportunity for the press to snap two big ugly centre-halves with squidgy noses which looked like a pair of American Tan tights were stretched over their faces as if about to rob a post office, wearing pink tutus. Allison also used rugby training techniques to improve power, impact and stamina.

But football is the entertainment business. When you reflect on the game in the 1970s you think of maverick players and a decent smattering of controversial characters like Allison. They were constantly on football shows as pundits and the chat show circuit. In his fedora, sheepskin coat, smoking a huge cigar, with his showbiz friends, inviting porn star pals into the changing room bath (which Palace would later sack him for), and drinking champagne, it might be easy to understand why fans at City and especially Palace loved him so much, and why directors were exasperated with him.

This public image detracted from and overshadowed his innovative approach to sports science. One of his players at City, Mike Summerbee, recalls, 'Malcolm was way ahead of his time. He had us on running machines with massage-based fitness sessions at Salford University back in 1965.' For many in the game, he was a maverick but to others, such as Don Revie, well, Revie thought Allison was a clown and an embarrassment.

Allison's coaching career began when he had to quit West Ham after losing half a lung to tuberculosis. He gained experience at lowly Bath City in 1963 then moved to Canada with Toronto City the following year. A spell at Plymouth was next, his apprenticeship complete before the experienced Joe Mercer took him to Manchester City in 1965, as his coach.

It was there with Mercer that it started to click as he proved the perfect mentor for the ambitious Allison. As Mercer's number two, Allison was responsible for training, tactics, ideas and methods. He would coach Mike Summerbee, Colin Bell and Franny Lee in a team considered one of the best in City's history. Their flowing, entertaining, attacking football saw them win the First Division title in 1967/68, the FA Cup in 1969 and the European Cup Winners' Cup and League Cup in 1970.

By 1971, Mercer moved upstairs and Allison became manager, staying in the role until 1973. His ill-fated signing of Rodney Marsh didn't work out, so he moved to Crystal Palace for three years. He would prove a better coach than a manager. Not surprisingly he became more famed for his action off the park, frequenting nightclubs and bedding Christine Keeler, pop stars, Playboy bunnies and two Miss UKs.

On the pitch, tactically, he was an early convert to the use of wing-backs. Allison, along with Terry Venables, drilled a 3-5-2 system with his Crystal Palace players, while playing in the Third Division, and this when a more robust traditional formation was the norm. They played with wing-backs, and defenders bombing up and down the flanks. The full-backs were trained to play like wingers and expected to get in behind the opposition. The players and fans loved it. At Crystal Palace over three seasons he implemented many changes, rebranding the club from the Glaziers to the Eagles and changing the side's strip.

Manchester City chairman Peter Swales lured him back for a second spell with a sizeable war chest. Allison kicked out City favourites Peter Barnes and Gary Owen while bringing in Michael Robinson from Preston for an over-exuberant £750,000 and signing Steve Daley for an eye-watering £1.45m from Wolves, a national record transfer fee. It didn't work out well. Allison had a brief second stint at Crystal Palace, two months with an unsuccessful attempt to save the club from relegation. The hyperbole and flamboyance would eventually run out, and as the drinking increased, alcoholism and depression took their toll.

Allison is best remembered for his two spells at Manchester City and Palace but he also managed at Middlesbrough and Bristol Rovers. He even had his European forays in Turkey with Galatasaray, and later Portugal with Sporting Lisbon in 1982, then between 1986 and 1989 he had spells at Vitória Setúbal and S.C. Farense. At Sporting Lisbon in 1982, he won the league and cup double. He also had a spell in Kuwait.

On his death in 2010, aged 83, the League Managers' Association chairman Howard Wilkinson said of Allison, 'An innovator who was ahead of his time and in his time, Malcolm was a legend. He was generous, humorous and a fantastic coach who lived life to the full. Malcolm was inspirational to all would-be coaches including myself and the likes of Terry Venables. A forward-thinker with a big personality who always had a smile on his face – I do not know anyone who did not like Malcolm. He will be truly missed.'

Object: White Teeth
Subject: Jürgen Klopp

Jürgen Klopp came to the English game as Liverpool manager in 2015 with a tactical interpretation of something the Dutch claimed and evolved in the 1970s, Total Football, and delivered what is known as gegenpressing to the EPL. He captivated the fans and the media with his positive attitude, his interviews and soon, his big teeth. He delivered the Champions League to the Reds in 2019 and a year later their first league title since 1989/90, but yes, let's repeat this, after a few months his big mad teeth were like the White Cliffs of Dover.

Sometimes you have to find the source. If those intrepid explorers of old could locate the source of the Nile, this alternative museum can locate the source of these huge pearly whites. The start of the big tooth bonanza, as is the way with such matters, happened after former Liverpool defender Martin Škrtel was involved in a training-ground accident and needed to visit his dentist.

When he reported back for training the others liked what they saw and they copied him. That's what footballers do. As the dentist was a diehard Liverpool fan, he made sure they got a competitive price in return for a selfie and a big game freebie. Footballers do what's known in advertising as mirroring. They copy each other. First, they copied the mad coloured boots, then wearing gloves with short-sleeved shirts, then hair weaves, and then tattoos. Now they have gone mad for the big white teeth. The pearly white gnashers can be traced to a dentist called Robbie Hughes, who has gone on to fix the teeth of numerous members of the Liverpool team, most notably Roberto Firmino, Sadio Mané and of course the boss. Others have had theirs done on the fly, such as Andrew Robertson and Jordan Henderson. They have been subtle and understated. Then we have this spreading out into the broader world of sport and showbiz. The defence calls Andy Murray and Rylan Clark-Neal.

Klopp was mesmerised by the whiteness of Firmino's gnashers and made haste to visit Hughes. 'When Jürgen came to see us, he basically said he liked Roberto's teeth,' Hughes said. 'He wouldn't want to go quite as white but he liked his teeth.'

Footballers are all at it; Ronaldo, Bale and Coutinho. Players are obsessed with a perfect smile. However, maybe there's a maverick trendsetter thinking ahead of the curve and how distinctive they would look if, instead of perfect white teeth, they could be fashionistas if they lost their front teeth after a crunching battle. Imagine a return to the gumsy days of Nobby Stiles? A team with players who were real men. Let's hear it for Joe Jordan, Paul Merson and Craig Burley.

The term gegenpressing could be used in my modern rethink of the hit quiz show *Call My Bluff*. In my show format, called *The Germans Have a Word for It*, gegenpressing sounds like the verb for pressing something into one's mouth (as in 'shut yer gegen') or in Klopp's case, it could be the moulds used to fix his big teeth.

Object: Ponytail
Subject: Roberto Baggio

Italians are normally immaculate, of unparalleled taste and coolness – then we had Bobby Baggio and his rat's tail. However, 'Il Divino Cordino' (The Divine Ponytail) played football in a way that provided hope, optimism and made people smile. Such was the ridiculous incongruence between his taste in hairstyles and his delightful touch, and the manner he played the game, he was forgiven for the ponytail. Here was an Italian whose instinct was to attack. He was the type of player fans rooted for, especially once they knew of his back story.

Having impressed for his hometown team Caldogno from the age of nine, he then signed to Vicenza's youth team aged 13. His prodigious form was such that two years, 120 matches and 110 goals later, aged 15, he signed for the senior Serie C side. His play and goals saw him awarded the Serie C player of the year prize at Vicenza and helped gain his side promotion to Serie B. Soon other teams were noticing and Fiorentina came in to offer £1.5m for him.

When 18, and two days before heading for Florence, in 1985, he ruptured both anterior cruciate ligaments and the meniscus, the thick shock-absorbing cartilage that protects the knee. Baggio was seriously injured and his right knee was so badly damaged that by the time he was cobbled back together and his ligaments reattached, there were concerns he would be unable to walk unaided, never mind play. He was told his career was over. The deal to Fiorentina had been approved and finalised and despite medical experts saying he would not play again, Fiorentina stuck by him, paid the transfer fee and paid for his surgery.

Baggio won hearts and, undeterred, fought back to fitness, making his debut in September 1986. But in the same month another major setback would see him out again, and this time his knee required 220 stitches to rebuild it. In two seasons he managed five games. He would endure everything though, and prove everyone wrong. Fiorentina would see him add his magic to their side. In one game, the first I remember seeing him play, came a goal scored against Maradona's Napoli. It was a wonderful free kick, perfectly placed. Forget the bad hair, what a player, he really could play.

In the seasons leading into Italia '90, Il Divino Cordino was on fire, making the squad and scoring one of the best goals of the tournament against Czechoslovakia. At first there were rumours but as the story started to prove true, it was eventually confirmed that Fiorentina president Flavio Pontello had accepted a world record fee of £8m for Baggio from Juventus.

Any footballer's move to the Turin side is always met with scorn and disdain in Italy. Due to their size, success and the widespread nature of their fan base (people all over Italy support them) Juve are not universally loved. When Baggio left Fiorentina after the UEFA Cup Final (they lost 3-1 to Juventus), riots broke out. Real riots, with bricks, Molotov cocktails and injuries; more than 50 were hospitalised and nine arrested.

From a footballing perspective, Baggio probably had to move to Juventus to improve his career and it worked. He inherited the number ten jersey worn by Platini and between 1993 and 1995 was at his peak. In 1993 he won the Ballon d'Or. Baggio, as a Buddhist, auctioned it off to raise money for Italian flood victims. He helped Juventus to domestic and European success and in 1994 dragged Italy to the final of the World Cup.

Domestically, Italian football always had sides peppered with names like Zico, Platini and Maradona but the Italian national side were still ruthless in their vision of defensive perfection. A medical student friend once told me of Baggio, 'He's unique. He's a footballer who doesn't have any knees. He will probably struggle trying to walk after training and playing.' And, more pointedly, he told me the player had a lifelong allergic reaction to painkillers. So he felt every ache and pain throughout his career.

For many reasons, Roberto Baggio is viewed in Italy as something of a national treasure. It's part courage, part perseverance but also the extraordinary grace notes and delight he brought to an Italian system famed for shutting down football. As a great technical player and set-piece specialist, he was renowned for his dribbling and curling free kicks. His position, as an attacking midfielder and second striker, yielded goals too – 220 in 490 league games. He played 56 times for his country, scoring 27 goals. Some of the goals scored for Italy were his most memorable and witnessed on the world stage. With an uncanny ability to arrive in the box at the right time, and read the game well, he had a great eye too for a curving shot over a goalkeeper only millimetres off their line.

Perhaps his best quality was his determination to keep coming back from career-threatening injuries, especially when so many medical experts and detractors continued to write him off. When Baggio is discussed, many focus on the crestfallen, broken man, with his hands on his hips after missing a penalty in one of the worst World Cup Finals, in one of the worst tournaments ever, against Brazil in Pasadena, in 1994. The same player had saved Italy throughout the competition, and when the game ended in a draw after extra time it was decided on penalties. No one remembers the redemption. He would score another World Cup penalty against Chile in 1998 in France.

After five years from 1990 to 1995 and 115 goals from 200 appearances with Juventus, he was told he no longer featured in their plans. They decided to focus instead on Alessandro Del Piero. Baggio headed to AC Milan, then Bologna, followed by a spell at Inter for two years, where he had the odd moment of brilliance. It was his final four-year flourish in Brescia that provided a wonderful reminder he still had it, even earning a return to the international setup. In one match, when playing against Juventus for Brescia, Andrea Pirlo found him from the halfway line with a perfectly flighted pass. Baggio brought it down on the 18-yard line, controlling the ball on the spin, and scored with his left foot past Edwin van der Sar in one fluid movement.

Baggio came through a career-ending tackle at 18 to star at two World Cups and play for the big three in Italy: Juventus, Inter and Milan. Yet for many, Baggio was a story of what could have been. To achieve what he did despite his injuries, there's always a niggling doubt that with more luck in terms of injury he could have possibly been the best Italian number ten ever – and that's an impressive place to be alongside the likes of Roberto Mancini, Gianfranco Zola and Del Piero. He was deservedly voted the fourth-best player of the 20th century in a public poll for FIFA.

On his retirement, after playing for an unbelievable 22 years, Il Divino Cordino was unequivocal and honest, telling *Corriere dello Sport*, 'When I hung up my boots for the last time, it was like being liberated.'

Object: Beatles Wig

Subject: Jogi Löw's Ball Readjustment and Sniff

Former German coach Joachim Löw had it all, cool, handsome and great mop top hair. He made it all look so effortless, although it wasn't always this way. Even that time when he needed to fix his pants, have a quick ball realignment and then have a quick sniff, and was caught on camera. Anyway, more of that later. Löw has come a long way and worked hard to become Germany's most successful coach.

His playing career at VfB Stuttgart, Eintracht and Karlsruher was hardly the stuff of legend. His most productive period was during his three spells in the second tier for Freiburg. His tough apprenticeship as a manager was similar, more about hard work and learning; one of continual improvement. He started out coaching while still playing. For the final three years of his playing career, Löw played in Switzerland for FC Schaffhausen, FC Winterthur and FC Frauenfeld. While at the last two sides, he was a player-coach and manager.

He would move to Germany in 1996, to VfB Stuttgart as assistant manager, caretaker manager and then manager over three consecutive seasons. Löw won the German Cup with Stuttgart in 1997 but was sacked. He headed to Istanbul for a year, managing Fenerbahçe to a third-place finish. He returned for a spell at Karlsruher before managing in Austria, first at FC Tirol then Austria Vienna. It was here Jürgen Klinsmann brought him in as his assistant for Germany. He would become head coach two years later, in 2006.

His style and approach are clear. Löw manages Germany as though he were a club manager. He kept faith in his players such as Miroslav Klose and Lukas Podolski. If the players have a dip in form, he believes they will play their way out of it and get back to their usual level.

He won the World Cup in 2014, and the Confederations Cup in 2017 but after the 2018 World Cup, it looked as if Löw's tenure as German national coach was over. However, the German FA, the DFB, stood by him as he tried to rebuild the next German world champions. He was given a contract through to the 2022 World Cup in Qatar but announced he would leave the job early, after the rearranged Euros in 2021.

Löw believed the team was in a transitional period and that's why, in March 2019, when he started the subsequent campaign he was unafraid to drop experienced players if he had to. He flew to Bayern Munich, along with his assistant Marcus Song and general manager Oliver Bierhoff to explain why the three World Cup winners, Jérôme Boateng, Mats Hummels and Thomas Müller, were no longer part of his plans. The three players had won 246 caps between them. 'I thank Mats, Jérôme and Thomas for the many successful, extraordinary and unique years together,' said Löw. 'This is the year for our new beginning. It was important I could personally tell the players and the bosses at Bayern about my thoughts and plans. It is time to set the course for the future in the national team, we want to give the team a new face. I'm convinced this is the right move. The youngsters coming through will have the room they need to grow. Now it's up to them to take on responsibility.'

During the 2018 World Cup, Hummels and Boateng were heavily criticised for the team's defending and Müller was accused of looking disinterested. However, instead of calling or worse still texting, he felt the need to speak to the players and their club, to explain his decision.

After a humiliating defeat to North Macedonia, Joachim Löw recalled Thomas Müller and Mats Hummels in May 2021. With a few months until the Euros and Timo Werner looking like he couldn't hit a cow's bum with a banjo, Löw was shrewd enough to realise he needed something.

Löw's place in the museum couldn't pass without mention of his fixing himself, then having a quick sniff check. So much was made of the scrotal readjustment that he had to come out and apologise for shoving his hands down his trousers live on TV and then sniffing his fingers after it. Joachim Ballsack more like. If he becomes bored in retirement and it doesn't work out and he wants to come and manage Scotland, he can scratch and sniff anything he wants all day on camera. Especially if he can win the World Cup and beat Brazil, 7-1, in Brazil.

In May 2021 it was announced former Bayern Munich coach and one-time national assistant to Löw, Hansi Flick, would replace him after the European Championship. Flick signed a deal that will run through until after the next Euros, held in Germany in 2024.

Object: Bracelet
Subject: Bobby Moore Jewellery

It is to Bobby Moore's eternal credit – and maybe a nod to his East End upbringing – that despite the chaos caused and the stigma attached to the alleged theft of a bracelet in Bogotá, he would not grass or furnish the true story. Moore swore to take the incident to his grave. He had, however, confided his unconfirmed version of events to his friend, journalist Jeff Powell. In Powell's book the player remained vague about the specifics of the incident while hinting at and offering some kind of explanation. The England skipper said, 'Perhaps one of the younger lads with the squad did something foolish, a prank with unfortunate circumstances.'

England were World Cup holders and Moore himself an iconic figure in world football. However, his reputation was left in tatters in the build-up to the 1970 finals. Sir Alf Ramsey, prone to understatement and agitation at anyone getting above their station, conceded going into the tournament that his side were better than the 1966 squad. He felt certain they could win it. The one issue which kept him up at night was not their opponents but the climate. Two friendlies against Colombia and Ecuador had been organised to help prepare for the high altitude and acclimatise the squad to the conditions they would endure in Mexico.

The alleged incident occurred when the team stayed in Bogotá. Moore had visited the gift shop called Fuego Verde (Green Fire) in the foyer of Hotel Tequendama along with Bobby Charlton, who was looking for a gift for his wife. Both men found nothing and left. The shop assistant followed them out and accused Moore of stealing an expensive diamond and emerald bracelet.

The pair had to make a statement to the police and thought it would be forgotten about. The touring press pack decided to keep quiet and the story remained out of the papers. On Wednesday, 20 May England beat Colombia 4-0, then four days later they beat Ecuador 2-0.

After this game, the proverbial hit the fan. A second witness came forward claiming they saw the robbery and backed up everything the shop assistant said. When the side returned to the same hotel, police were waiting for Moore. He was arrested, and while his team-mates flew off to the World Cup in Mexico, Moore was detained for four days. As the case escalated, it took an intervention from the prime minister of the day, Harold Wilson, before Moore would be released to play against Brazil in Mexico. Moore was forced to appear before Justice Peter Dorado in Bogotá and was questioned for four hours. The judge was so confused with the detail of the case he arranged a re-enactment of the incident, in which the shop assistant Clara Padilla's many conflicting claims were undermined.

According to Powell's book, the 'hi jinx' angle is backed up by the fact Moore and Charlton had their backs to the door of the shop and, in a statement, Moore had said there were several players out in the hotel foyer who were close to the door but he couldn't see anyone. Moore's then-wife would later dismiss this theory, remaining resolute to the received wisdom that the incident was an attempt to blackmail and extort money to keep quiet. The former Brazil coach João Saldanha came out to back Moore and England, stating that the same chain of events occurred when he was managing Botafogo and his side used the same hotel, and jewellery was planted on his players and money demanded to stop them going to the papers with the scandal.

It is now thought that the incident was a deliberate attempt to frame Moore and have England's most iconic player ruled out of the World Cup and lessen the team's chance of retaining the Jules Rimet Trophy. It didn't work against Brazil, Moore probably playing one of his finest games in an England jersey. Perhaps it was the relief of being free and the relaxing of tension. Moore was imperious at times, especially in two remarkable tackles against Jairzinho and Tostão. However, this is football and mud sticks, no matter how immaculate the reputation of the individual involved. If anyone wants a true measure of the man though, watch the footage or check the iconic photograph of a sporting Bobby Moore smiling in defeat and swapping shirts and embracing Pelé after that encounter.

Object: Hair Weave
Subject: Totò Schillaci and Italia '90

A World Cup based in Italy would surely provide a passionate, colourful, explosive carnival of delights? From the towering cauldron of the San Siro in Milan to the pulsating Olympic Stadium in Rome and Pavarotti's rendition of 'Nessun Dorma', none shall sleep. For many fans, Italia '90 did not live up to expectations and over time, when you look at the cold, hard facts, it's difficult to argue with that opinion. There were fewer goals per match, more red cards – 16 in total – and with the game still allowing goalkeepers to handle back-passes, many of the later knockout games were stifled to suffocation with four sides going through after penalty shoot-outs.

The 1990 World Cup promised a feast of football led by Diego Maradona, but as is the wonderful game of football, the script was subject to a major re-write and the narrative was changed by an unexpected character from the wings. Enter a certain Sicilian by the name of Totò Schillaci. The player's iconic and emotional goal celebrations, the crazed, euphoric expression as his body was filled with sheer, primal ecstasy and a passionate, frenzied confusion of relief, delight and disbelief. The charged emotion of the balding Schillaci was unforgettable, but check Totò now and you won't recognise him. He has had a weave as spectacular and astonishing as his four-week, career-defining tournament.

Schillaci captured the imagination of football fans across the globe. Here was a player included in the Italia '90 squad after one season playing for Juventus, seemingly coming from nowhere – he didn't. He was Juventus's leading goalscorer. The issue for Schillaci was his misfortune to be in a squad containing Gianluca Vialli, Roberto Mancini and Roberto Baggio. Football fans love a 'boy from nowhere' narrative, even if it isn't one. Schillaci was 25 before he played in Serie A. He came late to the big time, coming on as a sub and his life changed forever. For the purist, that is what football is all about.

The tournament had its moments. The football on show was often dramatic, probably serving up more tension and drama than moments of exquisite quality. One immediately spots the number of goals and chances that came from goalkeepers hoofing it up the park. Schillaci's against Uruguay and Niall Quinn's equaliser for Ireland against the Dutch spring to mind.

West Germany defeated holders Argentina 1-0 in one of the worst finals ever. A scrappy and cynical affair in which Argentina's tactics were to dismantle the opposition by strangling the life out of the game, then they became frustrated and didn't have the discipline to stick to their game plan. Andy Brehme scored from the penalty spot in the 85th minute of a turgid game. Argentina had two men sent off.

Perhaps, however, we are being unkind. World Cup and Champions League finals tend to have so much at stake and are seldom cavalier, free-flowing, high-scoring games.

Our hopes were raised with the mouthwatering prospect of Brazil, West Germany, Argentina and the hosts Italy. Then we had Scotland, England and Ireland there too, which meant every day there was something to look forward to, in the group stages at least.

The first game saw Argentina beaten 1-0 by a nine-man Cameroon side, thanks to Argentina keeper Nery Pumpido. This World Cup gave us a ruthlessly robotic West Germany with some finesse and class from Lothar Matthäus. It gave us Cameroon and Roger Milla, and Gazza's tears and Gary 'have a word with him' Lineker. The Pope met the Irish team, led by Jack Charlton. It gave us Scotland capitulating – again. But it gave us Totò's moment in the spotlight and his six goals. Now, you genuinely have to Google his lustrous hair. Toto take a bow.

Object: Brolly
Subject: Steve McClaren

For the English national team, it was another miserable failure to qualify. As befits the death of an international campaign there was much soul-searching, perdition and a long two years of qualifying for the 2010 World Cup in South Africa. It is viewed as a national disgrace if England don't qualify for every major tournament, due to their considerable resources and the quality of players at their disposal. This team included David Beckham, Steven Gerrard and Frank Lampard and expectations were high that they would reach UEFA Euro 2008, hosted in Switzerland and Austria. The over-confidence oozed out of every TV, radio and sports journalist. England might struggle against Spain in the final. Forget beating the eventual winners, a superlative Spanish side, who became only the second team (after France in 1984) to win all their group stage games and the tournament. England were left stranded at the airport but were flying off to the nearest beach.

It is 21 November 2007, and England boss Steve McClaren and his side are facing a crucial match against Croatia – in the torrential rain. The game took place in the new Wembley. The players were unhappy about the pitch – an NFL match had taken place there a few weeks before. Wembley, the home of football, was now a multi-faceted modern money-making stadium that could house not only football but the American version with guys in helmets and concerts from the Foo Fighters. The pitch also looked like Wembley staff were cultivating a sideline growing Maris Pipers, such was the way the players ploughed it up. That said, the pitch was the same for Croatia.

McClaren's tenure as England coach will always be defined by this game against Croatia, and, sadly for the amiable North Yorkshireman, it was self-inflicted. Needing only one point to qualify, he switched his keeper and brought in Scott Carson, and dropped Beckham for Chelsea's Shaun Wright-Phillips. In his defence, he had no defence – John Terry and Rio Ferdinand were injured and up front, both Michael Owen and Wayne Rooney were out. Even then, these players were replaceable. Crucially, he changed the formation to a more defensive 4-5-1, at home. Remember, qualification to Euro 2008 only required one point. His side were two down inside 14 minutes.

In such games consistency is required; the national coach has to remain calm, measured, eliminate errors, stick to the system. All the boring stuff. The coaches who remain consistent and boring are more successful. Those capable of ignoring outside pressures on team selection, who can connect with the squad, support those who fall from grace, handle the players and the media well, have a system, allow players to play, be a tactician, a diplomat, and gain the trust of the players. Hyperactive coaches like Jürgen Klopp or Pep Guardiola would make dreadful international coaches. They have too much time to contemplate and think, tinker and tweak. The perfect candidate is a studious, headteacher type, with the long-term application of good habits, shape, structure and a template. Gareth Southgate adopted all of the above in the summer of 2021 when he almost led his young squad to glory in the European Championship. It's about continuity. Coaches forever speak of 'the small margins' and 'playing the averages'. You don't gamble. England only had to win or draw. But why so much change? Was it an attempt to say 'I'm the boss'? Perhaps the pressure, or the brolly, had gone to his head?

On the umbrella, McClaren explained he picked it up to watch the warm-ups and noticed Croatia boss Slaven Bilić was wearing a ridiculous-looking beanie hat. McClaren told *FourFourTwo* in 2018, 'I always like to see the warm-up but I walked out and it was chucking it down with rain.' Then the crucial part, 'I saw Slaven Bilić with a beanie hat on and thought, I'm not going to wear one of those. I'll get killed for that! There was this FA umbrella lying around so I thought, I'll use that, support the FA and keep myself dry! After thinking I'd get killed for wearing a beanie, instead, I got killed for holding a brolly.'

It is a realistic assumption that McClaren thought he looked quite the dude, and cool and sophisticated. Why get the expensive suit, under a huge FA anorak, wet? The problem? The football world needs to see you get wet, drenched and applauding and jumping up and down; football messiahs need to jump, be more vocal and argue with everyone – how can you argue and complain while holding a brolly? You need both hands to gesticulate. McClaren needed to point at players such as Luka Modrić, who played for Dinamo Zagreb and was controlling the game aged only 22, with a career ahead of him that would lead to Spurs and Real Madrid. McClaren should have been pointing at his team to mark Ivan Rakitić, only 19, who had signed for Schalke but would eventually star for Barcelona. It was Niko Kranjčar who scored from a speculative long-range effort in the eighth minute. The shot bounced awkwardly in front of Carson. Ivica Olić made it two just six minutes later.

At half-time, McClaren brought on Beckham, who pulled England back into it. He then took the corner which led to the penalty that allowed Lampard to score. From Beckham's perfect cross, Crouch took it on his chest and perfectly finished to make it all square. All England had to do was hold out for the draw. They couldn't; substitute Mladen Petric was given time to tee up and blast home with a superb powerful left-footed drive.

You would assume the sub-editor of the *Daily Mail* channelled the spirit of William Butler Yeats, coming up with the word 'wally' to rhyme with 'brolly'. Fortunately, they had the sense to change the word umbrella to brolly. I was considering the academic heft to the line when I read it was Andy Townsend who was the source. The *Mail*'s head of sport, Lee Clayton, and the former Chelsea and Aston Villa midfielder are mates. He was watching the game and phoned his friend with the line 'the wally with the brolly'. To this day, if you hear those five words, you will only think of one game. Though such is the fickle nature of football, if McClaren had won and made Euro 2008, the FA would be selling out lucky brolly merchandise like there was no tomorrow.

Match-fixing, Tax Avoidance, Corruption and Bungs

Football is susceptible to anyone taking advantage of it. Throughout the years, many a cunning scam has cast a shadow over the game.

Object: Italian Betting Slip
Subject: Totonero

In 1980, Italian football was rocked with its first major fraud scandal, but sadly there would be more to come. The first, the Totonero affair, was a massive deal; an illegal betting scheme that involved widespread match-fixing and a syndicate who tampered with Serie A and Serie B games. The fallout was huge with multiple arrests, bans, and point deductions. Club owners, players and coaches were indicted. Champions AC Milan and chief protagonists Lazio were relegated.

Totonero centred around two Rome-based businessmen – Massimo Cruciani, a fruit and veg trader, and Alvaro Trinca, a restaurateur. Trinca's restaurant was a favourite of Lazio players and the owner befriended many of the team. It was here they came up with the idea of bribing Lazio players to influence games and, amazingly, some agreed to take money to fix matches.

In Italy, if you wanted to bet on football there were two options. You had the football pools, the legal, state-run method, called Totocalcio. This involved betting on a number of games, around 12, a way which makes it virtually impossible to manipulate, fix or cheat, due to the number of variations and outcomes. If you wanted to bet on the outcome of a single match, or who would win a title, you had Totonero, the illegal way, betting on the black market through an illegal bookmaker.

Trinca and Cruciani quickly realised this match-fixing malarkey was not as easy as it seemed. In their first attempt, a friendly against Palermo, the game was postponed because Lazio missed their flight. The following match was fixed for a draw and ended in an away win. By the third attempt they finally won some cash but were already in debt. 'Bookies' were already refusing to take bets from them. Also, one particular Lazio player caused problems. Maurizio Montesi refused to accept bribes and cheat. Montesi would later be suspended because he failed to inform the authorities about the match-fixing but many believe he was deliberately punished because he spoiled the fun by refusing to cheat.

The cunning scam was not going as planned and they lost a huge amount. At one stage, when a bet on a Milan v Lazio game failed to go the way they had paid for, the masterminds unbelievably became convinced they were being conned by Lazio players. This is when the plan veered off into chaos. In February 1980, a fixed match between Bologna and Avellino was the end. It had been fixed as a draw but Bologna won. Cruciani and Trinca were done. They had no more money to fix matches and were in serious debt to 'bookmakers'.

The instigators were squeezed to pay their debts; their families were targeted – one of the vegetable trucks belonging to Cruciani's father was set alight. Both Cruciani and Trinca hired a lawyer who then threatened the Italian Football Federation, stating that their players had cost his clients more than a billion lire and he was going to the press to tell them everything. When they were both caught and left high and dry, they released every shocking detail, every receipt, every payment.

On 23 March 1980, police hit each game simultaneously, at half-time, to prevent any alibis and collusion between other sides involved. Thirty-eight arrests were made, 33 players and five others including Cruciani, Trinca, and Milan's president Felice Colombo, but by December all were free. The football authorities handed out tougher penalties though, and Colombo was banned for life. Bologna's president, Tommaso Fabbretti, was banned for a year.

Player bans ranged from anything between six years and three months depending on the level of involvement. Ricky Albertosi, AC Milan's goalkeeper, got four years. Paolo Rossi received a three-year sentence, cut to two. Interesting stories started to emerge during the investigation. Legitimate bookmakers claimed it was commonplace for players to bet against their team as an insurance policy, especially older professionals who were closer to retirement.

The headline from the affair was Rossi's three-year ban. While Rossi was on loan at Perugia, he was accused of taking a two million lire (around £1,000) bribe from Cruciani and Trinca in a match fixed at 2-2, against Avellino. He always denied this and in a criminal court was found not guilty of aggravated fraud because the evidence against him was so weak. He claimed the Italian FA wanted to make an example of him because he refused to speak out against his team-mates. His ban was cut by a year which conveniently allowed him to play in the 1982 World Cup, in Spain, where he starred, scoring six goals, including a hat-trick in the classic 3-2 victory over Brazil. For Rossi, who passed away in 2019 aged 64, winning the Golden Boot in Spain was redemption from the accusations of his role in the scandal. Milan and Lazio were relegated to Serie B and 25 points were deducted from various clubs.

If what happened with Cruciani and Trinca wasn't so serious, the whole escapade bordered on the ludicrous and absurd. When they found how difficult it was to fix matches, they quickly accrued debts, the money they were borrowing to continue to pay bribes was soaring and when those they were bribing couldn't give them the promised score, they or their lawyers approached prosecutors to inform them they had been cheated out of the money by unscrupulous footballers who'd scammed them.

Object: Corner Flag
Subject: Bribery and Match-Fixing in Spain

In recent years, Spanish sport has come under pressure from the World Anti-Doping Agency due to its woeful attitude over drug testing in cycling and tennis. UEFA and FIFA were also accused of an alarming lack of professionalism after they had gone a year without any valid drug testing in domestic Spanish football. However, it turned out the Spanish football authorities had bigger issues to deal with: match-fixing.

In 2017, the head of Spain's football federation, Angel María Villar, along with his son Gorka and four executives from Spanish football's governing body, were arrested after a series of dawn raids. They were charged with embezzlement, fraud and collusion. Villar immediately offered his resignation as vice-president of UEFA and senior VP at FIFA. The 67-year-old denied the allegations. The investigation was led by Santiago Pedraz, a High Court investigating magistrate.

Concerns were raised that national federation money had been used to bribe regional officials to vote for Villar as federation president. Villar was one of the most powerful men in world football, second behind FIFA's Gianni Infantino. He was in charge of Spanish football when the national team was at its peak and dominating the world game.

In 2013, Spanish sports paper *Marca* published an article from an anonymous player, stating his manager instructed him to fix a game: 'I went to play against Levante and the coach, in the pre-match team talk, told us, "If we score a goal, they will equalise, and if they score a goal against us, we will equalise. If in the 85th minute, the scores are level, we give up and that's it." We both needed a draw. We finished 0-0.'

Enter one Javier Tebas, the former sports lawyer who was elected La Liga president in 2013, stating that illegal betting and match-fixing would be stamped out in Spain and made it clear that any players involved in match-fixing would go to jail. Detectives had been investigating the range and depth of the issue and in 2019, several players and officials were arrested by police. The Spanish courts are currently, in 2021, investigating some match-fixing cases, with a judge in Valencia hearing evidence from players involved in a Levante versus Real Zaragoza game from 2011. It took some time but clearly, La Liga were taking the claims of corruption and match-fixing seriously.

You may wonder why there's a corner flag used for this exhibit and what this object has got to do with Spanish football. Organised criminal gangs weren't only putting pressure on players to win or lose a game. The main cause of the match-fixing wasn't only the outcome or the result of the game. With online in-play betting, punters were gambling on every eventuality but one of the most popular, and easiest to manipulate for a player was the number of corners in a game.

Object: Monaco Postcard
Subject: Harry Redknapp & 'Rosie47'

Football, and society as a whole, was taken aback when in 2012 Harry Redknapp found himself in court. This was before Redknapp's elevation into something of a national institution after he became a reality TV star and had cameos on *EastEnders*. The details were scathing. Redknapp was Spurs boss at the time of the trial and doing well. His stock was high. He was in the running for his dream job as England's boss and was favourite to replace Fabio Capello until the scandal blew any chance he had of managing his country.

The charges were read by John Black QC, for the prosecution, who told Southwark Crown Court, 'The crown's case is that the money transferred to that offshore Monaco account was deliberately and dishonestly paid by Mr Mandarić [former Portsmouth owner Milan Mandarić, who had employed Redknapp at Fratton Park] and was deliberately and dishonestly received by Mr Redknapp with the intention of concealing them from the UK tax authority. The prosecution alleges both these defendants are guilty of cheating the public revenue.'

In layman's terms, they were accusing Redknapp of opening accounts to receive and hide bungs so he wouldn't have to pay tax. The facts were damning. He had flown to Monaco, notorious for its clandestine banking, to set up a secret offshore account. The account was named after his dog and set up to receive money from transfers to hide from the taxman. What did emerge from the trial was how skilfully Harry outfoxed international crime syndicates and hackers globally by choosing his pet's name 'Rosie' and his year of birth '47'.

Both Redknapp and Mandarić denied all charges. The use of the word bung is enough to make guys like Harry shudder. He claimed they weren't bungs but a bonus from his former boss. The accusations were damming and stark; £189,000 was paid into his accounts, cuts from Peter Crouch's transfer from Portsmouth to Aston Villa for £4.5m. Redknapp had a 'number of contractual bonuses' including a 'transfer bonus' based on the 'net increase' of a player's valuation, Black said. The case came to light through the inquiry led by former Metropolitan Police Commissioner, Lord Stevens. He was looking into illicit payments. The information found in the investigation was handed over to then-Premier League chief executive, Richard Scudamore.

When Redknapp moved from being Portsmouth's director of football to become head coach, his cut of transfer profits dropped from ten per cent to five per cent. Mandarić told the court he 'wanted to do something special for Harry' but denied it was a compensation payment for Crouch's transfer, calling it 'an investment for a friend'. After five hours of deliberation, Redknapp left the court and following his acquittal said, 'It's been a nightmare, it's been five years, it's a case that should never have come to court. I'm looking forward to going home and getting on with my life.'

The five-year ordeal hung over both Redknapp and Mandarić and cost nearly £8m. They were cleared of cheating the public revenue through untaxed bonus payments. Within minutes of being cleared of tax evasion, there were calls for his immediate appointment as England boss to replace Capello, who had stood down ahead of Euro 2012. Bookmakers stopped taking bets. Harry's moment had passed though, and he would not get the job. Football often puts people through the wringer and, as we are learning, it rarely forgives or forgets.

Object: Stradivarius
Subject: The Messi Tax Affair

The first observation, when you look at the dramatic courtroom photograph of Lionel Messi and his father, is how petrified they both look as they await the verdict for tax evasion. The second is the startling resemblance between Lionel and Jorge. The hair, the nose, the mannerisms. Lionel looks as if he is waiting outside the headmaster's office after his father has been called to the school because of his bad behaviour.

In 2016, both men received a suspended sentence of 21 months for tax evasion. The Catalan court heard that tax havens in the UK, Switzerland, Belize and Uruguay were used to hide earnings from the player's image rights. The player owed more than €4.16m in back taxes.

Since the sentence meted out was less than two years, and because the pair did not have a criminal record, apart from Messi junior's propensity to dive when tickled then plead and beg for opponents to receive a card like someone waiting for a kidney transplant, the sentences were suspended.

Messi's legal approach deployed 'The Full Manuel', and in truth, it was his only hope. 'The Full Manuel' is a cunning legal tactic that adopts the essence of a character from the John Cleese sitcom, *Fawlty Towers*, called Manuel, the waiter from Barcelona famed for his catchphrase, 'I know nothing.' It's a legal technique which states, quite categorically, 'It wasn't me, it was someone else. I know nothing whatsoever about this.' It tells the judge, courts and prosecutor that you are completely ignorant to the situation, or are at least claiming you are. The 'I know nothing' defence, about the whereabouts of more than €4m, to most would be hard to fathom. What

Messi did say was, 'All I knew was that we signed agreements with certain sponsors, for "X" amount of money and that I had to do adverts, photos and those things but about the money and where it went, I knew nothing.'

In 2020, when he fell out with Barcelona and threatened to quit, some of his contract details were leaked, according to French newspaper, L'Équipe, Messi's salary breaks down to a weekly wage of £2.1 million, £108.2 million a year. So, to him, this might be like spare change found down the back of a sofa. Tellingly, his father remained vague, taking the 'big boys told me to do it and ran away' approach, claiming he had been advised that the practice was legal.

Messi was fined €1.7m for the three counts of tax fraud, and his father €1.3m. Expert financial analysis of the Messi case was difficult because it was shrouded in such vagueness. Tax investigators zoom in on a lack of transparency. As soon as there's a lack of clarity or poor documentation, they can usually smell a rat. We know multinationals and huge conglomerates shell away money and it always feels wrong. When a footballer does it, there's something unpalatable about their actions. Pay up and stop the fiddling, your fans have to pay their taxes, why don't you? But when you start to hide information, it looks bad.

Robert W. Woods, in *Forbes Magazine* in 2017, put it best, 'A key element in Messi's case was the clandestine nature of the tiered entity arrangement.' Woods continued, 'The Spanish prosecutor made it clear that the opaqueness of the deal was key. Advisers and accountability matter too. Messi's father Jorge may have had a much larger role than his son in setting up the chain of shell companies at the root of the criminal charges … Signing a tax return requires some accountability.'

The Messi family's tax issues paled into insignificance compared to his then Barça team-mate, Neymar. He was fined £40m by a Brazilian court for tax evasion over several sponsorship deals. Cristiano Ronaldo, while at Real Madrid, was equally as bad; his case was similarly based on image rights and squirrelling away money in shell companies. He also refused to provide full disclosure and a complete set of accounts of the earnings from the image rights.

Here's a thought. Maybe it isn't them. It might be us. These three, Neymar especially, would beat up and rob his gran of her purse if it meant getting a win. It's hard for them to adjust to the reality of conceding anything, particularly taxes. Oh, and one more observation, if the Messi family were going to avoid tax, don't get a mention in the Panama Papers, an unparalleled database leak from a Panama-based offshore law firm Mossack Fonseca. Some 11.5 million files were obtained and released to the public revealing how the rich and powerful exploit tax regimes; the names included world leaders, politicians, celebrities and Leo and Jorge Messi.

Object: Poirot's Moustache
Subject: Forest, Anderlecht and the UEFA Cup Final

Imagine being at a game and you know the referee is having a howler. So much of a nightmare, it crosses your mind they were behaving erratically because they had been nobbled. As responsible people though, we try our best, despite the upset and pain, to remain rational and balanced. Each of us has bad days at work. But, years later, the current president of the club you played against in that same crucial semi-final admits that his father, while president, bunged the referee. You lost out on a major European final, the 1984 UEFA Cup Final, and your suspicions were proved correct.

Such was the situation Nottingham Forest fans found themselves in years later in 1997, when evidence came to light that the Spanish referee had taken a bung to fix the second leg of the semi-final against Anderlecht. Anderlecht's president Roger Vanden Stock confirmed that his father, Constant, had bribed the Spanish referee, Emilio Guruceta Muro, paying him one million Francs – about £20,000. He also claimed his father wasn't bribing the referee but giving him a loan. The story only started to unfold when Anderlecht came forward because someone close to the club had been subject to a blackmail plot and they had decided to come clean. They admitted they had paid off the official and won that semi-final 3-2 on aggregate.

Forest were 2-0 up after the first leg but were eliminated after going down 3-0 in the return in Brussels. They conceded on 20 minutes to an Enzo Scifo volley. On the hour, eyebrows were raised at the soft nature of the penalty Anderlecht were awarded. To say it was hotly contested would be like describing John F. Kennedy's headshot wound as a minor scratch. Anderlecht's penalty came after a 'challenge' by Forest's Kenny Swain when he tripped Kenneth Brylle, who converted the resulting kick. Forest team-mate Garry Birtles said, 'That penalty was the most embarrassing decision I have ever seen in football. The distance between Kenny Swain and their guy who went down was absolutely ridiculous.' Paul Hart takes up the story. 'I have seen footage of the incident and it confirms that their man took a dive as soon as he set foot inside the area. Ken was nowhere near him. In fact, I wish he'd been a bit closer. It was a disgrace.'

Anderlecht's third and winning goal, which came in the 88th minute from Erwin van den Bergh, was the killer. Then Hart scored the crucial away goal. 'We got a corner and the ball flew past Ian Bowyer's ear to me. I headed it straight in, but the ref gave them a free kick and ran off without offering any explanation.'

Sadly, Forest weren't only robbed, they were mugged and beaten up and nothing was done about it. Not only did Anderlecht have their free penalty, but Forest also had a definite goal disallowed, a crucial away goal, in the last minutes of the game. Hart is still vehement about the referee's performance, 'I was convinced at the time, and I have never changed my mind, that the referee was fixed for that game. Some of the decisions, including the one to disallow the "goal" I scored that would have put Forest through, were unbelievable. He said he awarded a free kick against me for pushing, yet I had scored from a free header.'

UEFA proved they were the epitome of a hapless sitcom organisation, an incompetent government department run by idiots. It emerged they had a dossier of evidence as early as 1992 which they failed to act upon. It took a criminal case in 1997 for the full extent of the bribe to come out. That's when the details behind the surreal refereeing were revealed, and Anderlecht admitted paying the referee.

The bungling football civil servants at UEFA claimed they didn't take action because the incident had occurred more than ten years previously. They must have become embarrassed with their procedures, as they decided to impose a one-year European ban on Anderlecht.

During the case, it was revealed that Constant Vanden Stock approached Brussels-based criminal Jean Elst, who spoke to a friend in Alicante, who made an offer to the ref, and he agreed to fix the game for 1.2m Belgian Francs. This was one of the most blatant and high-profile pieces of bribery in recent football history yet it has gone under the radar. Now it will remain in full sight, in this museum as a reminder. It is such a shame for Forest that they missed out on an all-English final against eventual winners Tottenham Hotspur. This is a tale of corruption, greed and the underworld. You always hope we are above cheating and this behaviour, but we should never become complacent about the integrity of the beautiful game.

Object: Plasma TV
Subject: German Match-Fixing

In 2005, Germany was embroiled in its own betting scandal when the scourge of match-fixing moved from Italy and Spain to another footballing superpower. This particular scandal was more intriguing because of the detail which emerged at the trial.

It was simple. Two referees, Robert Hoyzer and Dominik Marks, fixed games they officiated and were paid by a betting syndicate. They refereed outside the Bundesliga, focused mainly on Bundesliga II fixtures, cup ties and regional games. One of Hoyzer's matches, which was highlighted in court, was a German Cup tie between Hamburg and the regional side Paderborn. To give some background or even some perspective, in Germany the top three leagues are the Bundesliga, I, II and III, then below that there is the Regionalliga, which is divided into five regional divisions.

The underdogs, despite being two down, were awarded two dubious penalties and to help the result along, Hamburg's striker Émile Mpenza was also sent off. Paderborn won 4-2. We can laugh and joke about it, but any form of cheating, particularly at this level, is totally against the spirit of the game. It goes against most of football's fairness and sportsmanship but when a referee is bent, it's the worst of all possible scenarios.

After a four-week trial, Hoyzer, who was then 26, was jailed for two years and five months for fraud after being convicted of rigging games. However, both German football and the broader sports and news media were shocked at a prison sentence. They were expecting a suspended sentence because Hoyzer's testimony had been extensive, providing detailed information as he fully cooperated with the authorities. The co-accused, Dominik Marks, received an 18-month suspended sentence.

Hoyzer told the courts he was paid thousands by a Croat gambler named Ante Sapina. He was a compulsive gambler and sports bar owner, who was the 'brains' or the 'mastermind' behind the €2m scam. Sapina was handed two years and 11 months and his brothers Filip and Milan, who were also part of the scam, received suspended sentences.

It was revealed that Sapina raked in €750,000 from the Hamburg game. In December 2004, he also placed €240,000 and won €870,000 on a Bundesliga II match between Karlsruher SC and MSV Duisburg. Duisburg won 3-0 and Dominik Marks officiated.

The court case revealed that Hoyzer received €67,000 and a big spanking plasma TV for the nine matches he was involved in trying to fix. Marks made €36,000 for four games. As details of the case were released, it was revealed the syndicate communicated with the referee at half-time by phoning him, and on one occasion offered him €50,000 by text at half-time to fix a correct score. Quite how Marks got off so lightly escapes me, and credit must go to other referees as it was them who informed the authorities of their suspicions.

Object: Bulging Envelope
Subject: Marseille Match-Fixing Scandal

If you wandered along Marseille's most recognised street, La Canebiere, from Vieux Port – the port, to the Reforms, the old church – you would find it difficult to meet anyone with anything negative to say about their controversial former owner, Bernard Tapie. He remains much loved among the football-crazy fans of Olympique de Marseille.

The flamboyant and colourful millionaire made his money buying up bankrupted companies. You get the feeling he might be a bit of a Francois Del Garcon – a French Del Boy. He was born to working-class parents in Paris, though you would not assume so, as he was more like the son of a Hollywood movie mogul; dashing, charismatic and with great hair and that's crucial in football, for both player or owner.

Football clubs from the mid-1980s came with these characters attached. They were colourful and, when we say colourful, we are employing excessive overuse of euphemism. We had Silvio Berlusconi at Milan and Tapie at Marseille. It simply wasn't enough that they were successful businessmen, they were central to everything. They were businessmen, entrepreneurs, singers, actors, owners of vast media conglomerates, television hosts, politicians and one of them even stretched his skills to party planning. How they found the time to run a football club was remarkable.

It was the mayor of Marseille, Gaston Defferre, who suggested Tapie buy Olympique de Marseille. Tapie found success in 1984 when he used one of his acquisitions, a health food company called La Vie Claire, to sponsor a cycling team, formed by legendary French cyclist Bernard Hinault. They became one of the strongest teams in road racing, winning the Tour de France in two consecutive years.

Tapie bought Olympique de Marseille in 1986, and strove to great success in the late 1980s and 1990s. Most neutral football fans were taken by Marseille around this time and loved their cavalier, entertaining and attacking play. They had stars like Jean-Pierre Papin, Chris Waddle, Enzo Francescoli, Didier Deschamps, Marcel Desailly, Fabien Barthez, Jean Tigana, Alain Giresse, Rudi Völler and Alen Bokšić.

The Stade Vélodrome was an astonishing arena – pulsating, dynamic and bouncing, especially when the side were winning. By 1989, they had won their first title in 17 years and would go on to win the league five times in a row. They grabbed the headlines and glory from the millionaires of Monaco. Marseille were great to watch, exciting, powerful and quick. In France they were portrayed as the working-class heroes, the plucky side from the wrong end of the Mediterranean, taking on Arsène Wenger's mighty Monaco. Wenger did not like or trust Tapie. Marseille's fans were fervent and passionate, unlike the soulless Monaco, whose stadium in the principality felt like an anaemic corporate hotel car park.

Marseille's ambition and focus moved on to Europe and they were unlucky at first. They reached the semi-finals of the European Cup in 1988 and 1990 and the final on two occasions. They lost to Red Star Belgrade in 1991, but their fortunes would change in 1993.

They reached the first Champions League Final in the updated format when they defeated Glentoran and Dinamo Bucharest and qualified into a group with Rangers, CSKA Moscow and Club Brugge. They drew with Rangers at Ibrox, won the following two, and were top of Group A. Something though did not appear right. Questions were asked, especially after Marseille casually beat CSKA Moscow 6-0. Even allowing for players like Bokšić and Völler, the Russian side had beaten Barcelona in the previous round. It was around now that rumour and suspicion started to take hold. CSKA's manager Gennady Kostylev claimed in a newspaper interview that he was offered money to lose the game and that his players were out of sorts, something was wrong. In his 2006 autobiography, the player central to the match-fixing scandal, Jean-Jacques Eydelie, claimed members of the Marseille party used a syringe to squeeze something through the lid of the water of the CSKA players.

Glasgow Rangers were next for the treatment. Having won at home against Brugge, they were Marseille's closest rivals in the group. Mark Hateley revealed he received a strange phone call before the game and was offered money to not play. He refused but ironically, Hateley would be sent off against Brugge anyway and miss the game in the Stade Vélodrome. Rangers were on six points, with the French side on the same. The penultimate group game at the Vélodrome would have a big say on who made it to the first Champions League Final and ended 1-1. Marseille needed to win their final match against Brugge and they would be in the final. Bokšić scored from an obvious mistake and Brugges hardly showed up in a fixture that is one of real concern once you know what eventually unfolded and the behaviour of Tapie and his staff.

With the domestic title still in the balance, Marseille's fixture away to relegation-threatened Valenciennes interrupted their preparations going into the final against AC Milan in Munich. The approach to Valenciennes gave the game away. Tapie had Marseille general manager Jean-Pierre Bernès and Eydelie approach key players in the Valenciennes side and offer them cash to play poorly.

I have to admit at this juncture, I haven't tried to bribe someone. I'm not too sure of the etiquette, but I'd assume there would be some cunning and guile, some craft and imagination involved. A furtive look, a riddle, a crossword clue in *The Telegraph*, leading to a hidden bag in a deserted woodland containing 20 Rolex watches. Seemingly, there's no big mystery, you offer money and ask three of their better players to play poorly.

For Tapie the plan was simple. Valenciennes don't put in the boot, and Marseille win in an uneventful, injury-free game, stay ahead of PSG and Monaco chasing them down, win the title, with a nice easy passage to the final a few days later. Tapie denied the claims, only for Valenciennes player Christophe Robert to break ranks and come clean. He and the Argentine Jorge Burruchaga were charged. What pained me most about the whole affair was that the only player with the correct moral rectitude to do something, Jacques Glassman, was treated terribly and abused everywhere he played. Valenciennes' Robert confessed to his boss Boro Primorac at half-time in the game and two weeks after Marseille's historic win in Munich, a criminal complaint was lodged to magistrate, Éric de Montgolfier.

Marseille were stripped of their league title and banned from defending the Champions League the following season. PSG were awarded the championship but refused to accept it. Tapie, at first, appeared above suspicion as by then he was part of François Mitterrand's government but would eventually be collared, receiving a two-year sentence, of which he served only six months, for corruption and interfering with witnesses. Tapie's drive and ruthless ambition to succeed in Europe consumed him to the extent he would, eventually, be jailed. He bounced back and over time bought a French newspaper, and remained high profile.

In that first Champions League Final, Marseille beat AC Milan to lift the trophy with Basile Boli scoring the only goal of the game. This was an AC Milan side who had won every game in the competition until then and a win in the final would make it a perfect eight out of eight. Any side who were able to contend with the best striker in the world at that point, Marco van Basten, and breach one of the toughest defences to ever grace European football deserved the trophy. The Milan defence were skilled, powerful and robust. Even reciting their classic back four zings and sings with poetry – and stylish malice: Alessandro Costacurta, Paolo Maldini, Franco Baresi and Mauro Tassotti. After the glorious Champions League victory against Milan, Marseille's reputation would end in tatters.

This is a book about football, and we can't go into Tapie's still-ongoing 15-year battle with state-owned bank Credit Lyonnais over the sale of Adidas. He was awarded a settlement of €400m (£340m) by a panel who judged he had been the victim of fraud when in 1993, he sold his stake in Adidas to Credit Lyonnais, who deliberately undervalued the sportswear brand. We can't mention then French Minister of Finance, Christine Lagarde being found guilty of negligence. He is gravely ill as we write and in April 2021, hit the headlines when burgled, tied and beaten by robbers. It is a great shame the Marseille side of this era was mired and dragged into this match-fixing disgrace; they were so much better than that.

Fanorak Fact: Jacques Glassman, who refused to be bribed and reported it, received FIFA's Fair Play award in 1995 for blowing the whistle on the scandal.

Object: Romanian Folk Singer Costume
Subject: Cooperativa Cartel

Romanian football is a peculiar place. On one hand, you have the legendary Steaua Bucharest, who in the mid to late 1980s ventured on an unbeaten run of 119 games (they did not lose between 1985 and 1989), won five league titles and four Romanian Cups, and the European Cup. In their 1988/89 league run they won 31 of their 34 fixtures, scoring 121 and conceding only 28. In 1986 their European Cup victory was over Terry Venables's much-fancied and star-studded Barcelona side. Even the Seville stadium was full of Barça fans. Steaua were without their suspended captain, every member of the squad was Romanian and most came through the club's youth system. Coach Emerich Jenei was organised, well drilled, played to his strengths and had his side break up play and frustrate Barcelona. In the penalty shoot-out, Helmuth Duckadam saved all of Barcelona's penalties.

Then, on the other hand, you have Adrian Mutu, who in 2013 was banned from playing for Romania after he posted an image of Mr Bean on the face of his national coach, Victor Pițurcă, on Facebook. So you have this weirdness and ridiculousness. But we are going to cover the changes that took place after the Iron Curtain collapsed and capitalism replaced communism and when Romanian football turned into *The Sopranos*. Steaua and Dinamo Bucharest had control for half a century but when the Cooperativa, a cartel of around 12 clubs, came together in the late 1990s, they engaged in match-fixing and bribery. Romanian football became more like the Wild West.

Jean Pădureanu was considered the Godfather of the Cooperativa, along with his willing lieutenant, Gheorghe 'Pinalti' Ştefan of Ceahlăul, based in Piatra Neamţ. Pădureanu would lavish expensive food, alcohol, luxury clothes and jewellery on the wives. Gheorghe Ştefan was an expert money launderer. Pădureanu was 'boss' as in the Italian meaning of the word. He set the rules, established the guidelines and chose who was allowed in. The rules for engagement were the rules of corruption and bribery – if you did not contribute you were not allowed in, would rarely win and were relegated. The response on a handshake was, 'I win at home; you win at home.'

How were the wheels oiled? Gifts, holidays, prostitutes. Copious amounts of food and wine were delivered to the door of match officials. They had information on the officials too, so any indiscretions could be used to blackmail them.

Players too were showered with the same generosity and understood when not to give their best in matches. Players preferred money. Any players joining clubs were taken aside and told in no uncertain terms how it worked. Journalists were in on it too. For the Cooperativa to thrive and prosper, they were rewarded if they kept their match reports and interviews simple and vague with as few details as possible.

To make sure it worked, the head of the Cooperativa had the backing of the two most powerful football administrators; Dumitru Dragomir, the head of the Romanian Professional Football League (RPFL), and Mircea Sandu, the head of the Romanian Football Federation (FRF).

Before Ceahlăul played an Intertoto Cup tie in 2000 against Austria Vienna, Gheorghe Ştefan casually tried to bribe the French delegation with prostitutes. When the referee Stéphane Moulin was having none of it and took it the wrong way (i.e. the correct way) and was shocked with the brazen act, he let those in charge know. Ştefan claimed that they were not prostitutes but Romanian folk singers who were supplying sandwiches and it was a terrible misunderstanding.

When Moulin reported the incident to Sandu, instead of taking action, he responded by demeaning the referee for complaining. He then claimed that Moulin was a 'queer fish'. This showed how deep-rooted and systemic the problem was. It was part of their culture, it was not a shock. This was normal. The actions during communism were about survival. So what if it takes bribery and corruption to get through? This kind of behaviour, in a broader sense, had permeated into the psyche of the country.

Ceahlăul were banned from Europe for five years, although the punishment was then reduced to a year after an appeal. This mentality has evolved and blended into Romanian society, politics and business. The same approach for football was used to get a deal done. This might be normal behaviour for some but for sporting integrity, it was wrong.

At the request of the Romanian government, the World Bank released a paper in 2001, entitled *Diagnostic Surveys of Corruption in Romania*. They covered poverty, inequality, and looked across sectors like the judiciary, health, policing and state procurement. The blame lay on poorly implemented regulations. The biggest victims were poorer families, living in poverty who were more susceptible to bribes. But the headline from the hefty report was that two-thirds of the Romanian public believed that 'all' or 'most' officials were corrupt.

Object: Golden Whistle
Subject: Porto Scandal

The wonderfully nuanced codename by the judicial police, *Apito Dourado* (Golden Whistle), should not distract us from Portugal's damning and comprehensive investigation into corruption and bribery of match officials.

The long-running Golden Whistle investigation looked into alleged bribery of referees in 2003/04 and corruption in the Portuguese game. In 2008, Porto were stripped of six points and fined €150,000 (£118,000). The champions were also banned for a year from the Champions League.

The police, following tip-offs from unnamed sources, conducted extensive phone tapping. They were regularly hitting gold with their targets yet like everything else in Portugal's legal system, the process trundled along at an alarmingly slow pace. It was lengthy, cumbersome and far too mired down in detail. Yet despite the high profile of those caught, ranging from agents, lawyers, referees and club presidents, it came to nothing.

Then, by chance, the never-ending investigation flipped on its head when Carolina Salgado, the ex-wife of Porto's president Jorge Nuno Pinto da Costa (though he became eager to erase his spouse of six years from his history), made some serious accusations in her book, *Eu Carolina*. She claimed to have seen thick envelopes being passed to Augusto Duarte, Pinto da Costa's favourite referee.

When the authorities, again, appeared mired down in another ponderous investigation, along came these serious accusations, breathing new life into the case. The public prosecutor brought in Maria José Morgado and she ripped through the evidence and files. Pinto da Costa was soon charged on three counts of bribing referees dating back to the 2003/04 season, when José Mourinho's team beat Benfica in the league by 12 points and also won the Champions League. Mourinho was not involved or indicted.

Salgado's book mentioned that referees would call and ask for some 'fruit', or 'coffee with milk'. And they were provided. A check through the wire-taps confirmed the saga, 'They called to ask for fruit tonight. Can I take it to them?' António Araújo, the fixer, asks Pinto da Costa. The code names 'fruit' and 'coffee with milk' referred to three Brazilian prostitutes. They agreed to give evidence and were then allowed to leave and fly home to Brazil.

In her book, Carolina claims she was asked by her husband to arrange for a councillor named Ricardo Bexiga to be silenced. Bexiga had witnessed Pinto da Costa bribing someone and this would serve as a warning not to speak to anyone. 'Jorge asked me to make contacts, I did, the job was done and I paid them.' Bexiga was fortunate to escape badly beaten with just a broken arm, but Pinto da Costa's lawyer Lourenço Pinto reminded her, somewhat menacingly, that the job had not been done properly, as Bexiga was still speaking.

Jorge Nuno Pinto da Costa was and still is a massive figure in Portuguese football. The Porto fans adore him. The news emanating at the time from *Apito Dourado* must have come as a clear shock. To see their president behaving like some sort of gangster. Porto fans sing songs about him and affectionately call him '*O Papa*', translated as 'The Pope'. He is currently one of the longest-serving presidents in world football and has overseen the winning of countless domestic and European titles.

Despite fleeing at the time to Spain, to avoid being detained, Pinto de Costa was formally accused of corruption in June 2007. He accepted the six-point fine but vowed to appeal the two-year ban by the Liga Portuguesa de Futebol Profissional's Discipline Committee, promising to clear his and Porto's name. Despite the overwhelming evidence, eye-witness accounts and the transcripts from mobile phones, Pinto da Costa was declared innocent in April 2009, a decision which no doubt shocked most of Portugal, not least Pinto da Costa himself.

Object: Restaurant Menu
Subject: Roma v Dundee United
Ref Bung

There's a despicable photograph, following Dundee United's controversial semi-final defeat to AS Roma in the 1984 European Cup, which always stays with me. The lack of sportsmanship is abhorrent. Dundee United's manager Jim McLean and his assistant Walter Smith are walking past the Roma side. The opposition players are cursing and gesticulating. They look menacing as they provoke and intimidate McLean and Smith after they had beaten Dundee United. Smith and substitute goalkeeper John Gardiner were punched in the ribs and spine as they protected their boss not only from Roma players but from club officials too as they kicked and punched. What a contemptible way to behave, especially after your team had won. When news broke in 2011 that the referee in the game had been bribed, it only added to the distaste I felt. I was angrier than I should have been, but sadly, I wasn't shocked.

It was beyond anyone's wildest expectations that a provincial club like Dundee United would win the league and reach the semi-finals of the European Cup with a first-team squad of 14, but they did. Meeting them in the semi-final over two legs were the mighty Roma. It was a horrible and cold evening in Dundee, standard weather for mid-April. The Italians, full of stars such as Bruno Conti and Falcão, weren't up for it. The ground was small and old-fashioned, the pitch poor. Already the Terrors had got inside their heads, now they were in their faces. The first half was a bitty affair, the quality of football on show more tense than entertaining, but in the second half United clicked. Davie Dodds scored in the 46th minute and Derek Stark scored the second. The game was over and the dream was on.

For Roma the issue was two-fold. They would be humiliated if they were to exit to the rank underdogs and the final was being held at their home ground, the Stadio Olimpico. From the airport to the game, Dundee United were attacked, the 3.30pm kick-off switched to the hottest part of the day, hardly ideal for pale, redheaded Scots more used to April snow. Their hotel had security guards with dogs barking all day. The fans joined in on the evening before the game and Dundee United couldn't sleep. When they travelled to the stadium the bus was attacked. When they got to the park they had missiles thrown at them. Ralph Milne had a great chance not long after the start but by half-time, Roma improved and were two up, both goals coming from Roberto Pruzzo. In the 58th minute Roma were awarded a penalty which captain Agostino di Bartolomei converted.

McLean kept his counsel after his side were beaten 3-0. The tie was there for the taking if only the referee had not been so unpredictable, to the point of being crooked, but that's football and you take your medicine. Roma's third and crucial goal was a weak penalty. Scottish, indeed British sides, when playing in Europe, are naive, tending to accept bad refereeing and the concept that those officiating can make 'an honest mistake' instead of the unthinkable, that they have been bribed. Some years later, Jim McLean revealed that Ernie Walker, the SFA boss at the time, demanded a UEFA probe. He smelt a rat in the referee's performance. His suspicions would prove accurate. The referee Vautrot had taken a bung.

As Anderlecht's Constant Vanden Stock's son revealed his father's actions (see Chapter 19), Roma's president Riccardo Viola, son of the late Dino Viola, would also confirm that an 'alleged' bribe had taken place. He explained how his father had approached it. The tale sounded like a scene from a cheap but tense made-for-TV mafia flick. 'Spartaco Landini, the director of football at Genoa, came to see my father. He told him Vautrot was a friend of his and that we could get at him via another friend, but he would have to be given 100million lire [£50,000].' Speaking on the Italian pay per view sports station Mediaset Premium, Viola continued, 'He said a dinner would be organised with the referee on the eve of the game and a signal to show the deal had been done would be demanded. During the dinner, a waiter went up to the referee, saying, "Telephone call for Mr Vautrot." That was the pre-arranged signal. Vautrot left the table and when he returned, said, "My friend Paolo rang and he sends you his best wishes." Then I got up, rang my father and told him, "Message received."' Why even attempt to cheat? Viola explained they needed help because they were already two down and not making the final, held at their home stadium, would have had serious financial repercussions.

Watching the game back now, it's difficult to disagree with John Holt who played for Dundee United from 1973 to 1987, 'The referee was giving free kicks when we'd hardly touched a guy. I felt the referee was more for them than us. I didn't feel he was right down the middle. Every free kick, I thought, and there were a lot. It kept increasing the pressure. We all felt it at the time, no doubt.'

Aberdeen and Dundee United were impressive in this period. Between 1979 and 1987, Alex Ferguson's Aberdeen side, won the UEFA Cup Winners Cup, the UEFA Super Cup, three league titles, four Scottish Cups and the Scottish League Cup. Dundee United won the title in 1983, and the League Cup in 1979 and 1980. They reached the semi-finals of the European Cup in 1984 and the UEFA Cup final in

1987. They were called the New Firm because they took on Celtic and Rangers, reaching extraordinary heights for their size and budget. Aberdeen beat Real Madrid to win the Cup Winners' Cup in 1983. They reached the semi-finals of the competition in 1984 and were beaten by Porto. Two Scottish sides through to the semi-finals of major European competitions. It's a travesty to consider Dundee United were robbed of a chance to make the European Cup Final.

The Roma president confirmed on Italian TV in 2012 that they had bribed the referee, as they were so desperate to overturn the first-leg score because the final was in their stadium and would be too lucrative to miss out on. In the end, Bruce Grobbelaar's wobbly leg routine would be the talking point of the 1983/84 final when the game ended in a draw and Liverpool won after a penalty shoot-out.

Jim McLean was a visionary coach, tactical, and loved playing a certain way. He also had players such as Dave Narey, Paul Hegarty, Maurice Malpas, Richard Gough, Eamonn Bannon, Paul Sturrock and Ralph Milne to help. With time to reflect, John Holt remains adamant, telling *The Independent*, 'We were robbed. That's right, we were robbed.'

McLean was angry, though he was always angry. He passed away on 26 December 2020. He once punched a BBC journalist, live, during a post-match interview. It may have passed the attention of many that he even had the humour to pass away peacefully on Boxing Day. When hearing that the referee for the semi-final had been bribed, he was angered at Roma's lack of grace, 'Any individual or club that stoops so low as to go in for this tactic deserves to be nowhere near the game. It's an utter disgrace because I have always tried to believe football is honest. I'm pleased Liverpool won the final, even if we were denied the chance to play in it. I'm glad a bunch of cheaters didn't win.'

Object: Sim Card
Subject: Calciopoli

Most genuine fans of the game have always had a romanticism with Italian football. Maybe it's because Italy is a football nation, with the iconic blue jersey and great clubs such as Juventus, Milan and Inter. The country is football crazy. How many Italian cricketers, rugby players or athletes can you name? But you can reel off Italian footballers by the dozen.

Maybe it was the wonderful World Cup sights, or the Channel 4 show *Gazzetta Football Italia* presented by James Richardson from 1992 until 2002. It may even have been Maradona, Gazza and Maldini at Napoli, Lazio and Milan respectively that made us fall in love with Italian football.

Football loves to throw the metaphorical spanner into the works and serve up some colossal shocks but few have come close to the scale of the scandal referred to as Calciopoli (literally football-gate). Sometimes these moments, with so many great clubs, are difficult to process and fully take in. The scandal came to light while Italian prosecutors investigated allegations made about doping in the 1990s by a Juventus doctor. While looking into the Italian football agency GEA World, police stumbled upon phone conversations between football executives and referee designators.

They found Juventus general manager Luciano Moggi and director Antonio Giraudo attempting to influence designators to approach certain referees, who they thought would be more sympathetic to their team's cause. Transcripts published in the 2004/05 season by *Gazzetta Dello Sport* laid it all bare. The conversations were between officials of Italian football to influence referee appointments. Central to the Calciopoli match-fixing scandal were accusations Moggi and Giraudo created a network of contacts inside the Italian Football Federation. This allowed them to influence referees assigned to specific games and ensured key opposition players were booked and suspended ahead of matches with Juventus.

Moggi even accused referees Pierluigi Collina and Roberto Rosetti of being 'too objective' and wanted them 'punished'. Too objective? They didn't want them to coolly and calmly consider the facts and the circumstances, to arrive at the best possible and hopefully, the correct decision? No, they wanted the decisions to go to Juventus. After the investigations, both Collina and Rosetti were among the few to come out unscathed.

Moggi and other Juventus executives arranged for 'amenable' referees and assistants to officiate games involving their side and those of opposition sides who were allies of Juventus. The judges, one a former president of Italy's top court, gave Pierluigi Pairetto, one of two officials responsible for allocating referees for Serie A matches, a two-and-a-half-year ban. Moggi used Swiss SIM cards to avoid wiretaps from the police.

In July 2006, the Italian Football Federation's prosecutor Stefan Palazzi hit the clubs involved hard. He called for the main sides involved to face relegation. Juventus were accused of building a system to alter the outcome of matches. Moggi, Giraudo and referee designator Pairetto created it, and Lazio and Fiorentina copied it. AC Milan tried an alternative approach.

After appeal, the punishments given out were as follows: Juventus, one of the most illustrious names in world football, were stripped of their 2004/05 and 2005/06 titles and downgraded to the bottom of Serie A. Relegated to Serie B, they were forced to start in the second tier with a nine-point deduction. They were also kicked out of the Champions League. Moggi and Giraudo were banned for five years, narrowly avoiding jail sentences (they were acquitted in 2015). Crucially, they also lost many stars like Zlatan Ibrahimović, Patrick Vieira, Fabio Cannavaro and Lilian Thuram. However, Gianluigi Buffon, Alessandro Del Piero, Giorgio Chiellini, David Trezeguet and Pavel Nedvěd (who made his European debut against Airdrieonians) garnered some credit for remaining.

AC Milan remained in Serie A but were deducted 30 points for the 2005/06 season and eight for 2006/07, and were forced to play one game behind closed doors. They were allowed back into the qualifying rounds of the Champions League. Fiorentina were originally relegated with points deductions. They ended up staying in Serie A with a 15-point deduction for 2006/07, were forced to play two games behind closed doors and were also banned from the 2006/07 Champions League. Lazio were allowed to remain in Serie A, receiving a three-point deduction for the following season and were forced to play two games behind closed doors. They were removed from the UEFA Cup. Reggina were docked 11 points and received a €100,000 fine.

When something like this happens to a club, the actions of owners and general managers always filter down to the supporters. It's the fans who are always hit hardest and it always emanates from the soulless officials running things. They tarnish the reputation of these great clubs and swan off and once those responsible are gone, the fans are as always still left, loyally backing the team.

Fascism

The scourge of fascism affected millions and filtered into life, and, inevitably, into football.

Object: Pools Coupon
Subject: Franco Wins Spanish Pools Twice

When I first heard Franco enjoyed playing the football pools, my immediate thought was of the coupon man chapping his door on a Thursday night to get paid and collect. Then the pools agent would be made wait at the door, only to be told by Franco's Commander of Armed Forces, 'Sorry mate, he's on the phone to Hitler, can we pay double next week?'

In the halcyon days of abandoned games due to frozen pitches, ice and snow, did Spain have a pools panel who sat and debated the outcome of games? What would Franco be like with the pools panel if they chose a home win instead of his choice of a draw, did they face a firing squad on Monday? Surprisingly, Franco didn't lose out. He won twice. Yes, General Franco won the Spanish football pools, not once, but twice.

Fear not as he played under a cunning pseudonym, Francisco Cofran. Nothing untoward here, but you'd imagine the Spanish pools office didn't have many eagle-eyed crossword lovers seeing the name Cofran and thinking 'that's an anagram of something, but I can't see what it is'. Do you think the German football pools office would allow someone called Harold Flite to win twice?

I'm genuinely intrigued by Franco's love of the pools. It's surreal. Imagine Hitler loved bingo and Mussolini was obsessed with *Come Dine with Me*. For context, though, apparently even Hitler claimed Franco was boring. He said he would prefer to endure having his teeth pulled than spend more time with Franco, and Hitler knew some questionable dentists. By 1940, Hitler wanted Franco to join the Axis powers but he refused. This was after the Spanish dictator used Hitler and Mussolini's forces during the Spanish Civil War to defeat Republicans.

After the civil war in 1939, when Franco took control of Spain, he began an oppressive national centralising project. The last bastion to fall was Barcelona. In one week, 10,000 were executed in the city. Barcelona couldn't forget that their club's president, Josep Sunyol, had been murdered during the war by Franco's nationalist forces, which only heightened the hostilities. Franco also enraged Barcelona by executing 25,000 of the Republican side after a ceasefire. These executions lasted throughout the 1940s and 1950s. Barcelona hated Franco and by default, Real Madrid, and the bad blood continues.

Rumours of Franco's alleged interference were always rife, if difficult to confirm. One of the main accusations surrounds the transfer of Argentinian Alfredo Di Stéfano to Real Madrid in 1953 after Di Stéfano signed for Barcelona. It is more likely a myriad of contractual confusion which saw Di Stéfano become a Real Madrid legend. His route to the Bernabéu was worthy of a Netflix documentary. It is often cited as one of the most bizarre transfer negotiations in football. ·

In 1948, a strike hit Argentinian football and many star players, including Di Stéfano, Adolfo Pedernera and Néstor Rossi, defected to the breakaway Colombian league and signed for Millonarios. The league attracted top players because Colombian football was outside FIFA's remit and didn't have to pay transfer fees, allowing more lucrative salaries. The team was considered one of the best of this era and toured the world, including Spain.

In 1953, Colombia re-joined FIFA and Di Stéfano grew disillusioned with life, in debt, in Bogotá. Real Madrid agreed a deal with Millonarios but Barcelona approached River Plate, who held his contract and had always stated his move to Colombia was illegal. Di Stéfano eventually joined Barcelona. However, the Spanish football federation (RFEF) refused to recognise the transfer and made the bizarre decision to force the two clubs to share him over alternate seasons. Barcelona have always stated this was done with Franco's backing as the Spanish federation gave Madrid the first season, one in which Di Stéfano had a poor start and Barcelona were 'persuaded' to sell their rights to Real Madrid. That Madrid's director Santiago Bernabéu was a supporter of Franco and a right-winger who was part of the forces who stormed Barcelona added to the conspiracy theories of Franco's involvement. Bernabéu was desperate to move the power and success from Catalonia to Madrid. Di Stéfano and Real Madrid won the European Cup five times in consecutive years from 1956 to 1960.

Another more alarming tale was the 1943 cup game when Barcelona beat Madrid 3-0 in the first leg of the semi-final. Before the second leg took place, one of Franco's henchmen visited the team and it was suggested they were only allowed to play because of the generosity of the regime. They were warned to take their foot off the gas for the second leg, or there would be consequences. The Barcelona players fearing for their lives, or at least their careers, eased off and were beaten 11-1, the biggest win in any game between the Spanish giants.

However, we end this exhibit with one of the most curious Franco/football-related stories. This museum is here to find out the weird and wonderful and strange in European football and no one can argue with this. One of the most contentious dictators Europe has ever produced played the football pools. It's surreal, imagining him listening to the radio, checking his coupon. Oh sorry, did I say Franco? No, it was Francisco Cofran. But twice though?

Fanorak Fact: Alfredo Di Stéfano played for Argentina, Spain and Colombia, but his Colombia caps were earned before FIFA officially recognised the country's football association. Barcelona's László Kubala was voted the club's best-ever player (pre-Messi and Cruyff) and is officially the only player to play for three countries. His parents were Czech, he was born in Budapest and played for Czechoslovakia, Hungary and Spain. Josef Bican represented Austria, Czechoslovakia and the region of Bohemia-Moravia.

Object: Coffee Cup
Subject: Matthias Sindelar

In the 1930s, Vienna was a beautiful, bustling city. It was vibrant, full of coffee houses, concert halls, a culture of higher thought, intellectuals, concertos, operas, artists, philosophers, great minds and enlightenment. To top it off, they had a football side the world was starting to take seriously, the *Wunderteam*. The Austrian national football team had players like Josef Bican, Walter Nausch and Josef Smistik but the star of the show was their captain and striker Matthias Sindelar. Then Hitler came along and ruined it for everyone.

Sindelar was nicknamed *'Der Papierene'* ('The Paper Man') because of his slim build. He spent his entire career playing for FK Austria Vienna. He was a football superstar, a bona fide hero, and was recognised across the world. He advertised suits and cars, and being a footballer he enjoyed spending and living life to the full, ticking the usual boxes such as womanising and gambling. Football had made Sindelar independently wealthy. Reports from the time suggest he was an extraordinary footballer, one of the best his country produced; he was the captain of the Austrian national side and a 1930s Maradona, Pelé or Cruyff.

His game mirrored those great intellectuals of Vienna; he read the game superbly and was able to out-think opponents. If that didn't work, his intelligence on the ball allowed him to dribble around opponents. He was part of the *Wunderteam*, managed by the strict disciplinarian and stickler for detail, Hugo Meisl. The coach was also a referee, so you can imagine what playing for him was like. Sindelar made his international debut in 1926 but would, through his indiscipline – on the park – be dropped by Meisl. It took an intervention from leading journalists, coaches and the Austrian FA to plead with Meisl to bring Sindelar back, and it delighted the nation when it happened. His first game back was a friendly against Scotland, then lauded for their style of play. Scotland had beaten Germany, Netherlands and France before facing Austria. The Scots were annihilated 5-0 in Vienna.

In the years leading up to the 1934 World Cup, Sindelar's men beat Germany twice, 5-0 and 6-0, Switzerland 6-0, and they hammered Hungary 8-2 (Sindelar bagged a hat-trick, scoring the first three goals). They won the equivalent of the European Championship in 1932, the Central European International Cup, when they beat Italy 4-2. Going into the World Cup in 1934, they were one of the favourites.

In the tournament, they entertained the public, played beautiful football, won hearts, beat Hungary in the quarter-finals and faced hosts Italy in the semi-final. Much was made of the poor weather conditions, which didn't help their slick, quick passing game. More alarmingly, questions and suspicions were raised over the efficacy of referee Ivan Eklind. He allowed a controversial goal after the Italians shoved the Austrian goalkeeper over the line. Then it was goodnight Vienna. The Italian organisers (and Mussolini) liked his work so much that he was awarded the final too, which they conveniently won.

In 1938, a game was organised to 'celebrate' Austria being annexed into the German Third Reich. Branded the 'Reconciliation Match', it would take place against Ostmark (Austria's German empire name) and Germany. There was huge pressure placed on the players to play a sporting draw and unite.

Top players like Sindelar could not be told before a game how it should end. So he deliberately missed easy chances, match reports claimed, especially in the first half. The fans understood it; he was mocking the Germans. He played not to entertain but to ridicule. He showed off, belittling the Nazi officers watching in the stands.

In the second half, with his point made, when he grew bored and insulted, he flipped into proper competitive mode and decided to score, then setting up his team-mate for a second. He used this high-profile game to make a brave protest. The Austrians in the crowd applauded and cheered as this was a slap in the face, a wonderful insult to Hitler and Nazism. When Sindelar dared to dance an ironic waltz in front of the German VIP box full of prominent dignitaries, the crowd were ecstatic.

With Austria annexed, Sindelar was approached by Germany's manager Sepp Herberger but repeatedly refused to play for the unified Germany-Austria side. The player said he was too old, while those closest to him claimed it was a refusal and a protest to play for the Nazi regime. This 'Mozart of Football' refused to take any part in the Third Reich's propaganda machine. Sindelar had many Jewish friends and knew that the newly formed Nazi regime had disbanded Austria's professional league and expelled its Jewish clubs. Sindelar's side, Austria Vienna, were the bourgeois Jewish club. So he saw what was happening first-hand.

He decided to retire and bought a café in Vienna from a Jewish owner, Leopold Drill, who had been forced to sell under Nazi regulations. Drill was within his rights to sell it for half the price because Sindelar, despite the Gestapo's suspicions, was not of the Jewish faith; he was Catholic. Sindelar refused to do that and paid the full asking price out of principle. The Gestapo made a note and monitored anyone who had sympathy for the Jewish cause.

When Sindelar and his girlfriend, Camilla Castagnola, were found dead in her apartment, their death was viewed with suspicion. The official cause of death was accidental carbon monoxide poisoning yet for many, that postulation always felt too convenient. There were rumours of murder and suicide because of gambling debts and fear of facing a concentration camp. Conspiracy theories took hold, that the Austrian who refused to play for the Nazi regime was killed after upsetting the Germans. To others, his death felt too convenient, especially when he and his partner were friendly with prominent Jewish people. But it was put down to an accident. It was known that a few of the chimneys in the block they lived in didn't work so carbon monoxide could have been a contributing factor.

Sindelar, in print, is often framed as something of a spiky, opinionated and obdurate character but he was 100 per cent opposed to the annexation of Austria. The truth is hard to pin down. Sindelar's death has been caught up in a myth, and the facts have been left behind over time. Police said he was accidentally killed by asphyxiation by carbon monoxide fumes from a faulty heater, though later they told a newspaper the heating worked fine. Some of the myth-making and lack of transparency could be down to this, and the fact public officials doing a more in-depth and thorough inquiry, held by the public prosecutor, were forced by the Nazis to close down the case. Sindelar's death was a huge story and 20,000 people lined the streets for his state funeral.

Sindelar made his international debut in 1926, scoring against Czechoslovakia, and would register 26 goals in 43 games. *Der Papierene* and his legend live on.

Object: SS Blindfold
Subject: Alexandre Villaplane

It's difficult to know where to begin with Alexandre Villaplane, but begin we must. Villaplane was France's first World Cup captain, who led his side in Uruguay in 1930 to a 4-1 win over Mexico and, at the time, was his country's finest centre-half. But he was also a traitor, gangster and murderer, who collaborated with Nazis and stood by watching women being raped, prisoners burnt alive and Jews sent to prison camps. He was shot by a firing squad in Montrouge fortress on Boxing Day in 1944. His official charge sheet read 'high treason and acts of barbarism'.

We do not expect this from our footballers, that they might be sadistic monsters, and if they are, they would normally leave it on the park and be gentlemen off it. This level of evil is difficult to comprehend but Villaplane was a psychopath seduced by power and money. This is a tragic story; one at times difficult to process.

Villaplane was a fine player with energy and pace who was robust in the tackle, a prodigious header of the ball, and an intelligent player with an eye for a killer pass. Here was a prodigious talent, an impressive player and leader, who sounds like the modern centre-half. Villaplane was born in Algeria in 1905 and would go on to become the first player of North African origin to represent France. Having moved to live with relatives in the south of France aged 16, he played for the local team, FC Sète. He had been spotted by a coach named Victor Gibson, one of many British coaches living and working in European football. Gibson had played for Morton, Falkirk and briefly for Espanyol before showing up at Sète, where he was player-manager between 1914 and 1924. Gibson was a Celtic fan, and had the side play in green and white hoops, which they wear to this day, and he quickly promoted Villaplane to the first team.

Villaplane had signed for Sète but after 18 months forced the club's hand when he left for a more lucrative offer from a second division side, Vergéze, who were financed by Perrier. Then he returned after Sète made a better offer. This one incident should have been a warning sign. Here was a player unafraid to hold a club to ransom. He may have been the uneducated son of immigrants but he was streetwise. He also realised that with Gibson's coaching, he was becoming a valued centre-half.

The trimmings around the game were already turning his head. Villaplane knew that the setup at the time, which was still amateur, was ripe for bribery and corruption. Cash was king and there was loads for the taking if you were cute enough. Clubs would secure the best players by offering fictitious jobs. By 1925 he was rapidly improving and, having guided Sète to the semi-final of the French Cup, was selected to play for a North African XI against France B. The national scouts for France spotted him straight away and he was awarded his first cap for France against Belgium in April 1926. Villaplane established himself as the country's best centre-half. When he was out, the nation suffered. He came back to save the day, played 20 times, then at the age of 24, in 1930, his career abruptly stopped.

The player was a mercenary, continually moving for cash: Séte (1921–23), Vergéze (1923–24), Sète (1924–27), SC Nîmes (1927–29), Racing Club (1929–32), Antibes (1932–33), OGC Nice (1933–34) and Hispano-Bastidienne (1934–35). The move from SC Nîmes to the high-spending and ambitious Racing Club was the beginning of the end. The temptations in Paris became too much for the player who, euphemistically, 'fell in with the wrong crowd'. His money was blown at the racecourse, the casinos, clubs, bars and restaurants. Villaplane enjoyed flaunting his wealth, lording it up and fraternising with the underworld. The wrong crowd suited the versatile Villaplane. He quickly adapted and realised he could be as corrupt as the others, effortlessly entering into the criminal fraternity. Unsurprisingly, his international career came to a sudden halt at this time.

When professional football was introduced to France in the 1932/33 season, Villaplane moved to FC Antibes. The inaugural professional league was split into north and south regions with the winners of each ten-team group meeting in a play-off. Antibes won the southern division and Lille the northern. Rumours started to emerge that the play-off against Lille had been bought. Antibes were stripped of their title and the coach banned for life, but Villaplane and two former Sète team-mates who were suspected of orchestrating the scam were moved on. Villaplane headed for OGC Nice. Undisciplined, unfit and constantly fined, he was kicked out. He teamed up with Gibson again at second division Hispano-Bastidienne in Bordeaux but Gibson sacked him. The player then received the first of his many jail sentences, this time for fixing horse races in Paris.

When Paris fell to the Nazis in June 1940, it was like the Gold Rush for criminals and gangsters. The war became an opportunity for racketeering and blackmailing. The Germans needed help and the French Gestapo's Henri Lafont emerged as the main man, thriving as others cowered. The Nazis needed someone to hunt down and torture the Belgian Resistance and Jews, and Lafont obliged.

With more influence he would recruit willing psychopaths from the Paris prisons. He teamed up with disgraced police officer Pierre Bonny and eventually recruited Villaplane. They set up at the notorious headquarters, 93 rue Lauriston, probably the most notorious address in Parisian history, the home of the gang that became known as the French Gestapo.

Hitler had been funding an Arabic-language newspaper that depicted him as a heroic liberator. He wanted Lafont to form a squadron drawn from France's immigrant population. In February 1944, the German authorities created the Brigade Nord Africain (BNA) to cleanse the Périgord region. Villaplane was a made-man now, and well rewarded as an SS sub-lieutenant in charge of the BNA. He excelled and his cruelty and sadism gained notoriety.

When Paris was liberated, the SS and BNA were rounded up and tried. The judge said, 'They pillaged, raped, robbed, killed and teamed up with the Germans for even worse outrages, the most awful executions. They left fire and ruin in their wake. A witness told us how he saw with his own eyes these mercenaries take jewels from the still-twitching and bloodstained bodies of their victims. Villaplane was in the midst of all this, calm and smiling. Cheerful, almost invigorated.'

Object: Pauper's Grave
Subject: El Patricio

I was ashamed to say I hadn't heard of Patrick O'Connell, not until 2014 when Johan Cruyff and other high-profile football people spoke out in a campaign to raise money to build a memorial to him. O'Connell captained Ireland and Manchester United, managed Real Betis to their first La Liga title and effectively saved Barcelona from bankruptcy. However, in the United Kingdom and Ireland, few, if any, had heard of him. He died destitute in 1959 and was buried in an unmarked grave in St Mary's Cemetery, Kensal Green, north-west London.

The Dubliner worked as a baker. He was spotted playing junior football in 1909 and signed for Belfast Celtic. His impressive displays caught the eye of many English sides and he signed for Sheffield Wednesday. He was unsettled in Sheffield, where his career failed to take off, so he moved to Hull. His form there saw him selected for Ireland (still a united Ireland, in 1914) where he excelled, captaining the side to victory in the British Home Nations Championship. O'Connell would join Manchester United from Hull City in 1914 for a transfer fee of £1,000.

Even the outbreak of the First World War would not stop the completion of the 1914/15 season. It would end controversially, mired in a betting scandal. On 2 April 1915, Manchester United faced Liverpool at Old Trafford. Liverpool were safe but United needed to win to avoid relegation. They won 2-0 with both goals from George Anderson. O'Connell skippered United and took and missed a penalty. The crowd and officials were unhappy with how it was played. They were correct; bookmakers had reported there was a huge bet placed on United winning 2-0 at 7/1. Chelsea and Spurs were relegated. Liverpool canvassed for Spurs to be reinstated but Arsenal's director, the Tory MP and prominent freemason Sir Henry Norris, persuaded and influenced the league to allow his side into the top tier. They had finished fifth in the second division. Chelsea were edged out. The FA ordered an investigation and four Liverpool and three United players were found guilty and given lifetime bans. An ex-United player who was now at Liverpool, Jackie Sheldon, was the ringleader. When, at 2-0, the Liverpool player Fred Pagnam hit the crossbar and his team-mates chastised him, the referee came close to abandoning the game.

Football would be put into cold storage until 1919. During the war, O'Connell lived in his brother's flat in London and worked in a munitions factory. He struggled to find a club in England but played a season in Scotland for Dumbarton. He ended his playing career at Ashington where he would also begin his coaching career.

O'Connell must have been going through some kind of emotional turmoil as soon after his spell at Ashington he disappeared, leaving his wife and four kids. The first time they heard anything from him was when letters containing money arrived from Spain. In 1922 he had taken a coaching job with Racing Santander, winning five titles before they were invited in as part of the newly formed Spanish league. O'Connell had met and married another woman, an Irish woman, also called Ellen, the same as his first wife. From Santander he moved to Real Oviedo, but a successful three-year spell at Real Betis saw him appointed Barcelona manager in 1935.

It was with Barcelona that O'Connell cemented his reputation but the man must have thought he was born under a bad sign. This time fate had thrown the Spanish

Civil War in his face and, as coach of Barcelona, he was front and central to the Catalan cause and up against Franco. The club's president and outspoken Catalan activist and radical, Josep Sunyol, was killed. FC Barcelona were badly hit in 1929 by the Wall Street Crash and were left in dire straits – the club's founder Joan Gamper had committed suicide in 1930. The club was dying, and by 1934 was close to folding.

With the club pushed to the brink economically, their overseas stars were told to stay away from Catalonia. O'Connell, who was home on holiday in Ireland, was advised it was too dangerous to return, but he did. Soon the national league was suspended as full-scale civil war broke out. The club managed to defiantly play on in a regional division, to let Franco know they wouldn't be silenced, but the players had no salary, and the club had no money coming in. The war had become bigger than football and looked like it would end the club. On the brink of bankruptcy, hope would come from a Barcelona businessman now resident in Mexico. Barça were invited over to do a lucrative tour in the socialist country, which was also largely against Franco.

While on the tour, many players chose to seek asylum, refusing to return from South America or jumping ship in France to escape the civil war. In the end, O'Connell had four players left. The club though was spared, thanks to the money earned on the tour from six games in football-mad Mexico and exhibition matches in New York.

What a sorrowful and tragic story. Football is full of these quiet legends; people held in high esteem in far-flung places yet barely known in their backyard. The Irishman known in Spain as El Patricio will not, thanks to some recent high-profile backing, be forgotten and that's some solace for his surviving family.

Eccentrics and Eccentricities

Football has had its share of weird and wonderful
characters with strange habits.

Object: A Hen

Subject: Gigi Meroni, the 'Italian George Best'

It may have been the swinging 1960s elsewhere in the world, but in austere, conservative and Catholic Italy, it may as well have been the 1930s. This was not a country for a young, flamboyant, art-loving footballer. That he lived in sin with an actress, Cristiana Uderstatd, did not help. Enter one Luigi 'Gigi' Meroni, the 'Italian George Best'.

Meroni had shaggy hair, stubble and an eye for fashion. The country was infatuated with him. He was idolised by his club's fans, mocked by opposition supporters and, with his unconventional behaviour and rebelliousness, left the rest of Italy reeling as they refused to accept such blatant displays of freedom and expression. Long hair and stubble was proof you were a revolutionary communist and mates with Che Guevara and Fidel Castro.

Here was a dedicated follower of fashion who was not like anybody else in his country's game, hence the later comparison with George Best. The star was an eccentric when his generation and team-mates were uniform and regimented. Meroni was a funny, bright, intelligent person who saw the world differently. Growing up, he loved poetry, jazz music and literature. When interviewed he once said he liked football but loved painting. He thought his real vocation was as an artist and he had worked in garment factories as an apprentice, designing and creating silk ties, before opting for football. Meroni would see someone walk their dog, so would put a lead on his pet hen and take it for a walk around Lake Como. On one occasion, as he knew the press would be following him, he dressed it in a bathing suit.

He started his career turning out for the local Serie B side, Como. His rangy body, speed, skill and quick wing play started to attract attention. He joined newly promoted Genoa who, in 1962, paid 40 million lire (£23,000) for him. Despite becoming a firm favourite with the fans at Genoa and helping them to narrowly avoid relegation by one point, the move would be underpinned by the volatility in his high profile relationship with Uderstatd. She left him to marry an older man but realised her mistake and left having not consummated the marriage. After running off, she returned to her true love, Luigi, evoking a full tirade of moral outrage across Italy.

Then there was the doping scandal. With the start of mandatory drug tests, three footballers were caught after testing positive for using amphetamines. Meroni claimed he forgot to submit his sample. The star received a five-match ban.

In the summer of 1964, Meroni signed for Torino for 300 million lire (£171,000). Torino were once a dominant side but after an air disaster in 1949 they were on the wane. Fresh hope had arrived with former AC Milan coach Nereo Rocco, one of those Italian coaches straight out of central casting, famed for his catenaccio. However, experience had made him a pragmatist; mavericks like Meroni won you games.

Meroni always wanted to beat defenders and attack, when the style of football at the time was rigid. Teams were set up not to lose; the art was in defending, it was about negative football, teamwork and effort. Like George Best, he would also be subject to brutal treatment from the press and opponents alike.

When he was called up for international duty, the strict disciplinarian coach, Edmondo Fabbri, demanded

Meroni cut his hair. Meroni refused. You would think he was in the Grateful Dead with his flowing locks. His hair was longer than most team-mates' styles but it made him stand out. Such was the excitement around this colourful individual who refused to conform that once, when he decided to shave his beard, it made the news. Turin's *La Stampa* ran with the headline *Meroni Has Shaved Off His Beard*. Of course, to those in Turin, that wouldn't have made much sense so they would have probably written 'Meroni si è tagliato la barba'.

When Juventus made a bold bid of 750 million lire – around £435,000 – for Meroni, and Torino's president Orfeo Pianelli accepted it, the Italian press shifted into overdrive. Torino were struggling financially and needed the money. When news filtered through of the offer from their bitter rivals, Torino fans launched a mass protest taking to the streets, heading to the homes of Pianelli and Gianni Agnelli. Meroni was so popular that workers in the Fiat factory threatened to go on strike. The deal collapsed, and Meroni remained at Torino.

From the Romans, through to a teenage Puccini banging out his first aria, Italians have always loved drama. Life is seldom, if ever, perfect, and that flawed imperfection means tragedy also befalls football with depressing regularity. After a 4-2 victory over Sampdoria on 15 October 1967, Meroni and team-mate Fabrizio Poletti decided to go for a final few drinks to a favourite bar, near Meroni's apartment. To get to Bar Zambon, they had to cross two lanes of chaotic traffic coming in both directions. Tragically, both players were hit by a car; Meroni was struck and thrown over to the other lane and later died in hospital of his injuries. Bizarrely, the car that killed Meroni was driven by one of the club's biggest fans, who would eventually become chairman. Meroni was dead aged 24. Italy was devastated and 20,000 mourners brought Turin to a standstill for his funeral.

After his death, one slightly unhinged fan broke into his tomb and stole Meroni's liver to confirm he had died.

Fanorak Fact: The Torino side who were killed in an aircraft crash were piloted by a man called Luigi Meroni, though no relation.

Object: Mantelpiece
Subject: The Life of C.B. Fry

Where to start with Charles Burgess Fry? The best place would probably be his party piece. Fry would leap from a stationary position, standing backwards, on to the mantelpiece. Facing the mantelpiece, he would be crouched, leap up, turn in mid-air, land on the shelf and take a bow. I would suggest that nothing, despite his implausible sporting prowess and achievements – and there were many – can beat this feat. Stop for a second and try to envisage even attempting that.

I always thought of Fry as a character from *Ripping Yarns*, written by Michael Palin and Terry Jones of Monty Python fame, someone ripe for parody. He was a gifted sportsman; between 1892 and 1921, as a cricketer, he hit 30,000 first-class runs. He was also described as looking like a Greek god, 'the most handsome man in England', and had a career as a nude male model. He turned down a claim to the throne of Albania and attempted to become an MP but narrowly lost the parliamentary seat of Banbury. If he was hanging around Muswell Hill in the early 1960s, The Kinks may have written the song 'Davy Watts' about him.

As a footballer his career was brief; although he played in defence he had blistering pace. He captained his school team and played in the FA Cup aged 16 for the amateur team, the Casuals. He won four Blues playing at Oxford. He joined Corinthian in 1891, playing 74 times. To gain international honours, he knew he would have to turn out for a professional side and his nearest club Southampton agreed to sign him. He won the Southern League title during that 1900/01 season. He worked on his game enough to gain an international call-up, playing for England once, against Ireland in March 1901, incidentally at Southampton. The following season Southampton faced Sheffield United in the FA Cup Final, which ended in a 1-1 draw. Southampton lost 2-1 in the replay – it was the same final in which William 'Fatty' Foulke starred for the Blades. In the same year, Fry also hit six successive first-class centuries.

The Saints had to release Fry as his cricket commitments meant he was seldom available. He then signed for rivals Portsmouth, playing as an amateur three times before retiring due to injury. None of the injuries were caused by his party piece. Imagine what the reaction would have been if he had played in the 1980s. You see how livid managers became when players played golf, so what would they have been like if they heard their star man was monkeying about on mantelpieces?

Fry excelled at cricket, captained England, and scored a century in the Oxford v Cambridge Varsity match but his talent didn't stop there – he also equalled the then world long jump record. Academically, he earned a first in Classics at Oxford.

As is the way with such talent, magnificence and genius, Fry suffered mentally. He endured the first of many nervous breakdowns when still at Oxford. In 1898 he married Beatrice Holme Sumner, who was ten years his senior. The marriage was fraught and his wife a cruel, domineering and terrifying person. Maybe she had to be to stop him attempting his party piece every time he saw a fireplace. As his mental issues became more of a problem, his sporting prowess and great life started to slowly fall apart.

When he was well, his many achievements away from sport continued. He set up *Fry's Magazine,* saved a prestigious naval training school from closure and was pivotal in the setting up of the scouting movement. He excelled as a writer of great versatility, from his book *Batsmanship* (in 1912) to his hugely popular column in the *Evening Standard,* to his autobiography; *Life Worth Living* – few could argue with his talent as an entertaining and sharp writer.

In between bouts of mental illness (said by Fry's children to be exacerbated by their mother), he would resurface, and in 1934 he fell in with the wrong crowd, most namely a chap called Adolf Hitler. The Fuhrer and Joachim von Ribbentrop were impressed at his mantelpiece routine and his constant pushing for the Germans to take up cricket. Then there were serious discussions about moving to Hollywood to star on the silver screen. Later, C.B. Fry would eventually sink into full-on mental illness, dressing outrageously and suffering from paranoid episodes, and he was once found running naked on Brighton beach.

But when he was well, what a man – and what a life.

Object: Coracle
Subject: Fred's Coracle

These days, ball boys are usually part of the club's youth setup, brought in to quickly and efficiently retrieve the ball. But in my day it was different. There was fun to be had as we hurled abuse at ball boys while pretending we weren't jealous, as we watched the sons of board members freeze and struggle in their tracksuits in sub-zero conditions. All for the price of a half-time pie. The real prize was seeing the game up close, for free, and the chance to throw the ball back to one of your heroes on a Saturday afternoon. Better still, if the game was against a decent side or maybe a big cup tie, there was a great chance of being on TV.

One of the more charmingly eccentric items from this wing of the alternative museum is the coracle belonging to Fred Davis. For years, at Shrewsbury Town's Gay Meadow stadium, Fred and his family retrieved any errant balls kicked out of the ground and floating off on the adjacent River Severn. When a centre-half would blooter an expensive Mitre match ball out of the ground, Fred would quickly get up, pick up his lightweight boat, put it over his back, and run up the tunnel and out of the ground to retrieve the ball. This would be accompanied by a huge roar from the fans present. Sometimes it was more exciting than the game itself.

One of the coracles eventually ended up in the National Football Museum in Manchester until they decided it wasn't cool enough for them. Shrewsbury moved out of Gay Meadow at the end of the 2006/07 season, to what would be the New Meadow stadium on the outskirts of town. The previous ground, as the name suggested – the meadow part at least

– was surrounded by parkland and trees but chiefly by the River Severn. This meant the stadium was regularly flooded, especially in autumn and winter. The changing rooms and offices were damaged, and costly to repair.

Well known locally, Fred hit the big time in 1975 when he was filmed by BBC1's high rating daily network show of the time, *Nationwide*. Viewers were intrigued and amazed by what appeared to be an elderly ball boy running out to get a ball. Then we realised that the ground backed on to a river, hence the need for a boat. The coracle now resides in the Montgomery Waters Meadow Stadium, and this imaginary alternative museum.

Object: Bell

Subject: Helen Turner's Bell and Manchester City

A TV crew beat Amazon Prime with fly-on-the-wall sports documentaries in the 1970s when BBC1's primetime show, *Nationwide*, the day's *The One Show*, followed Manchester City for a season as they struggled and toiled. It is important to remind everyone, especially younger readers, there was a time when City were in the doldrums and not very well off financially. In the 1980s they were twice relegated from the First Division. This wasn't a side followed by glory hunters. City fans earned their stripes. As recently as 1999, City played in the third tier of English football. Maybe the true football fans among them sensed it was a temporary measure, down to financial mismanagement and the wrong coaching appointments.

Their fan base, however, remained loyal. They weren't happy about it, but it was their team and they continued to support them. Despite suffering relegation to the Second Division (still the third level – the divisions had been renamed in 1992 when the Premier League began) their crowds were still more than 28,000. Football fans often looked at the turnout and thought it was as if City supporters were being nice out of badness. You could be forgiven for thinking the hardcore fans revelled in the mediocrity of being in the wilderness. Perhaps, like true supporters, they knew their club needed them in their hour of need? So with this in mind, it is difficult to begrudge them any of their recent success.

Most fans of a certain vintage, who delight in football unconventionality, when asked to mention City would know about the woman behind the goal at Maine Road. Fans knew her as Helen the Bell. Helen Turner was generally regarded as an unofficial mascot and Manchester City super-fan. She epitomised loyalty and devotion and followed the side through thick and thin, mostly the latter. She would ring a huge brass bell when she felt the fans needed to be roused and get behind the team. Sometimes when the team or the crowd were flat, the fans would sing to her, 'Helen! Helen! Ring the bell!'

In 1976 she was invited on to the Wembley pitch as part of the lap of honour when City won the League Cup. She was asked on by her friend, Joe Corrigan, to whom she would give a sprig of lucky heather before each home match. You could spot Helen from the blonde beehive, a big Bet Lynch hairstyle, ringing that bell at Maine Road. Through the years the bell rang – but by the mid-1980s she was in a wheelchair and suffering from arthritis. She still showed up, though.

The lucky heather would have been easy to come by as Helen was a flower seller with a stall outside Manchester Royal Infirmary and, in between sitting in the Old North Stand, was an active charity fundraiser. When City left Maine Road in 2003 for what was then known as Eastlands, Helen was given a standing ovation. (It was renamed the Etihad in 2011). When she passed away aged 85 in 2005, the club, players and fans perfectly observed a minute's silence.

Her passing marked the end of the era, the end of a time when football was not all glamour and glitz and super stadia and big-money moves, but full-on dedication to the cause, one at times to which even St Jude, the patron saint of lost causes accepted defeat and headed off to the pub at half-time.

Helen Turner is here as a reminder of the reason we fell in love with football and the colourful characters who make the game fun. They are in the museum to represent the millions of fans, volunteers and helpers who give so much to football without their contribution being recognised.

Fanorak Fact: Helen's bell was bequeathed to Manchester City and they occasionally lend it out for supporters to ring. Helen will always be remembered fondly and with a smile.

Object: Zimmer Frame
Subject: Harry Lowe

This Zimmer frame is a warm-hearted doffing of the cap to an English footballer born Horace Lowe, the oldest ever player to play in Spain's top division. He turned out for Real Sociedad aged 48 years, seven months and 14 days.

I love players like this. This towering colossus, all 5ft 7in of him, also played centre-half. He may have been a spectacular reader of the game, the Cannavaro of his day. What is evident is that here we have a man who simply loved the game. In his 12-year career with Spurs, from 1914 to 1926, he appeared in only 72 league games. He managed to play three league games for Fulham. It's hardly the stuff of legend yet he still had the drive and desire to continue.

After playing in England, he moved to Spain to coach Real Sociedad in 1930. He stayed there from 1930 to 1935 before moving to take on the same role at Espanyol. Lowe entered into La Liga and world football's record books because of what happened in one game in 1934/35. The unexpected call to action came after one of his Sociedad players had to pull out after falling ill before facing Valencia. Enter Harry, who got his boots on and slotted in to play centre-half. These were the days before substitutes, so he stepped into the breach.

Interestingly, the early decades and formative years in the development of Spanish football are full of British influence. The oldest club in Spain, Recreativo de Huelva, was set up in December 1889 by Scots Robert Russell Ross and William Alexander MacKay, who were working overseas in the Rio Tinto mining company in Andalusia. The club still plays in the Spanish second division and was formed to quench the workforce's love for football but also to offer fitness, exercise and recreation for the staff. Their first game was played in Seville in 1890 and the game itself was effectively made up of British-based players, workers and engineers from the mines.

I'm sure at the time that Harry wouldn't have given it a second thought and was stepping in because it was an emergency and he was needed. However, when Harry turned out against Valencia and his team were hammered 7-1 he would have been blissfully unaware he would be going into the record books. He was also adding to an impressive list of British influence in the narrative of Spanish football. Harry played one game in Spain and has become immortal. How wonderful is that? After all those years of dedication to the game, training hard every day without being selected, he finally got his reward.

Object: Scorpio Star Sign
Subject: Raymond Domenech

I'm unsure if the French have an effective translation for 'your jacket's on a shaky peg'; if they have, it will no doubt be literal and poetic. By June 2010, the career, tracksuit and coat of French national coach Raymond Domenech hung precariously from one. Thanks to his apparent fondness of horoscopes, Domenech no doubt would have seen it coming.

Unfairly vilified for the performance of his team in 2010, after a disastrous World Cup he was always an easy target and of course, if the media wanted to ridicule him further they threw his interest in horoscopes into the mix. Football, as we know and will continue to repeat, is unforgiving, and, as far as fans, press and media were concerned, he's portrayed as a fruitcake and that's that. This object is here because Domenech will be forever entwined with star signs, even if it isn't necessarily true or accurate. This is football though and *bâtons de merde* – shit sticks. Addressing a press conference like this did not help, 'When I have got a Leo in defence, I have always got my gun ready, as I know he's going to want to show off at one moment or another and cost us.'

While successfully working as a pundit for French TV or on the après-dinner circuit, Domenech cracks jokes and asides about not being public enemy number one after returning from the South African World Cup; he was number two, after Nicolas Sarkozy. His child's first words on his return were to ask if he was going to prison. Raymond Domenech is an off-kilter French coach who was guilty of nothing more than thinking outside the box.

At the World Cup in 2006, barring the odd Zidane headbutt, Domenech and France were unlucky, losing the final to Italy in a penalty shoot-out. France made it to Euro 2008 but failed to get through the first round. His side struggled to South Africa in 2010, controversially qualifying after beating Ireland in extra time in a play-off with Thierry Henry's outrageous handball setting up William Gallas. There was a feeling the Irish had whipped up a hurricane of a million rosaries and novenas to the patron saint of bad karma, which hit Domenech and the French players. The trouble started in the qualification stages but the humiliation continued at the 2010 World Cup. There was more to come. The situation in the French camp reached an astonishing level of idiocy and farce.

We had one of the most shocking chains of events in the history of French football. At half-time during the Mexico match, Nicolas Anelka told Raymond Domenech, 'Go fuck yourself, you son of a whore.' A charming way to speak to your gaffer. Anelka refused to apologise and was sent home. The squad went on strike and, in a mass protest at the FFF's decision to send Anelka packing, refused to train.

It became theatrical with talk of traitors – Patrice Evra fought with fitness coach Robert Duverne and it was Domenech who had to intervene, in front of an audience there to watch the team train. Evra, now appointed shop steward, told the coaching staff the players weren't training because of the way Anelka had been treated. The federation stayed resolute and hit back, saying Anelka's behaviour was unacceptable. Jean-Louis Valentin, the French team director, resigned. Bizarrely, after being cursed at, Domenech looked like he was a hostage with a gun pointed to his head as if forced to read a statement on behalf of the players. 'All the players without exception want to declare their opposition to the decision taken by the FFF to exclude Nicolas Anelka from the squad,' Domenech read. 'At the request of the squad, the player in question attempted to have dialogue but his approach was ignored. The FFF has at no time tried to protect the squad. It has made a decision without consulting all the players, on the basis of the facts reported by the press.'

The players hated Domenech, the fans loathed him, even the then-president of the FFF, Jean-Pierre Escalettes, didn't want him – he wanted Laurent Blanc. As a player, he was no pushover and nicknamed 'the Leg Breaker'. In the 1980s he even sported a moustache that was the very essence of a Colombian drug cartel enforcer.

Sometimes managers don't play by the rules. They don't follow the well-trodden path of clichéd managerial conformity, act the way they are expected to, protect the squad and remain consistently on message.

So to the horoscope issue, and the rumour that Robert Pires wasn't selected because he was a Scorpio. Domenech defended the comment as a flippant remark while admitting that as a bookworm and theatre lover, it was his curiosity and inquisitiveness, an interest in how human nature works. He didn't pick Pires because of his poor form and because he was a divisive influence. He should have kept quiet about his interest in horoscopes but was honest, and it stuck. Immediately he was cast as some mad wizard and the stage was the 2010 World Cup. It's okay for coaches to think about any detail that gives an advantage but horoscopes? This was becoming preposterous.

Domenech had kept his hand in but had not coached seriously since 2010, only taking the Brittany select side from 2016–19. In 2013 he wrote a best-selling book. In the aptly titled *Tout Seoul* – French for *All Alone* – he didn't play the game, and the adage of *what happens in the dressing room stays in the dressing room* was blown to smithereens. He singled out the troublemakers Anelka, Samir Nasri and Franck Ribéry when describing their spoiled, moody and delinquent behaviour. Once the public realised the extent of the players' and the FFF's conduct, their opinion changed significantly. They were also enjoying his work as a pundit and with his book, there is a feeling he has unloaded everything and moved on.

But there was a sting in the tail. Domenech was too idiosyncratic and eccentric, and far too intelligent to deal with players who struggle with a tweet, so forget reading a book. Seldom has one international coach received such disdain and hostility. Promoted from the under-21s, he was not taken seriously by his players or the nation. Do the French have the Pierre Principle? The Peter Principle, when someone is promoted to their own level of incompetence?

While France's under-21s coach, Domenech took some players – including Zinedine Zidane, Claude Makélélé and Lilian Thuram – to see Samuel Beckett's *Endgame* before a crucial match. *Endgame* is a heavy, dark play and Beckett was a lover of the Theatre of the Absurd, which focuses on existentialism and communication breakdowns and the story usually comes back to where it started. How apt. The whole debacle in his final scene as a coach could have come straight out of a Beckett remake called *Endgame: Scorpio*.

In January 2021, Domenech was unexpectedly named coach of Nantes. With Nantes struggling financially, a volatile president and an unrealistic fan base, it was not going to be boring. Domenech failed to win once in seven matches and was out of a job after six weeks, replaced with Antoine Kombouaré.

Object: Old Bicycle
Subject: Stefan Kovács

This rickety bicycle is here to represent Stefan Kovács, the serene, avuncular coach of Ajax. It is most likely you have not heard of him. In the opening scene of *Nummer 14*, the documentary movie about Johan Cruyff, directed by Martin de Vos and produced by Cruyff's father-in-law and agent, Cor Coster, the film shows the top names of the day arriving for work in their 1970s super sexy cars, speeding into the Ajax car park. Ruud Krol, Wim Suurbier, Johan Neeskens, Piet Keizer and Arie Haan get out of their cars. Then we see Kovács arrive on his bicycle, immaculately dressed in a blazer, shirt and tie. More like a charming vicar or civil servant than a top football coach.

The Romanian's appointment was typical Ajax; not the best, but the best of the cheaper candidates. In the history of European football he is spectacularly ignored, yet he guided Ajax to two of their three European Cup victories between 1971 and 1973 and helped in the formation of France's world-renowned national football centre, Clairefontaine.

When Ajax were at their peak and had won their first European Cup, in 1971, Rinus Michels headed for the sun and money of Barcelona. Kovács was then appointed. He was always depicted as a soft touch, an easily manipulated coach out of his depth with a team full of strong-willed, opinionated players, a powerful and tight group, yet he would guide this side to seven trophies in two seasons.

His appointment hardly came with great fanfare; most Dutch football fans were left asking Stefan who? At first, the Ajax players assumed he would be like that woodwork teacher forced to take a maths class who they could take the piss out of. Footballers being footballers, they would take their freedom too far.

Despite winning two Dutch titles, two European Cups, the European Super Cup, the Intercontinental Cup (the forerunner of the World Club Cup) and a KNVB Cup, his managerial approach was continually questioned. Footballers smell weakness. They knew he lacked the authority and the fury of Michels, and would test him. Kovács was nobody's fool and was ready for them. He had guided Steaua Bucharest to a league title and two cup wins before taking up the offer at Ajax. He would laugh off any idea of intimidation and knew how footballers behaved and what he was getting into.

Kovács spell as Ajax manager tends to split the room. Those who suggest that with such a talented dressing room including Cruyff, Haan, Krol and a forever complaining and impatient Johnny Rep, anyone could have coached them to success. The other is that Kovács sensed they were playing with too much rigidity, as if still playing under the strict disciplinarian, Michels. The Romanian encouraged them to relax and stick to the same Total Football system but play without fear and tension and more expression and flair. With the fear factor gone, the players would prove even better. They loved it and he was right.

In 1972, with the league nearly in the bag after beating rivals Feyenoord 5-1, and making the KNVB Final, then making it through to the European Cup Final by beating Benfica 1-0 over two scrappy games, the board wanted to fire him. The excuse was flimsy – the directors were hearing reports from his assistant coach and medical staff of problems with ill discipline. The players, though, with Cruyff's sway and influence, stood by Kovács, threatening to revolt, ironically proving that their ill-discipline was the problem.

Whatever their vices or approach, the players were pragmatic enough to know they were playing the best football they ever had.

People forget that the Ajax who blew the football world away with their style of play was the Kovács side, a team freed from the shackles. The wily Romanian stayed close with Cruyff and allowed him and the rowdy dressing room leeway. As much as they probably thought they were playing him, he was equally playing them. Party time comes with a price. You have to express yourself on the park. Kovács proved the doubters wrong when he won the European Cup for the second time, the club's third consecutive win in the tournament. He had convincing victories over Bayern Munich and Real Madrid along the way to beating Juventus in the final. This run saw Ajax become a real European superpower.

The Romanian didn't have a tough enough nature though and questions were asked about why he stuck with experienced club legend Sjaak Swart instead of Rep, mainly by Rep himself. It was only when Cruyff interceded that Rep would come in. Paradoxically, this level of power would see the team turn on the prince, when Cruyff also fled to the sun and money of Barcelona. Kovács was clever enough to move on before the following coach, George Knobel, struggled with the departure of Cruyff and inherited an Ajax side who thought they were the Stones on tour. Their inappropriate behaviour became too much to handle.

Kovács left to manage France but the move didn't quite click. It wasn't unfruitful though. Along with French Football Federation president Fernand Sastre, Kovács was convinced the country needed an elite academy. Kovács helped set up Clairefontaine, established in 1976 but not opened fully until 1988. Kovács instilled the principles where individual skills were channelled for the collective. Players could be wonderful and creative but only as part of the team. They produced and created stars from Thierry Henry to Kylian Mbappé. Kovács would also have brief spells in club management with Panathinaikos and Monaco. Not bad for a serene, happy chap from Romania on that rickety bicycle.

Object: Moat
Subject: Crocodiles of Romania

For many who love the indie rock oeuvre, *Crocodiles* is a seminal album from 1980 by legendary Liverpool band Echo and the Bunnymen. Such was the behaviour of hooligans in the Romanian fourth division in 2003, that plans were made to deter fans fighting and rioting by creating a moat around the ground and filling it with crocodiles, as you do.

Lowly Steaua Nicolae Balcecu, with an average crowd of 100, were facing expulsion from the league if they didn't sort their fans out. The problem arose after multiple pitch invasions, fights and repeated spates of violence. The local football association for Vâlcea County had warned all clubs to curb their pitch invasions or they would be banned unless they put in place sufficient measures.

The club's owner, local communist vice-mayor Alexander Cringus, had the answer. He had a 'moat', although in reality it was more like a big ditch, built around the perimeter of the pitch. The ditch was far too wide to cross unless you were an Olympic long jumper or expert at the pole vault. To make it more of a challenge, he wanted crocodiles too. 'This is not a joke. We can get crocodiles easily enough and feed them on meat from the local abattoir,' he said. Cut to aghast assembled news media. Cringus continued, 'The ditch is planned to be wide enough that no one could manage to jump over it. Anyone who attempted to do so would have to deal with the crocs. I think the problems of fans running on to the pitch will be solved once and for all.' If you listened carefully enough you could hear the sound of his evil Bond baddie laugh.

The moats were far enough from the playing surface in case the opposition striker dived for a penalty in the rain and couldn't stop and fell into the crocodiles. Oh, and the moats would be fitted with electric pipes to keep the water hot for the crocs in the winter. What could possibly go wrong?

Cringus was in full communist vice-mayor mode when he explained, 'I was in Rimnicu Valcea when I saw a crocodile in a pet shop. I asked how much it cost, and when I found out they are only €470, I went straight to local businesses to sponsor them. As soon as it is warm enough, I will introduce them to the ditches. No fan will be brave enough to jump across the ditch. I don't think we'll have any trouble with pitch invasions now.' Again, cue spoof evil dictator laugh.

Steaua Nicolae Balcecu and their communist vice-mayor owner are certainly a football curiosity. The Romanian media can't get enough of their quirky psychosis. They also have a superfan who is an 83-year-old priest (who is also the village vet – don't ask). He is celebrated across the nation for a speedy mass, especially when his side are playing at home.

The club has no dressing rooms and change in a pub, yes, owned by Cringus. I wonder if it's called The Crocodile's Legs?

Object: Hedge Trimmer
Subject: Brechin Hedge

It sounds lovely and picturesque and Glebe Park, home to Brechin City in Angus, Scotland, genuinely is. But imagine if your team were more famous for its hedge than for football? The pitch is stunning and always immaculate. In the surroundings, a church spire overlooks the main stand. The stadium has been added to over the years, but when it opened in 1919 Brechin had one stand – a portable one, from the Perth agricultural show. When the club joined the Scottish Football League in 1929 a pavilion was erected and the Cemetery End terrace was covered. The old stand was replaced in 1981.

Brechin caused a bit of a stooshie when they received a grant from the Football Trust of £210,000 and, along with funding from the house building company Stewart Milne Group, they constructed a stand – the Trinity Road end of 1,228 seats (later named after the club's chairman for two decades, David H. Will, who was a UEFA Executive Committee member, honorary FIFA vice-president and president of the SFA, and passed away in September 2009). As the stand was so big in comparison to the average Brechin home gate, there was much consternation from non-league clubs in England, who wanted money to fund their grounds as their larger crowds could fill that size of stand easily.

Brechin, over the years, had some brief moments in the spotlight, including a 1973 cup tie against Aberdeen when they were beaten 4-2 with the record crowd of 8,123, but, by and large, they are best known for their wonderful hedge.

At Glebe Park, this hedge covers half of the opposite end from the main stand. In front of that there's a small terracing of two or three steps and behind that runs this beautiful hedge. Anyone with a love of British football stadiums and an Instagram account should make the effort to score it off their must-see stadium list. If possible, make it to a game as it's a lovely ground and has great people.

Some investigative journalism and in-depth espionage took place to confirm unsubstantiated claims that the board were throwing out mouldy bread and charging the birds who nest in the exclusive five-star accommodation, bed and breakfast.

In 2009, though, the BBC reported that Brechin could be forced to extend the width of the pitch, which met SFA rules but not European ones. The playing surface at Glebe Park was three metres short, and it would cost Brechin £100,000 to comply. But, and here's the big but, extending the width of the pitch would mean having to move the hedge.

To gain the licence, clubs have to cover many criteria from facilities, health and safety, equality, fair pricing for fans, finance and coaching. If it was me, I would ask to play at Tannadice or Pittodrie if the side made it to Europe. Aberdeen reserves played their games at Brechin for years. Maybe the club were missing having David Will at the heart of UEFA? Alternatively, they might want to pay £100,000 from a hedge fund.

The hedge was in the news when Rangers played there in 2012. It was their first competitive game back and the Glasgow side brought a colourful and defiant vocal support. Their business and assets were sold to a company called Sevco Scotland and the old club liquidated. Rangers started their trip back after 112 years unbroken in the top league. Their club, in whatever shape or form, was at its lowest point and as always, it was the real fans who showed up. It was a memorable moment when a Dorian Goian clearance ended up on top of the hedge, then had to be shaken down to a bigger cheer from the fans.

Fanorak Fact: Brechin City has a streaming TV service imaginatively called Hedge TV. They were relegated from the Scottish league at the end of the 2020/21 season.

Object: Steam Train
Subject: TJ Tatran Čierny Balog

Imagine the scenario. It's a tough, end-to-end encounter, a pulsating game of football. Suddenly your team break up the park when the referee blows for what you think might be a penalty. You say it *might* be because, at that precise moment, the world in front of you has suddenly turned into a J.M.W. Turner painting. The steam from a locomotive engulfs you, stinging and billowing out, slapping you back to your senses; the noise is a cacophony of pistons and steam power. But what happened? Did the ref give a penalty? Welcome to life as a fan of amateur Slovakian side TJ Tatran Čierny Balog.

It is not uncommon to see football parks surrounded by running tracks but this is the only one in the world that has a railway track running down the stand side. A real rail track, a railway line between the stand and the football pitch. The ground even has a level crossing too.

If I mentioned the words football and trainspotting, you might think of Irvine Welsh's novel based around Leith with Hibs fans. No, no, this is way more tranquil. A closer look at the surrounding area gives you a clue as to the purpose of the railway. It's a heavily forested area with trees everywhere. The narrow-gauge railway was built in the early 1900s to enable the transportation of timber from Čierny Balog to Hronec.

As much as this is the ground of an amateur side, surely when they play in the cup they need an official running the line? When the train passes through, you would pity any match officials when they are asked to work on the stand side and run the risk of getting struck by a locomotive. Though the way some of them officiate, it's probably the least they deserve. If you thought a fourth official holding up a digital board was bad, then try a steam train puffing past you.

It may look quaint but Čierny Balog is a conglomeration of some 13 villages. This line was part of an extensive railway that ran for 132,000km transporting wood up and through Czechoslovakia. The area was also prominent in the Second World War as a centre of the anti-Nazi Slovak National Uprising, and anyone who is anti-fascist is all right in this book.

When you take the time to pore over photographs of the ground while a game is being played, the only wizard flying down the wing is perhaps Harry Potter on the Hogwarts Express. The railway line operated as a passenger service between Čierny Balog and Hronec until 1962. The line itself was closed back in 1982, but train enthusiasts begged for its reopening, and it has subsequently been granted national heritage status.

The railway fanatics also painstakingly helped fix and repair the line, which was officially re-opened in 1992. The heritage railway has become a must for trainspotters who love football. Spectators are known to sit in the stand and applaud and take photos of the train going by and ignore the football. This line is 17km in length and loops between Chvatimech, Hronec, Čierny Balog and Vydrovo.

I have not witnessed anything like this on or near a football pitch. I once played football for a side in Caldercruix, and the game was stopped for an Orange Walk. On another week, a match was stopped because cows ambled on to the pitch, but I have never seen a steam train go down the touchline while playing or watching football.

With each of those beautiful trees being chopped down and tonnes of coal-burning to power the steam engine, why don't they invite Greta Thunberg to come in as an honorary club president?

Object: Mirror

Subject: Mourinho, 'The Special One'

José Mourinho arrived at Chelsea in 2004 and during his introductory press conference gave a quote that would set the narrative for the rest of his managerial career, 'Please do not call me arrogant because what I'm saying is true: I'm a European champion, so I'm not one out of the bottle; I think I'm a special one.'

A translator for many years for Sir Bobby Robson, Mourinho had learned the game from the inside out but he had, ironically, made an error in translation with his metaphors. He was comparing himself to a selection of wines from a wine cellar and trying to say something along the lines of 'I think you have got someone better than the average bottle of wine, this [me] is a special bottle.'

Characteristically, Mourinho turned the minor slip around and revelled in playing the part. As far as football, the media and the press are concerned, though, he was a big head who loved himself. It was arrogant and portrayed an image of his character that the media loved to use.

Starting out, Mourinho had the drive, ambition and attention to detail. He decided to merge the coaching theory with motivation and psychology and it worked. This would see him on an extraordinary journey starting at União de Leiria, Benfica, Porto, Chelsea (twice), Inter Milan, Real Madrid, Manchester United and until April 2021, Tottenham Hotspur. A week after he left Spurs, Roma offered him a three-year deal to take over in time for the 2021/22 season.

At Porto he won two Primeira Liga titles, a Taca de Portugal, the Champions League and UEFA Cup. This earned a move to Chelsea where, over two spells, he won three Premier League titles, the FA Cup, three League Cups and a Community Shield. In his first season at Inter Milan he won the league title and in the second year had a clean sweep, winning his second Serie A title, the Coppa Italia and the Champions League. At Real Madrid, the Special One delivered *Los Blancos'* first La Liga title in eight years and a Copa del Rey.

Mourinho also drew substantially from his looks and the Special One persona with lucrative commercial deals with American Express, Heineken, Jaguar, Adidas and Paddy Power. Then there's his first love, Hublot watches. That said, this exhibit could have featured any watch; José has a penchant for timepieces. When he wins a trophy he removes his watch and places it in a safe box, like a player would with their medals or shirts. The special watch is stored away and he refuses to wear it again (they will eventually go to his wife and kids). Such is his love for watches, he has even designed one for Hublot.

Many have suggested that in recent years he's struggled after only winning the Europa League, League Cup and Charity Shield with Manchester United. Apart from a conceit of himself and a vanity that would leave Dorian Gray embarrassed, José also has one fatal flaw, like one of those special wines; he's also expensive. This also brings added pressure.

In 2020, Spurs sacked Mauricio Pochettino and brought in Mourinho. At the same time, Spurs had invited a film crew in to follow the coaching staff and players. The idea was to capture their true personalities. So they acted differently and didn't train or work on any tactics while the Amazon Prime documentary team were around. As we know, Mourinho was sacked in April 2021, when the European Super League debacle hit peak rage. A low-key exit for a high-profile, glamorous and entertaining appointment. Neither the football nor the players lived up to the Special One's moniker.

Despite his trophy success, Mourinho is close to being remembered more for his severance pay, and the skill of his agent, than his coaching. After his sacking from Spurs, his total pay-offs have accumulated to £80m. He has been sacked by Chelsea, Manchester United and Spurs in the last six years. As former PM Tony Blair is remembered for being a successful property developer, so José is less the Special One and more the Severance One.

Anger Management

Anger is an energy. Competitiveness can often spill over. Sporting superstars can explode and whether we want to admit it or not, we love it, really love it, when they do.

Object: Boots in Glass Case

Subject: Goikoetxea, 'The Butcher of Bilbao'

When we speak of hatchet men, none come close to Athletic Bilbao's notorious Andoni 'Goiko' Goikoetxea. Goikoetxea is the patron saint of hatchet men. He wasn't known as the 'Butcher of Bilbao' because he sold jamón ibérico, chorizo and salami in a Bilbao market. He was a legendary hatchet man who made Ron 'Chopper' Harris, Claudio Gentile and Roy Keane look like the Soggy Bottom Boys. Goikoetxea has a trophy room in his home and pride of place in it is a glass box containing the boots he wore when he broke Diego Maradona's ankle. The tackle occurred in a league game between Barcelona and Athletic Bilbao. In the build-up, both clubs and more specifically the managers provoked each other in the press. Bilbao's Basque coach Javier Clemente figured that Barcelona's Cesar Luis Menotti, the Argentine, was on the wane, a busted flush after winning the World Cup in 1978. By kick-off, the hostility between Basques and Catalans had escalated to the extent that the game itself became a powder keg.

Another intensity-fuelling subplot involved Goikoetxea's previous assault. In 1981/82 he had applied his butchering skills on Barcelona's West German midfielder Bernd Schuster, destroying his anterior cruciate ligament, ruling him out for the season and the 1982 World Cup.

With Schuster out, Barcelona paid a then-world record fee of £5m to bring in Maradona from Boca Juniors. The tackle on Maradona was brutal – from behind, studs up, premeditated and one of the worst ever committed in Spanish football. You immediately sensed that the magnitude and maliciousness of the tackle was greater than football. By injuring Maradona, Goikoetxea was not only killing off part of the beautiful game itself, but it mirrored where Spain as a nation was politically at the time.

The media viewed the tackle on Barcelona's star as an act of Basque terrorism. To many, it was also the end of an era at Barça. At the time, it looked as if Maradona's career was over. We could ask where the referee was and why only a yellow card was issued. Then, referees looked spineless, intimidated by the reputations of those they were officiating. Barça boss Menotti wanted Goikoetxea banned for life. The Spanish FA realised that they had better get off the golf course and deal with the situation, and decided to give Goikoetxea a ten-match ban.

Goikoetxea was part of a legendary defence at Bilbao. They were less a defensive line and more a security detail. Goikoetxea didn't mind the jibes of 'anti-football' or 'football terrorist', he revelled in them. His enforcement brought La Liga titles in 1982/83 and 1983/84 and a Copa del Rey in 1984. The success of the Basques in Spanish football was put down to an unusual set of advantages; being bigger, stronger and don't laugh, it was often said they played so much better in the rain. In a sunny, hot, dry and arid Spain, they revelled and delighted in home games with the rain from the Atlantic.

We should be grateful that Spain and football have moved on from this style of play. The game can occasionally have its moments of violence but the scarcity makes it more enjoyable when the odd brawl flares up. Football should always be honourable, fair and sporting, but on occasions it's prone to exploding into a civil war. For the most part, bitter rivals have always, even during the darkest days, been able to knock the living daylights out of each other on the park yet remain best mates off it.

Object: Head Phones
Subject: Kevin Keegan Would 'Love It'

Picture the scene. It's 29 April 1996; a period in the season perfectly described by Alex Ferguson after Manchester United's race with Arsenal in 2003 as 'squeaky bum time'. The Premier League was having quite a run-in. It was, as they say in the hyperbole adopted by commentators, pundits and scribes alike, 'going down to the wire', well almost. It was until Newcastle's challenge hit the buffers. These were the classic Premier League days and a season in which the team leading capitulated and the team chasing them down had the power, goals and mind games to catch up and in the end, would win the title by four points.

The Toon Army had a former Liverpool legend at the helm who played football with abandon, and his teams played with an all-out attacking style, scoring goals. Unfortunately, the defence leaked like a Frank Lloyd Wright roof (the legendary architect pushed the envelope but few of his architectural masterpieces remained habitable with leaking roofs). Kevin Keegan, like Lloyd Wright, knew that being creative engendered risk. Initially, the approach was starting to work. Keegan attacked, kept it simple, played players in their natural positions and everyone worked hard. With players like Les Ferdinand, Peter Beardsley, David Ginola and Keith Gillespie, it looked like it could happen. The two wingers and the playmaker gave the striker the ammunition.

Keegan had Newcastle on the march with nine wins from the first ten games of the season. By January they were 12 points clear. Before we knew it, they had won 20 matches from 26. The Toon was buzzing, the football he played had galvanised both the north-east and the country, and those watching the drama slowly unfold on TV were loving it too, absolutely loving it. Context again is everything: a few years previously, Newcastle were languishing at the bottom of the second tier of English football and were now at the summit of the top level. It was a remarkable turnaround. This was Newcastle's first serious title challenge since the days of Hughie Gallacher captaining the side to the First Division championship in 1926/27 with 36 goals in 38 league games.

The often highlighted 12-point advantage Newcastle had was brief, but it looked like Keegan's side were coasting to the title race. Alex Ferguson's Manchester United, though, were experienced; they knew if they were in the running after Christmas they could chase down any lost cause.

United had begun 1995 with Eric Cantona's infamous incident at Selhurst Park. When the 1995/96 season started, Cantona was still suspended. Ferguson had offloaded some big names in Mark Hughes, Paul Ince and Andrei Kanchelskis. Cue the Alan Hansen line, used after that season's opening fixture defeat to Aston Villa, about 'winning nothing with kids'. By October, Cantona was back but by December he was most certainly back. Ferguson kept pushing his side, telling his players the Newcastle side were vulnerable and would crumble. United had their 'kids' from the class of '92 but they also had Steve Bruce, Roy Keane, Denis Irwin, Gary Pallister, Peter Schmeichel and the mercurial Frenchman.

In February, over two games in a week, a Wednesday and Saturday, Newcastle lost 2-0 to West Ham then drew 3-3 with Manchester City. Manchester United walloped Bolton 6-0 to narrow the gap. Yet Newcastle still had that game in hand. Then the two sides faced each other, and, in keeping with the hectic and chaotic nature of the season, it was Newcastle who bossed the first half, and Schmeichel was the star. In the second half, after an undoubted bollocking and turbo-boosted hairdryer treatment, a much improved Manchester United showed up. They won it with a Cantona goal in the 52nd minute. Cantona was pivotal to the title race, scoring nine goals in ten games between the end of January and April. Six of his goals were the only ones scored in the game, yielding five wins and a last-minute draw.

Keegan was always the type of player who showed his true colours. He was an emotional man. Football likes that. What you see is what you get, everyone loved him as a player apart from the odd Leeds United player, in the 1970s. Ferguson knew that with some perfectly chosen post-match comments, he could get to him. Ferguson (before the knighthood for services to winding up fellow managers) directed his attention to Keegan, using the cut and thrust of the post-match interview to play mind games, and it worked.

United had played Leeds, beating them 1-0, when Ferguson commented, 'For some, it's more important to get a result against Manchester United to stop us winning the league than anything else, which to me, they're cheating their manager. That's all it is. Of course, when they come to Newcastle, you wait to see the difference.' Ferguson's deployment of psychological warfare and trying to unnerve and get inside the mind of his rivals was perfectly timed by suggesting that Leeds, Newcastle's next opponents, would lie down and not try as hard as they did when they faced his side. Ferguson also referred to Newcastle's penultimate game of the title race. They were facing Forest, their game in hand on Thursday, when also playing a testimonial game for Stuart Pearce five days after the season was over. The subtle inference was Newcastle would have an easier game from Forest.

Then, in one of the most memorable outbursts on Sky Sports, Keegan flipped. Newcastle beat Leeds 1-0 and

Keegan, wearing his big headphones, was doing his post-match interview. He was happy with the result, appeared upbeat, then began to slowly unravel. When you listen to Keegan's rant, it is the moment he speaks about Pearce (and Ferguson's dig about the testimonial) that he loses it.

Livid at Ferguson's suggestion Leeds and Forest wouldn't try as hard against Newcastle, he snapped and his emotional side came out. His voice was starting to crack and break as he let rip, 'No, no; when you do that with footballers like he said about Leeds, and when you do things like that about a man like Stuart Pearce, I have kept really quiet, but I'll tell you something, he went down in my estimation when he said that.' By then Keegan had clearly had enough and wouldn't cower to Ferguson like most did, so he kept going, 'We have not resorted to that but I'll tell you, you can tell him now if you're watching it, we're still fighting for this title, and he's got to go to Middlesbrough and get something, and ... and ... I'll tell you, honestly, I will love it if we beat them, love it!'

Keegan had vented his spleen but he had revealed a weakness; he had allowed Ferguson to get inside his mind.

On the day before the rant, Manchester United had hammered Forest 5-0. Newcastle still had Forest and Spurs to play. United had to face Middlesbrough, where a win would confirm them as champions. Newcastle could only draw both of their games, and United beat Middlesbrough 3-0 to win the title.

Object: Crash Helmet
Subject: Zidane's Headbutt on Materazzi

The moment Zinedine Zidane headbutted Italy's Marco Materazzi, in Berlin's Olympic Stadium in the final minutes of the FIFA 2006 World Cup Final, you immediately knew that was it. His playing career ended there. It was over.

Not only had Zidane dragged his side to the competition, but once there he drove them to the final. The French team had struggled to reach the tournament, with their coach Raymond Domenech under pressure. His side looked disinterested, except for Zidane, Lilian Thuram and Claude Makélélé, who had decided to come out of retirement to aid their country.

By the final, it was looking like a perfect career-ending fairy tale. Zidane had ten minutes left on the pitch. This would be his final game and that was that. France had reached the final with too many unconvincing performances.

Materazzi had an eventful game. He brought down Florent Malouda in the box and conceded a penalty to France. Skipper Zidane scored from the spot with a prodigious Panenka-style effort, proving at that point at least, he was able to stay cool under pressure. Materazzi then scored the equaliser. The game went into extra time at 1-1 and there for the taking. Then in a moment of madness, Zidane headbutted Materazzi in the chest and was shown the red card by the referee, Horacio Elizondo. Italy won the tournament in the penalty shoot-out.

Italy's coach, Marcello Lippi, had managed the star at Juventus, so knew his temperament was suspect and ordered Materazzi to mark him. The incident itself became one of the most controversial moments in World Cup history as it appeared to explode out of the blue. Most people were following the game and didn't see anything. There was confusion, noise, then silence, a strange moment of tension – had someone collapsed on the pitch? Then came whistles and boos from those in the stadium. The noise most fans dread; was it an off-the-ball incident or had someone run on to the pitch? Italy goalkeeper Gianluigi Buffon saw something and he was complaining and running to the fourth official. For this tournament the fifth official had a TV monitor but was not permitted to intervene, although the fourth official witnessed the incident and informed the referee who, to make sure, watched the replay.

When the rest of the Italian side noticed Buffon fuming they joined in. They didn't know what had happened, that was just a side issue, they wanted in on the action to influence the officials. At first, everyone thought it was Trezeguet. The cameras focused on him and the crowd were hostile; something had clearly happened. Materazzi was on the ground, had he been punched? The match commentators were confused. Millions around the world were waiting for a replay to see what happened.

It had looked to the casual observer like two players closing out a game with some verbals, both knowing their fates looked certain to be sealed from the penalty spot. Bang. Suddenly, everything was chaotic. One action flipped the game on its head. Materazzi had his arms around Zidane, the way players do when marking someone at a corner. Then he pulled at Zidane's shirt, there were more verbals between them as play moved up the field, then came the headbutt.

It's so memorable because you realise that as soon as the red card is brandished, Zidane's football career is over. It wasn't meant to end this way.

Before the end of the 2006 season, the Real Madrid star had announced he was retiring. It was over for him, 'I have to listen to my body and I cannot carry on for another year. I think it is better to clarify the situation now. I have been thinking about it for a long time. It's been three years since we won anything and in two of those, I have not played as I have wanted. I am not going to play any better than I have done in the past. I don't want to just play for Real Madrid for the sake of it.'

Keen-eyed fans were remembering Materazzi when he was on loan at Everton and managed to get three red cards in 27 games. He was usually the one being sent off, so he knew how to play it. The rumours and comments at the time always alluded to Materazzi insulting Zidane's mother. However, in 2020 on an Instagram Live Q&A a fan asked him what he had said about Zidane's mother. Materazzi was candid; he didn't insult his mother as having lost his own when he was young he wouldn't have done that. No, he was gallant. He had instead insulted Zidane's sister, 'I wasn't expecting it at that moment. I was lucky enough that the whole episode took me by surprise because if I had expected something like that to happen and had been ready for it, I'm sure both of us would have ended up being sent off.'

The player's version was that Zidane acted like he was the big shot superstar while Materazzi did his job, marking him. Materazzi said, 'There had been a bit of contact between us in the area. He had scored France's goal in the first half and our coach [Marcello Lippi] told me to mark him. After that first brush between us, I apologised but he reacted badly.' The Italian continued, going into detail, 'The late tackles, altercations and exchanges continued until 110 minutes, when things came to a head. After the third clash, I frowned and he retorted, "I'll give you my shirt later." I replied that I'd rather have his sister than his shirt.'

Big Zizou lost it, and so did France. Trezeguet missed his penalty and Italy were world champions. Game over.

Object: Spittoon
Subject: Rijkaard Gobbing at Völler

The beautiful game at times can be like a wonderful overture, a magnificent piece of art, an existential experience; then in an instant it can be tarnished and scarred and transformed into one of those distorted plastic surgery disaster faces.

This event unfolded in Milan's San Siro, in the exhausting and draining heat of Italia '90. The Netherlands were facing West Germany in the last 16 of the World Cup when Dutch player Frank Rijkaard twice spat at West German striker Rudi Völler.

The Dutch and Germans don't get on. Wars, defeat in World Cup Finals; the rivalry can, at times, be fierce and tetchy. This match always felt like it could boil over. Football fans have a strange relationship with spitting. Such is the warped and twisted logic that a scathing tackle from behind or an elbow to the face, though nasty, are more acceptable. Even a blatant old-fashioned punch, if merited, will be forgiven, but any pro who spits on someone – football doesn't like that.

Spitting or gobbing or howking up and launching at a fellow pro is despicable. To do so is beyond the pale. It is up there with heinously attempting to con the ref and blatantly diving for a penalty in the box. To some, spitting is even worse than feigning injury and cheating and having an opponent sent off.

Rijkaard may have done the spitting but West Germany won the game and eventually the World Cup. West Germany romped into the tie, winning their three group games. In contrast, the Netherlands were struggling and only scraped through on three points after three draws. Their group, which also included England, the Republic of Ireland and Egypt, became the tightest in World Cup history. After the first two rounds of fixtures had all been drawn, the four sides had each scored and conceded one goal. Nothing could separate them as they played their final group game.

Against the Netherlands, Ireland played to their strengths and launched it to the big lad up front, while the football aristocrats continued to look as though they hadn't woken up in the competition yet. When told England were beating Egypt 1-0, they played out a 1-1 draw, edging out Egypt. All three teams progressed; the Netherlands would face West Germany.

When Völler broke, Rijkaard hacked down the German and was booked. It was his second of the competition so he knew he would be out if the Dutch reached the quarter-final. This affected him, and as Rijkaard ran past Völler to pick him up for the incoming free kick, he spat at the front man. Völler complained to the referee but for some reason he was booked. When the resulting free kick came in, Völler appeared to handle the ball and then went down, too lightly in Rijkaard's opinion, as the defender and his team-mates thought he was cheating and looking for a penalty.

Later, Völler claimed he went down to avoid injuring the Dutch keeper Hans van Breukelen. Rijkaard by now was trampling on Völler's ankle and twisting at his ear. The referee, Argentina's Juan Carlos Loustau, then decided it was time to show how useless he was and, fearing it might escalate into a barney, red-carded them both and sent them to bed with no supper. As he was running off, Rijkaard spat again at Völler, leaving the German looking crestfallen as he trudged away with the spit dangling from his hair.

Those in the game rallied around the Dutchman and said it was out of character. His coaches, team-mates and those close to him didn't expect him to do that. The decision to spit was an awful move, one he immediately regretted and apologised for after the game. Völler accepted Rijkaard's apology. They would later do a commercial together and gave their fee to charity.

With Ajax, Rijkaard won the Dutch league five times, the Dutch Cup three times, the European Cup Winners' Cup and the Champions League. At Milan he played in a side with Costacurta, Baresi, Gullit and van Basten. He won two Serie A titles, and the European Cup twice. He scored the winner in the European Cup Final in 1990 against Benfica. At international level, he won the European Championship in 1988. As a coach at Barcelona he won two La Liga titles and the Champions League. But the wider football community rarely forgets. No matter what he thought of Völler's ridiculous perm, a full phlegm barrel volley at the German was unforgivable and his wonderful career as a player and a manager will forever be defined by that moment.

Object: Boot

Subject: David Beckham's Cut Face

Sir Alex Ferguson was clearly at the end of his tether with David Beckham, and it all kicked off with a massive dressing room bust-up in February 2003 after Arsenal beat Manchester United 2-0 in the fifth round of the FA Cup.

In the game itself, United were up against an Arsenal side that had Thierry Henry and Dennis Bergkamp on the bench yet still they struggled against the Gunners. Beckham committed the cardinal sin, in Ferguson's eyes at least, of ball-watching and not trailing back when Edu set up Sylvain Wiltord for Arsenal's second.

Beckham knew this was Ferguson deliberately trying to undermine him and make him the scapegoat. As far as Beckham was concerned, he had a decent game. He was nowhere near the worst player on display. Ryan Giggs had missed an easy chance, Roy Keane, Paul Scholes and Nicky Butt were booked yet it was Beckham who Sir Alex furiously launched into. But Beckham had enough and stood his ground.

In the heated post-match fracas, Sir Alex kicked a row of boots in the dressing room and one clattered the then-England captain above his left eye.

Ferguson accused Beckham of slacking and of taking his foot off the gas. He said that Beckham thought he was a superstar and believed the player's form had dipped and he wasn't giving enough to his team-mates. Beckham had been linked with a move from United and Ferguson sensed his chance. He knew the player's power and popularity in the dressing room could easily undermine him. For Alex

Ferguson, as soon as a player threatened your authority in front of the team, you were done.

It did not help that Beckham was married to Victoria Adams of the Spice Girls, who Ferguson thought was turning his head. The press and media surrounding them both was too high profile for the boss. Even the player's management were too powerful and showbiz for Sir Alex. The boot incident set off a combination of events that would see Beckham end up in Madrid.

Ferguson knew Beckham was becoming too big for Manchester United. He liked to know everything his players were doing. Beckham didn't let him know he was flying out to Ireland to see Posh. He arrived home early enough to make training but Ferguson had spies everywhere.

On another occasion, Beckham showed up for a training team meal and pre-match warm-up wearing a beanie hat to hide a shaved head. At that point, Ferguson knew he had lost the player to another level of fame and showbiz and Beckham knew he had driven another wedge between himself and his mentor. Beckham was unceremoniously benched but figured it was no more than a brief falling-out. He would accept being removed from the team by the gaffer to teach him a lesson, but then Ole Gunnar Solskjaer replaced him.

Beckham was shocked when he was sold to Real Madrid in a £24.5m deal. So shocked and hurt that he could not watch United on TV for three years. He was made an example of. In 2007, Beckham raised a few eyebrows, even the one he had split by Sir Alex, when he left Madrid for LA Galaxy. Many questioned if it was too early in his career to scale down to play 'soccer' in the States. His two loan spells during this period at AC Milan, then PSG, proved he may have thought so too. Of course, at the time, Beckham could also see what sort of deal his agents had arranged with the Los Angeles side, who were willing to pay £128m for a five-year deal. The moral of the story is that in his time as manager of Manchester United, no one was bigger than Sir Alex Ferguson. As soon as any player acted like they were, they were sold or moved out.

Object: Stretcher

Subject: Schumacher's
Assault on Battiston

Schumacher's Hip may sound like a constellation in the night sky, only visible around December with a powerful telescope, but in this case it refers to the scathing assault by West German goalkeeper Harald Anton 'Toni' Schumacher on French midfielder Patrick Battiston. We love football but the beautiful game has a brutal side. It can, for example, veer off unexpectedly and, in the blinking of an eye, go from slick and skilful football to brutal, career-ending tackles. This game was an attacking, exciting, end-to-end World Cup semi-final that served up six goals, went into extra time, and was decided in a penalty shoot-out (the first in the history of the finals). This was one of the finest matches in World Cup history. Sadly, it has been overshadowed by Schumacher's challenge on Battiston.

It is also one of the greatest misnomers as people keep referring to the incident as a foul. It wasn't a foul as the referee didn't give one. This particular tackle, masquerading as an assault, occurred at Sevilla's Estadio Ramón Sánchez-Pizjuán on 8 July 1982, with the game tied at 1-1. Battiston had been on the park for ten minutes after replacing Bernard Genghini, and was full of energy. He was found with a perfect pass from French skipper Michel Platini. Battiston was through and only had the oncoming Schumacher to beat. The ball was sitting up perfectly for Battiston, at which point he was poleaxed and wiped out clean by Schumacher.

This was more befitting of a street brawl attack. Pure and simple. If this happened in any street in Europe, the assailant would be charged. This was no accident but a deliberate leap and twist for maximum effect, with his hip, at a player following the ball, and running at speed. It was cowardly. Battiston was left with cracked ribs, damaged vertebrae, three of his teeth broken and looked like he'd been hit by a train. He was left unconscious but the most alarming moment and my strongest memory of the attack was how his lifeless arm hung from the stretcher. He looked as though he was dead. At the hospital, he was drifting in and out of a coma.

Anyone with a basic grounding of the rules of association football could see this was a red card, even allowing for the leniency and levity granted to most goalkeepers. But the experienced Dutch referee Charles Corver missed the incident as he was following the ball. He asked Scottish linesman Bob Valentine if he saw anything and, as is the tradition of Scottish refereeing, he saw nothing. Schumacher remained on the pitch, no foul was awarded, and a goal kick was given to West Germany. The sporting gods have a bewildering rational and a propensity to obliterate fair play to another level; Schumacher saved two in the penalty shoot-out with West Germany making it to the final.

Most fans accept players are human and would hope the offender would be contrite and seek forgiveness, showing some concern for the player. Not Schumacher, and when asked how he felt about Battiston, he sarcastically suggested he would pay for his dental bill.

It turned out the big bad monster had a heart after all. As time passed, Schumacher revealed his bemusement and nonchalance immediately after the challenge was an act, and one of cowardice, as he had feared it would be far worse for Battiston and was afraid to visit him in hospital in case he was in a coma. His ruthless appearance was an effort to stay in the zone. They did meet up soon after the tournament.

In 2007, on an official UEFA World Cup video, Schumacher said, 'When he was lying there I knew he was injured. When he was stretchered off, I knew it was something serious … The most important thing for me was I got the chance to apologise to Patrick. It doesn't matter what people or the media say, Patrick accepted my apology. I'm just happy we put the incident behind us.'

Even now, the challenge is still uncomfortable to watch – brutal, unpleasant and unsporting. It highlights several issues; the cold, harsh level of professionalism even in a World Cup semi-final and why wasn't mandatory drug testing available – for the referee and his assistants? What were they on?

Fanorak Fact: The World Cup's first penalty shoot-out had occurred in January 1977 in the first round of African qualifying, between Tunisia and Morocco.

Object: Fireworks

Subject: The Madness of Balotelli

In Italy, wild rocket is called Rucola Selvatica. It might also be the most apt description of the bizarre, unpredictable and wayward Mario Balotelli.

'Why always me?' was the question emblazoned across his compression vest under the Manchester City strip after he scored the opening goal in a 6-1 win against Manchester United in the derby. Why always you? Because you have lit fireworks indoors to see what would happen because you're a total and complete rocket (he got booked for that, too; not the fireworks, lifting his shirt over his head).

Let's have a quick look over a showreel of Mario's highlights. For example, the time when all hell broke loose during training after he fought with his manager at Manchester City. Roberto Mancini repeatedly warned him about the way he was tackling his team-mates. When Balotelli disregarded the instruction and went through Scott Sinclair, Mancini lost it and ordered him off the park. Balotelli refused and chaos ensued. By ignoring his manager, he was undermining him, not only in front of team-mates and staff but the fans who were able to watch the team training every day.

During a pre-season friendly against LA Galaxy in 2011, Balotelli decided to perform for the crowd, with some showboating by pirouetting and back-flicking the ball into the goal. He missed the target by another galaxy. Football turned on him, fans booed, commentators became hysterical and Mancini yanked him off. Further chaos ensued. Why always me?

Balotelli was only two weeks in at Manchester City when he was stopped by the police after he crashed his car near to City's former training ground at Carrington. The police asked why he was carrying £5,000 in cash and Mario responded, not with the arrogance of a footballer but the innocence of a child, 'Because I am rich.' Mancini was not alone in struggling to deal with the mentality and nature of Balotelli. José Mourinho and Brendan Rodgers struggled too.

When he started out at Inter Milan under Mourinho, there were many occasions when José lost it with him. The coach had arranged a meeting with Balotelli at 2pm. Instead, he chose to take in the Italian Grand Prix at Monza. When Mourinho called him and asked where he was, Balotelli told him, quite calmly, that he can come to his office any day but the Grand Prix was only on once a year. Mourinho laughs it off now. He says he could write a 200-page book about Mario but it wouldn't be a drama, it would be a comedy. Footballers, eh?

On one such occasion, before a huge Milan derby, he appeared on a popular satirical TV show wearing an AC Milan shirt. Mario thought the cameras were off. They weren't. Why always me?

The Inter fans were not too enamoured and he was promptly sold to Manchester City for £19m.

It's interesting that once they had moved him on or the managers had changed, they speak fondly of the player. It's clear he was kind-hearted, familiar to those in need, for example going around Manchester giving money to homeless people. Mancini is on record as going as far as to describe Mario as one of his children and someone he loved. He did, however, say that as he sanctioned a move to AC Milan.

During a short spell at Liverpool in the 2014/15 season he struggled, because he slowed the side's play down. Rodgers described his move as a gamble yet he too speaks fondly of Balotelli despite his wayward behaviour.

He was and still is a character, a bona fide star. When he was focused, fit and on it, Balotelli was one of the best but when he wasn't in the mood, forget it. Who remembers the game against Norwich for Manchester City, when he scored a goal by volleying the ball in with his shoulder?

Then there was that glorious goal against Germany when he scored for Italy in Euro 2012 only to reveal his torso for the world to see. Super Mario.

Moving to Nice in 2016, he signed a year-to-year contract, in and out of form, and in two and a half seasons, in 61 league appearances he scored 33 goals. It was enough to earn an international recall, yet after three seasons, returning late, out of shape and incurring the wrath of Patrick Vieira, his contract was terminated. He was released during the winter transfer window of 2018/19 and moved to Marseille.

Memorable moments playing for Marseille? Yes, there was that time after a spectacular overhead kick against Saint-Étienne when he had his phone sitting at the sidelines and picked it up and took a team selfie and posted the footage live on Instagram.

Balotelli appeared to finally find some solace playing for his hometown club, Serie A side Brescia. In December 2020, Balotelli signed a seven-month contract for ambitious Serie B club Monza. In July 2021, he signed for newly promoted Turkish side Adana Demispor.

SAN MAMES

Memorial to Athletic Bilbao striker Rafael 'Pichichi' Moreno Aranzadi (1892–1922). Since the 1950s, the Spanish sports newspaper Marca *has awarded the Trofeo Pichichi to the top goalscorer in La Liga.*

FC Barcelona's Lionel Messi and his father Jorge, accused of defrauding the Spanish Tax Agency of €4.1m by using tax havens to conceal image rights earnings.

Porto's long-serving president Jorge Nuno Pinto da Costa, who the fans nicknamed 'The Pope', was embroiled in the damning Apito Dourado (Golden Whistle) investigation into bribery of match officials.

Matthias Sindelar, the Austrian superstar, part of the Wunderteam, 'The Mozart of Football' refused to play for Germany and belittled Nazi high command in a reunification game.

The French side captained by Alexandre Villaplane (back row, far right) at France's first World Cup in Uruguay, 1930. His fall from grace was one of the most shocking in European football history.

Luigi 'Gigi' Meroni, the Italian George Best, in Turin, 1967.

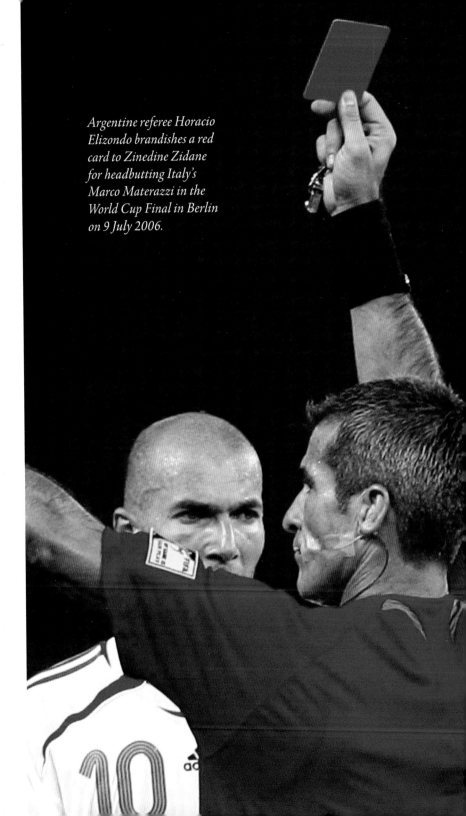

Argentine referee Horacio Elizondo brandishes a red card to Zinedine Zidane for headbutting Italy's Marco Materazzi in the World Cup Final in Berlin on 9 July 2006.

Roy Keane sprints to help team-mate Eric Cantona before he infamously kicks a Crystal Palace fan in January 1995.

Perugia's colourful president Luciano Gaucci presents Al Saadi Gaddafi, son of Muammar Gaddafi to the press, in 2003. Gaucci's friend Silvio Berlusconi hinted it would 'help repair relations' with Libya.

Lazio's Luciano Re Cecconi signs autographs at the World Cup in 1974; l'Angelo Biondo, the Blond Angel, would die tragically in January 1977.

Günter Netzer, West German superstar of the 1970s, one of the first German players to cultivate a playboy image. A maverick on and off the field, he loved Ferraris and opened a nightclub, called 'Lovers Lane'.

Robin Friday with Cardiff City's manager Jimmy Andrews. The striker left Reading to sign in December 1976.

Object: German Top
Subject: Koeman Wipes Bum with Thon's Jersey

The Dutch and Germans have always enjoyed a bit of banter back and forth. It would be fair to say they have some previous. This might be best typified by Dutch manager Rinus Michels's comment after the Dutch won Euro '88, held in West Germany, 'We won the tournament but we all know the semi-final was the real final.' The Dutch won the semi-final 2-1, a game when one of their players used an opponent's jersey as a sanitary wipe.

Though quite what Ronald Koeman thought he was doing when he faked an arse wipe with a West German shirt he'd exchanged with Olaf Thon is anyone's guess. You're supposed to wash them and have them framed. Such diplomatic incidents can rapidly escalate to a response of fighter jets and aircraft carriers and lead to World War Three.

Koeman himself is something of a contradiction; big, powerful and robust yet the epitome of the modern Dutch player while being versatile, equally comfortable in defence or in midfield and often playing as a sweeper. His scoring ratio wherever he played was high, down to power and accuracy from long range, as well as taking free kicks and penalties.

By the time of this semi-final, with thousands who made it over the border on 26 June, the match had been hyped to fever pitch. An unprecedented TV audience of more than ten million (the Dutch population is 17.2 million) watched the encounter.

Koeman sprayed passes to Ruud Gullit and Marco van Basten; he was the engine room in an amazing performance.

Perhaps he was giddy. After the Dutch had conceded to a Lothar Matthäus penalty in the 55th minute, it was Koeman himself who scored the equaliser from the spot. The huge scoreboard told the story, 'Torscutze in der 74 Minute Ronald Koeman.' It was all square. When Wouters played a low pass into the box, Marco van Basten stretched to score a dramatic winner in the 89th minute.

The modern West German players had grown up ashamed, trying to forget and hoping they would be forgiven for the war, yet many Dutch players still refused, hating their opponents. Apart from the war, there was an absolute annihilation in October 1959 when West Germany destroyed their neighbours 7-0 in Cologne thanks to a wonderful performance from hat-trick hero Uwe Seeler. And there was 1974 when the world tuned in to see the Dutch and Total Football, with Cruyff, Rep, Neeskens et al, take a lap of honour thinking they had won the World Cup – only to find they were up against one of the best strikers who ever lived in the shape of Gerd Müller.

On 15 August 2021, Bayern Munich announced the death of Gerd Müller, a player who Rinus Michels wanted to sign before Cruyff, at Barcelona.

This dirty West German shirt would have to remain in Koeman's bag until after the final, which the Dutch eventually won. Koeman was caught up in the moment and was over-exuberant in his celebrations. However, he had performed brilliantly to beat the hosts.

For most, such ribald behaviour could be the sort of incident that could kill a career stone dead. Koeman moved on to an extraordinary playing and coaching journey and played for Barcelona between 1989 and 1995, scoring their winner in the 1992 European Cup Final at Wembley. He would be appointed as the club's manager in 2020, replacing Quique Setién who was sacked after a humiliating 8-2 demolition by Bayern Munich in the Champions League.

As a coach, Koeman served his time as an assistant to the Dutch national team. His first managerial position was at Vitesse Arnhem, then Ajax, where he won two Eredivisie titles. He was less successful at Benfica and then PSV Eindhoven before winning the Copa del Rey in Spain with Valencia. Back home, he had a horrendous time at AZ Alkmaar, losing seven of the first 16 league games. Then he was at Feyenoord for three years before coming to the Premier League with Southampton, where he found success by taking the side to sixth in 2015/16. He then moved to Everton but was sacked after a disastrous year. Then came the stint as the national boss for the Netherlands, where he guided the team to the Euros. The jury is out over the move to Barça, but we can only assume 'he interviews well' as his managerial record points to someone players don't always buy into. How soon will he be wiping his backside with Messi's shirt? The player is keen to go elsewhere to get away from Koeman.

In August 2021, Barcelona announced that due to financial difficulty they couldn't afford to keep Messi. La Liga had also imposed a salary cap. In an emotional press conference, Messi bid a tearful farewell, thanking the club and fans he'd served for 21 years. Within 48 hours it was confirmed he was moving to PSG, in a two-year deal with an extra one-year option. Thankfully the side are bankrolled by the state of Qatar and able to afford the rumoured £29.6m salary.

Object: Kung Fu Suit
Subject: Eric Cantona

Eric Cantona scored 82 times for Manchester United, winning the Premier League four times and the FA Cup twice. However, leap over the advertising hoardings and attack an abusive, racist Crystal Palace fan, and for some reason that's all they remember.

On 25 January 1995 at Selhurst Park, football was abruptly rocked off its axis when Cantona jumped into the crowd and attacked a supporter. The image was broadcast and beamed around the globe. Photos existed. It did happen. It was so unbelievable that we needed proof and confirmation that someone hadn't put something in the half-time Bovril. Did we just witness that? There was a surreal realisation seconds after it happened; you knew you were watching one of the most notorious moments in Premier League history.

When Cantona kung fu kicked (and don't forget the amazing right hook) the supporter, that moment, like José Mourinho's 'Special One' press conference, defined his career, personality, mercurial nature and his life. The event occurred after Cantona was red-carded for going through Crystal Palace defender Richard Shaw. Cantona was incensed at the number of heavy, unchecked tackles by Shaw and Chris Coleman on both he and Andy Cole, which he felt were ignored by the referee.

Barely into the second half, Cantona snapped and retaliated. As he left the pitch, the Frenchman was insulted by a quip, some witty repartee, questioning a return to his country of birth and his parentage, the usual racist diatribe. Matthew Simmons had run from a seat 11 rows back to jovially share the rejoinder, 'Fuck off back to France, you French motherfucker,' no doubt assuming the stewards and the hoardings would be enough of a barrier to protect him. They usually were, but not tonight, Josephine.

When Cantona signed from Leeds United for £1.2m in 1992, everyone knew he came with baggage and the reputation of a troublemaker and, as such, was a gamble for Alex Ferguson's side. This was a high-risk move, yet Ferguson believed he would be able to handle the Frenchman, not by affecting his mentality but by understanding his nature and managing to get the best out of him. Or so he thought.

After the assault on the fan, who Cantona always called 'the hooligan', United moved quickly and decided to suspend him for the remaining four months of the season. The FA intervened, extending the ban to the end of September. Then criminal charges were brought against Cantona, who received two weeks in jail, reduced to 120 days of community service. He was also fined the maximum two weeks' wages, totalling £10,800.

Eric's trawler, that of the seagulls following it, came when he was in a press conference. 'When the seagulls follow the trawler, it is because they think sardines will be thrown into the sea.' This quote occurred during Eric's fishy philosopher's press conference, held after he won his appeal against a two-week prison sentence. He would now spend his community service teaching kids in Manchester how to play football and defend themselves with kung fu kicks against abusive racist idiots.

The newspapers hardly mentioned the game, only Cantona's assault. United dropped two points despite David May scoring his first goal for them as Gareth Southgate scored the equaliser for Palace. The aftermath was predictable. *The Sun* kept it blunt with 'YOU THUG' plastered across their front page, while the *Daily Mail* chose 'THE SHAMING OF SOCCER'. *The Mirror* squealed, 'THE NIGHT FOOTBALL DIED OF SHAME', with a back-page headline, 'IS THIS THE END FOR THE MADMAN?'

When Alex Ferguson grew perplexed and frustrated over the whole debacle, it was his wife Cathy who rallied her husband, 'It's not like you to give up so easily, particularly against the establishment.' She encouraged him to follow his instincts and he made a secret dash to Paris, had a restaurant close for the evening and pleaded with Cantona to stay. Mercifully, he returned. These days Cantona would be held up as a hero, an advocate of kicking racism out of the game, though maybe not so literally. Speaking about the attack years later, Cantona considered it his best moment in football. He seems to have processed and applied his idiosyncratic logic to it. 'When I did the Kung Fu kick on the hooligan, because these kind of people don't have to be at the game, it's like a dream for some, you know, sometimes to kick these kinds of people. So I did it for them.'

Maybe the final word should go to a fuming Ferguson, who claimed the coverage was wall-to-wall over the ensuing 48 hours and that there were 93 showings of the kick. You can imagine his nose getting redder as he counted every news channel and Sky Sports News clip as he shouted, 'That's more repeats than the films of the JFK shooting.'

Object: Munch's *The Scream*

Subject: Bayern's Unfriendly Farewell to Cruyff

When Dutch superstar Johan Cruyff shocked the football world by announcing he was retiring from the game aged 31, his previous club Ajax organised a farewell game and a chance for the club's fans to show up and say thanks to a player they produced and developed from the age of ten, who became one of the best footballers to ever live.

The match took place on 7 November 1978 against the mighty West German behemoths, Bayern Munich. It was held at the Olympic Stadium in Amsterdam, to allow 55,000 fans to say goodbye to Johan. Love was in the air. Bouquets were handed out, while happiness, appreciation and goodwill overflowed in an emotional tsunami of gratitude. It had started so well. By the end, missiles, cushions, parts of chairs and anything fans could get their hands on rained down on the players.

Instead of employing testimonial rules and showing off with some fancy flicks, entertaining passes and superb goals, Bayern had their game face on as if competing in a European Cup Final. That wasn't quite cricket, was it? Where was their sense of fun? They hammered Cruyff's Ajax team 8-0. The result proved the club's worst score since 1913. What a way to see off a legend.

The Ajax players were relaxed and had a game plan; every time one of them received the ball they would give it to Johan and let him do his stuff. They were expecting a high-scoring, entertaining draw and were angry at Bayern behaving so disrespectfully, for wanting to win. After the game, in the dressing room, Ajax players were angered at the behaviour of their opponents, with some needing to be held back. Bayern had discarded the long-held etiquette of the farewell match or testimonial, which decreed that the star of the evening have their moment and go out with a delightful memory of their special game.

Before the game, Gerd Müller was sweetness and light. In one delightful photograph, he and Cruyff are caught sharing a moment of genuine respect and warmth. Sixty seconds later he had rattled home the first goal. After he scored, Müller looked a bit pumped up and aggressive for someone scoring a goal, albeit a great effort, in a farewell bounce game. Later, there would be claims the German side were called 'Nazi pigs' – Müller was neither. Karl-Heinz Rummenigge made it 2-0 after 41 minutes.

Instead of relaxing in the second half, Bayern intensified with some spellbinding football. Paul Breitner made it three, two minutes in, but Bayern's fourth involved some neat interplay and saw a familiar name, Martin Jol, back-heeling to Bernd Dürnberger, who set up Rummenigge. Breitner then capitalised on slack Ajax defending to make it five, and we hadn't hit the hour mark yet.

For all Bayern were powerful and formidable, Ajax were unfocused, careless and making too many mistakes. Müller scored the sixth, his second of the match; Breitner made it seven, then played in Rummenigge to make it 8-0 in the 75th minute. Then and only then would Bayern allow themselves to take their foot off the gas. There was a party planned after the match for Cruyff but Ajax took the immature step of not allowing Bayern in, and instead got drunk and more bitter.

Ajax subbed Cruyff in the 85th minute, and Müller again gave the star a warm handshake before the departing Dutch icon was hoisted into the air with more flowers – well it was Amsterdam. The crowd even held a ceasefire to applaud Cruyff, who by this time just wanted off the park to get to the party.

Over the years, there have been several reasons held up as to why Bayern slaughtered Ajax – mainly Breitner's claims that the Dutch fans were calling their players, especially him, a Nazi pig; he wasn't a Nazi or porcine. He was a Maoist. Another reason was that the Bayern entourage were angered at not being picked up at Schiphol Airport or met by anyone from Ajax (I don't buy this one).

Then they had to deal with a terrible hotel where home fans partied outside most of the night (I don't buy this one either; Bayern were an experienced European side and were hardly impoverished; if they were unhappy with the accommodation they could easily have gone elsewhere, or phoned the police). What is seldom highlighted is that clubs like Bayern have winners in their team, who had won the World Cup, because in their mentality they 'don't do friendlies'.

The senior players on both sides had also demanded a real, hard game. This was a powerful side, with a strong winning mentality and ego. Breitner had announced his retirement from international football after winning the World Cup at the age of 22. They weren't short of self-esteem, confidence or an opinion. Breitner had returned to Bayern after four years at Real Madrid, in a side with Günter Netzer and won two Spanish titles. At this point, Bayern were toiling domestically and going through a transitional period.

Those in charge at Ajax may have been better inviting Barcelona or a World XI if they wanted a showbiz farewell. Bayern remained true to their character and values, they were professional hitmen, but the result would only fester into the next generation, and lead to far worse events between both nations in competition on the European and world stage.

As for Cruyff, due to some financial misdemeanours when he was scammed of his fortune by a conman and found himself nearly bankrupted, his retirement did not last too long. He was forced back to play in the lucrative but short-lived North American Soccer League. His agent set up a money-spinning gate fee percentage deal when he returned to Ajax and he was still box office. After Ajax refused to grant him a valedictory year, angered at the gate money deal, they deliberately offered a standard player contract. Cruyff ended his career at rivals Feyenoord in a sensational final season, winning the league and cup double, and more importantly allowing a successful re-write of his final chapter.

TV, Media and Technology

We live in the modern era, one of 24-hour rolling news and dedicated sport. We also have a video assistant referee and idiots with phones. What could possibly go wrong?

Object: Laptop
Subject: VAR

Most football fans, when told that this innovative, cutting-edge technology called VAR was going to stop referees making horrendous mistakes, were excited by the prospect of a brave new world. VAR, though, has caused no end of anger, rage and debate since its introduction. Ironically, the biggest anti-VAR exponent was Sepp Blatter, the deposed FIFA chief, now living in exile and penury in one of his many villas. The poor ex-dictator was proven correct. When Blatter at first opposed VAR, he was accused of self-interest and being a dinosaur, a Blattersaurus Rex, for refusing to move with the times and accept technology. His biggest gripe was that it would interfere with the spirit of the game.

Football fans and pundits alike were sick of referees getting it wrong and at first, were keen to embrace the idea. They thought this was the white heat of technology and would stop incompetent referees from making game-changing wrong decisions. Now it's gone too far. Blatter's great skill, apart from winning votes by gifting bags of loot to obscure member states, was the slowing of bureaucracy. FIFA, under Blatter, like most governing bodies, were expert at slowing down the implementation of laws when it suited them. VAR trials began in 2016, when the International Football Association Board (IFAB), the powerful legal wing of FIFA who oversee and implement the laws of the game, allowed the change. VAR focused on four points: goal decisions, penalty decisions, direct red cards, and cases of mistaken identity.

The results from the trials were ignored until Blatter was finally removed from office, and only then was VAR able to roll out. Despite the barrage of criticism that came his way, Blatter's views on the effect of VAR and the spirit of the game proved accurate. Initially, when he suggested referees should be allowed to get it wrong, he was viewed as an embarrassing, out-of-touch, sexist and racist uncle at a party. Blatter also believed that fans enjoyed the idiocy and incompetence of decisions as it meant they had something to complain about. This is why Blatter felt it might be better to avoid technology and allow human error.

England's Premier League introduced VAR in 2019 and, after a few weeks, there were calls for its immediate shutdown. England knew they had to embrace it and couldn't remain out of the loop. Yet once they were in, there was no going back. VAR was originally devised during the KNVB (Dutch Football Association) 2010 Netherlands Referee 2.0 project. Tests and mock trials were used in the Eredivisie in 2012/13. It was a success, so the KNVB pitched it to IFAB to see if they would allow a law change to use and review video footage during games. With Blatter out of the way by 2015 after FIFA's corruption scandal, Gianni Infantino, Blatter's successor, loved VAR and sped it through. The case was simple. Fans in the ground had technology the referee didn't. VAR would help the referee. The system was tested in major football nations such as the Bundesliga, Serie A and the Portuguese Primeira League. The Premier League were nervous and still unsure but the FA started trials in the FA Cup and League Cup.

The issue, and it is a big one, is that no one can pull out of VAR. Once the genie is out of the bottle, there is no going back. Though with such huge changes to the game – arguably some of the biggest changes since the penalty or offside rule were introduced – these advances might need time to settle down, and not stop at every decision. The VAR system and its implementation might need some fine tweaking. It's undeniably here to stay.

I can't see the point of VAR. There's already one referee, two assistants and a fourth official, so surely that's enough to officiate a game? It's as though having another four looking at the game in HQ only adds more confusion. The concept of referees sitting miles away in a place called Stockley Park sounds more like a BBC sitcom. Let me introduce the premise.

Chief Inspector Stockley Park is a detective in the quaint village of Crunchy Puddles. For such a quiet and peaceful village, he is central to countless heinous crimes. He solves them with the help of CCTV by staring at the screen, for ages, until he works out the culprit. At the weekends, the quiet, genial Stockley dons his referee uniform and becomes an uncompromising official in the cut and thrust world of the Brooks and Bonhof Insurance League. He's not universally loved for his obdurate and ruthless refereeing style. He also has a VAR tattoo.

No? Be honest, it's a winner. OK, let's call him Jack and get Bill Nighy in.

Object: ITV Mic
Subject: Big Ron's Slip

Ron Atkinson was one of the more enlightened, forward-thinking managers, who was unafraid to play black players years before everyone else. His gifted black stars loved him. He looked after their wellbeing and encouraged them to express themselves. Ironically, he had been protective towards them due to the level of racism in this era. This is a hugely important point to make, a crucial part of his career as a manager, the fact he was so well-respected for giving black players a chance. So, for many, to see him sacked from his high-profile job for his comments was difficult to take.

Atkinson was a popular ITV pundit and co-commentator, bringing years of experience, including spells as a manager with Atlético Madrid, Manchester United and West Bromwich Albion, to the role. This was a huge story and surprised many. Atkinson resigned immediately after he made a racist comment about the black Chelsea player, Marcel Desailly, in April 2004. 'If you look at my track record as a manager,' Atkinson said, 'I was one of the first managers in the game to give black players a chance.' Which begs the question why, after a poor performance by Desailly, did Atkinson even think, 'He's what is known in some schools as a fucking lazy thick n***er.' Let alone say it. But there it was, all his great work, and reputation was undone.

The comments were made once Atkinson thought the microphone was off, but he was unaware he was still live to millions in the Middle East. The game, a Champions League semi-final, was the first leg between Monaco and Chelsea. The official ITV statement read, 'We don't in any way condone the comments in question, which were not broadcast as part of ITV's [UK] coverage but were made in an off-air conversation after the game. It was a regrettable lapse by a respected and experienced broadcaster. He immediately offered his resignation which we have accepted.'

Atkinson was shocked too, mostly at his stupidity, 'I made a stupid mistake which I regret. It left me no option but to resign. At the moment I can't believe I did it.' The self-inflicted nature of the comments show how easy it is to slip. Atkinson made the comment aged 64 and has, say for the odd appearance on *Big Brother* or an awkward pairing up with Tessa Sanderson in *Celebrity Wife Swap,* been off the mainstream channels, and out of football.

His record and legacy as a manager at the top sides and pioneering work with black players was gone in an instant. Again, football is unforgiving. People don't remember his work at West Brom or Manchester United. Ron is a racist. Guys like Atkinson were brought into the commentary box because they were colourful, flamboyant and like old-school comedians. Part of Atkinson's undoubted charm was his refusal to conform. He was not what we would consider 'woke', nor was he particularly au fait with political correctness. But these comments proved he was desperately out of touch. No matter who you are, anything racist or homophobic is wrong. And that's how it should be.

Object: Ejector Seat
Subject: Danny Baker's BBC Sackings

This ejector seat is here for the broadcaster Danny Baker, who has been sacked so many times by the BBC that it's easier to leave it primed in the studio and set up for his return. Baker himself has something of the Marmite about him. People either like or dislike him. I've always had a soft spot for him, especially his journey, from working on punk fanzine *Sniffin' Glue* and then the *NME*. I liked his attitude and the speed his mind moved at. However, it may be fair to say the latter is indeed the issue which has found Danny in the dock, or in this case, up in front of his bosses so often.

Before we get to the main point, his on-air meltdown at a referee in 1997, as recently as May 2019 he was dropped from his high-profile and popular Saturday morning BBC radio show for allegedly being racist about Harry and Meghan. He tweeted a joke about the latest royal birth. Baker denied that the tweet was racist but was hammered online by the moral majority. I believed Baker when he suggested he didn't know Meghan was black. He posted an old photograph, one with a chimpanzee dressed in their Sunday best and one used to highlight privilege. He tweeted 'royal baby leaves hospital' but once that was processed through the febrile world of Twitter, it came back as a racist slur at the latest royal baby.

Soon it was 'Danny Baker fired by BBC over royal baby chimp tweet' then a tweet from the man himself, 'Just got fired from BBC 5 Live. For the record – it was red sauce. Always.'

Off he flew on the ejector seat.

In 2012, after cancelling his show, BBC 5 Live's controller Jonathan Wall had emailed staff telling them of his decision to sack Baker after he had taken to both Twitter and used his show to criticise the BBC, and gone against the integrity of the corporation.

Off the ejector seat jettisoned again.

Our football-related controversy occurred when Chelsea played Leicester in an FA Cup fifth-round replay, a televised match, in 1997, at Stamford Bridge. Chelsea won 1-0 after they were awarded a dubious penalty in the 116th minute. The first tie at Filbert Street was an eventful affair with Chelsea 2-0 up before Leicester came back into the game to earn a replay.

Baker's show was often controversial with a bit of edge but was always a fans' show and popular because of that. He used his platform on national radio to have a belligerent rant at the referee Mike Reed and his decision to award a penalty. Reed had awarded Chelsea a penalty in the 116th minute when Chelsea's Erland Johnsen fell over without being challenged. The fact the game was televised live on terrestrial TV only served to fuel the flames.

Baker encouraged fans to make the referee's life hell. His tirade included a memorable pop at referees, calling them 'the maggot at football's golden core'. Unbelievably he slagged off his producer, accusing him of selecting calls that didn't agree with him instead of callers who supported his rant. He also called for a former producer to return to replace the current incumbent.

It wasn't a penalty. When Baker became incensed on air about the referee's decision he was fired from 5 Live. The reason? His bosses accused him of inciting and threatening behaviour in his outburst. The penalty was controversial, the decision to attack the referee on-air crossed the line. He was sacked by then-station boss, Roger Mosey.

Off the ejector seat rocketed, again.

Baker has been written off and bounced back from far worse than BBC bosses. Reset the ejector seat. He will be back, although he has now found a natural broadcasting home as a podcaster. A place where he can go off on one and is even allowed to swear, and no BBC bosses can sack him.

Fanorak Fact: Bayern's DNA doesn't do friendlies, in August 2019, they thrashed amateur side FC Rottach-Egern 23-0 in a pre-season game, that's a goal in just under every four minutes.

Object: Waterloo Bridge
Subject: Blackouts, Macca, and the Big Yin

When we hear the word blackout we normally think of the Blitz, and officious air raid wardens straight out of *Dad's Army* leading half of the East End down into the underground to start a sing-song and a version of 'We're Going to Hang Out Our Washing on the Siegfried Line'. This particular blackout is a reference to the televised football blackout of 1985.

For some background, in August 1985 the football season began without a TV deal in place. The Football League had rejected a joint bid from the BBC and ITV of £19m for a four-year deal. The offer hit the buffers over the split between live games and recorded highlights. Club owners were fearful they would lose fans coming through the gates if matches were broadcast live but were happy with recorded highlights. The feeling within the game, mostly from those directors, was that live coverage would kill football.

This meant that the 1985/86 season began with no coverage. There was no footage of Manchester United setting the pace with ten straight wins. More crucially for our story, there was no record of the 18 goals the West Ham United striker Frank McAvennie had rattled in before Christmas, to eventually give John Lyall's men their highest ever league finish, when they ended the season third behind Liverpool and Everton in the First Division.

McAvennie was signed from St Mirren by West Ham for £340,000. It was just as well he and Tony Cottee clicked as few Hammers fans had even heard of him, but that soon changed. McAvennie became a bona fide legend at West

Ham, probably because there was no footage of him, and since his goals could only be seen by the fans at the game his daring deeds made him even more mythical.

Yes, but why the Waterloo Bridge you may ask? Well, such was the excitement at seeing any football on our TVs whatsoever, that *Saint and Greavsie* became one of the few outlets for football chat. On one occasion, the ITV producers sent out the current Sky Sports commentator Martin Tyler to walk around London with McAvennie to see if anyone recognised West Ham's star striker. As they crossed Waterloo Bridge, the crew stopped and asked passers-by, 'Do you know the name of this footballer?' People shrugged, said no and kept going. They didn't know who he was because he wasn't on TV. Then, by coincidence, the next person to walk by, out for a wander, was Billy Connolly. When asked, Connolly said, 'That's one of us – Frank McAvennie.'

Speaking in *The Independent* in October 2011, Tyler told Simon Hart, 'Not many people recognised him – only a taxi driver did. Amazingly, when we walked back down to the South Bank to the studios, Billy Connolly walked out and he recognised Frank!'

Football in the 1980s was so far removed from the constant EPL games we have now. The Heysel ban had kicked in. Crowds were down. Yet something was in the air at Upton Park and it wasn't just bubbles. John Motson, the esteemed former BBC commentator, said, 'I commentated on the first live game back on television in January 1986 for Charlton v West Ham in the FA Cup, and when McAvennie appeared on screen I said, "Now you know what he looks like."'

With a TV deal met, McAvennie would soon become a household name with 26 goals in this season. West Ham approached the last game of the campaign knowing that if Chelsea could beat Liverpool and they could beat

Southampton, they would win the First Division. Liverpool's player-manager, Kenny Dalglish, scored his side's winning goal to take the title back to Anfield. West Ham played Everton in a play-off for second place and were beaten 3-1, but the Hammers wanted the title and were past caring about being second. They had made their point. People knew who Frank McAvennie was. He was the talk of the town and had gone prime time, even appearing as a guest on the popular BBC chat show, *Wogan*.

Object: GPS
Subject: UEFA's Wonky Geography

Anyone with a rudimentary understanding of football and location will tell you UEFA have a somewhat complicated take on geography. Those bumbling bureaucrats running the game need to sit down in front of a map and be taught many of the countries their member clubs play in and what constitutes Europe and Asia.

We are not talking about the familiar incongruences like Las Palmas, who play in the Spanish league, on the Canary Islands, off the west coast of Morocco and closer to Western Sahara. They are a three-hour flight from Madrid. Then there's Monaco, who play in the French league despite being a principality, a sovereign city-state, and not French. Berwick Rangers, formerly of the Scottish league, are based in England but play in Scotland. Many Welsh sides, most notably Swansea City, Cardiff City and Newport County play in England. Northern Irish club Derry City play in the Republic of Ireland's League of Ireland. These are pardonable as they are geographical and political.

Vaduz, from Liechtenstein, are a classic UEFA geographic/logistical misnomer. They are one of seven sides from Liechtenstein who play in Switzerland because their country doesn't have a professional league. Yet they do have a cup competition so they play cup games in their own country. Conveniently, Vaduz win the cup all the time which allows them time to secure a lucrative place in Europa League qualification.

In UEFA's world, sides like Neftchi Baku from Azerbaijan and Maccabi Tel Aviv are part of Europe. They love a geographical anomaly in the wonderful world of UEFA but one club might highlight our point: let's discuss FC SKA-Khabarovsk.

Russia is part of the UEFA region yet 77 per cent of Russia is in mainland Asia. Most, 75 per cent of the population, live in the European part. Meanwhile, back at UEFA's wonky geography lesson, in 2017 FC SKA-Khabarovsk gained promotion to the top tier of the Russian Premier League. They are based in Khabarovsk, in the east of Russia, and when we say east we mean the east. Find a map or a globe (that's a paper version of GPS and a spherical model of the earth for those too young) and look south from Khabarovsk and it is above Korea and Japan. It is 19 miles from the Chinese border.

So, say you were based in St Petersburg and facing an away game against Khabarovsk, the flight takes seven and a half hours. The clubs are 5,442 miles and seven time zones apart. If you have a Dennis Bergkamp in the side, who has a contractual loophole permitting him not to fly, then it will take 111 hours to drive there. Most of their league rivals would have been relieved when the side were relegated after only one season.

When pushed about their strange take on geography and arrangements, UEFA explain it away by calling Azerbaijan, Georgia, Kazakhstan, Russia and Turkey transcontinental states. This is another name for countries with bits that are in more than one continent. Countries like Armenia and Cyprus are part of Europe 'culturally and politically'. Then again, if you go to parts of Buenos Aires, Toronto or New York, they are like parts of Europe culturally and politically. How loose are these rules? Then we have the sides from Asia who were once members of the Asian Football Confederation; Israel and Kazakhstan for example. Israel were allowed to join UEFA after they were banned from the Asian Football Confederation in 1974.

The blame may have nothing to do with UEFA, but cartographers from the mid-17th century who decided the border between Europe and Asia would be based around the Caucasus and Ural Mountains. The modern border means that countries like Georgia and Azerbaijan, despite most of their country being in Asia, still have parts of their country in Europe. The borders themselves are only defined by convention and are more do with a historical, political and cultural construct.

The Turkish capital Istanbul is a transcontinental city, lying in both Asia and Europe, and is split by the Bosporus. For many champions of smaller nations, trying to qualify for the Champions League can be like an Istanbul scenario: a kick in the Bosporus.

Game-Changers and Tactics

Since the rules of the game were set down in 1863, football has had many creative thinkers who changed the game for the better and forward-thinking coaches and individuals who helped shape it.

Object: Old Notebook
Subject: FA Rules

It's difficult to process the significance and eventual global impact a group of people meeting in a pub would subsequently have. Imagine being in the room when someone came up with the rules of association football? Was there the usual dour-faced, grumpy, parsimonious person in the company who would shake his head and keep saying it will not catch on? I've often sat down with friends in the pub and tried to come up with a fresh concept or idea but by the end of the sentence, I'd already forgotten my genius plan.

Those present at the Freemason's Tavern in Holborn, London, on the evening of Monday, 26 October 1863, had the idea of having inaugural common rules set down, and, to implement them, they formed the Football Association. Representatives, mostly the captains and club secretaries of 12 clubs who until then, were playing their own version of football, met 'for the purpose of forming an Association with the object of establishing a definite code of rules for the regulation of the game'.

A further six meetings would take place over 44 days to firm up suggestions and implement them into laws. The FA was formed at the first, the rules at the second and the rules re-drafted at the third and so on. The main protagonist was a London solicitor called Ebenezer Morley who, apart from having a great name straight out of a Dickens novel, also formed Barnes FC in 1862. He had written to the popular paper of the day, *Bell's Life*, with a letter stating football should have rules the same way Marylebone Cricket Club had for cricket. This idea created more interest and eventually led to the meeting.

Until then, football was played in confined villages, towns and cities, by packed riotous mobs who violently fought with each other. You were also still allowed to pick the ball up. The public schoolboys who had joined forces with Morley were used to the great open playing spaces of Eton. There had been many attempts to bring together a more uniform set of rules, chiefly from Cambridge undergraduates who tried, in the late 1840s, to make the game more orderly and organised. Maybe their timing was wrong, or perhaps they were too ahead of their time. Maybe their rules weren't as in-depth.

One of the more interesting laws Morley and his friends introduced from 1863 was the original offside rule (nothing like the one we have now). I'm sure it would have been as thought-provoking and controversial. Before this rule, like rugby, anyone who was ahead of the ball was offside and any advancements came through a mixture of scrimmaging and dribbling. The FA changed that to the three-player rule where the attacker was offside if he was in front of the third to last defender, now football had become about the passing game.

It's extraordinary that someone writing a letter to a newspaper could lead to a few meetings which would evolve into one of the most played and viewed sports on the planet. This was the basis of our beautiful game. I wonder what the founding fathers would think of VAR? Or for those few inglorious days in April 2021, of the failed European Super League?

Fanorak Fact: Originally, referees weren't used. The sporting integrity of the game was down to the players and if there were any disputes they were originally settled by the two captains. However, as the game grew, drawing larger crowds, and with more at stake, this became more difficult. With penalties eventually awarded, a proposal by the Irish Association was passed and it was agreed that a referee was allowed on to the field of play.

Object: Burst Ball

Subject: European Super League

Betrayal is a treacherous thing. The European Super League (ESL) was the ultimate act of betrayal to football's integrity and its supporters. On Sunday, 18 April 2021, news of the ESL started to filter out. Initially, it was met with incredulity, then the realisation slowly started to dawn – this meant that football as we knew it was facing an existential crisis. The spirit of the game and sporting integrity was in danger of being robbed and hijacked by billionaires.

By Sunday evening the story began to take hold of the news cycle. England's supposed 'Big Six' – Manchester United, Manchester City, Liverpool, Arsenal, Spurs and Chelsea – were joining Europe's so-called elite in a breakaway league. The owners had been secretly plotting to take their clubs into a perpetual cash generator where no one was relegated. To them, it was a business dream, a corporate utopia, a land of milk and honey. It was a closed shop of 12 corporate giants.

Their proposals meant no pyramid and no chance of entry. This was a private club and the likes of you and I and our team were not allowed in. This was a closed shop. It should have been *Open All Hours* but ended up like *Fawlty Towers*.

Within days, the ESL crashed and burned in one of the most embarrassing capitulations in recent football history. At the heart of it lay two issues. One, the owners were blatantly firing ahead without consultation, and two, their actions were those of billionaires desperately ignorant of the emotional connection fans have to their club.

The super league was a super scheme, hatched by the dirty dozen, for super clubs, like super Spurs who last won a trophy, the League Cup, in 2008. Spurs are a great club, with a wonderful history and great support but are they there because of their stadium and infrastructure?

The European Super League was theft. The theft of a dream. If you were a club six divisions down and you won your games, you were promoted fairly and squarely, up the football pyramid. The billionaire owners came in and removed jeopardy. Now we had pundits babbling on about adopting the Swiss or German model. Metaphors ran for cover to escape former pros. They were everywhere, explaining that football was at a giant crossroads and chairmen and owners were falling on their swords.

By Wednesday, it was over. Club owners failed to gauge the vehement level of outrage and intense public outcry. They underestimated the power of the fans and quickly realised they had made a huge error. Football came together, accusing the owners of deliberately trying to speed the European Super League through as they hid behind the Covid-19 pandemic, blaming the financial hit from it but also moving quickly as fans were not allowed near stadiums to protest. The clubs thought they could push through the league and fans wouldn't mind but here, football was central to the identity of the nation.

Liverpool's owner, John W. Henry, made a statement and acted like he was originally part of a heist and had been temporarily blinded by greed but people power, and the public, made him see sense – once he was caught. Most apologies rang hollow, corporate mea culpas with an eye on the share price.

The story was so big, European giants Spurs decided to bury bad news among the hubris and sacked José Mourinho. Poor José had to play second fiddle to the mass murderers of the European Super League. He left the club with his belongings in carrier bags for a life of misery in one of his five Portuguese properties and his place in Belgravia.

You know it's a weird day when both UEFA and the man who pulled the UK out of Europe, Boris Johnson, have the moral high ground or at least are trying to claim it. Johnson saw it as a useful distraction to jump aboard, anything to make him popular while he ignored the global pandemic, dodgy texts to inventors of a vacuum cleaner to promise to 'fix' a tax issue and claims of secret payments from donors to renovate his Downing Street flat. The main protagonist, the ESL's real big wig, was Real Madrid's Florentino Pérez. He claimed he was trying to save football. Both they and Barcelona were in dire financial straits.

By Tuesday the six English sides decided the optics didn't look great and made a big song and dance about making the wrong choice and begging for forgiveness as they hoped season ticket sales wouldn't be hit too badly.

As the week controversially progressed, UEFA started to make threats. They would consider sanctions on the 12 clubs. President Aleksander Čeferin promised that renegade clubs would suffer the consequences of their mistake. Čeferin had a pop at the main instigators, Real Madrid, Barcelona and Juventus, who by Thursday were the only three left. Manchester United's executive vice-chairman Ed Woodward was thrown under the bus by the Glazers. Apologies looked like embarrassed pleas for forgiveness from the accused after getting caught with their grubby hands on the gold bullion during a heist. By Wednesday, Andrea Agnelli of Juventus accepted it was over, but there were still three sides involved. It was the supporters who made the ESL die on its feet. Most noticeably, German teams Bayern Munich and Borussia Dortmund, in a country where fan power and the concept of artificial football clubs is anathema, had nothing to do with it.

UEFA continued with the hard line, saying the clubs involved could be banned from the Champions League. By Friday, it broke that Madrid *would* be allowed to remain in the competition, despite all the trouble the club had caused. That same day, ESL financiers JP Morgan came out all apologies, admitting they had made a mistake in their €3bn deal to fund the project. They had vowed to 'learn' from the debacle.

The ESL had tried to overrule fans and then, once they were caught out, agreed that sporting merit was crucial. Another issue for me was the branding. When I hear Super League, I think of rugby league. In the end the ESL's dazzling cash cow turned out to be a pig in a poke. Though the one thing they did get right, was their inspirational and rousing anthem: the theme from Laurel and Hardy.

Object: European Cup
Subject: Gabriel Hanot,
L'Equipe and Wolves

Imagine this scenario; the football editor of France's leading newspaper, one devoted entirely to sport, has an idea for a Europe-wide football competition to find the continent's best side. Gabriel Hanot of *L'Equipe* is convinced his continent-wide tournament is a winner. His idea will bring together the finest teams from each country, united in the spirit of the beautiful game – but no one else is interested. Undeterred, he continues to plough on, and with colleagues Jacques Goddet and Jacques Ferran from *L'Équipe* continually harangues his connections, using his influence and his newspaper's high profile to pitch it.

Hanot was an outspoken, formidable figure in France and carried considerable heft. He had played football for France, making his debut on 8 March 1908 against Switzerland. He won 12 caps, captaining the side in his last game. He became a war hero, when injured while piloting a plane. After the Second World War he became both a football journalist and national team selector and coach. He used his newspaper to call for the coach's sacking, in effect sacking himself. I'm unsure if today we could have someone comparable. Not only did he select the French national side, but he also helped set up the country's professional league. You could say he was qualified for the job.

By 1955 the tournament was finally conceived in Paris and became known as the European Champion Clubs' Cup, more commonly referenced as the European Cup. With hindsight, it was such a simple, obvious and wonderful idea.

The germ of the idea came when he grew tired of Wolves manager Stan Cullis bragging continually that his team were the 'Champions of the World' after they had beaten Honvéd (a side containing Puskás, Sándor Kocsis and Zoltán Czibor) in a few friendlies.

Wolves had installed floodlights and the novelty had allowed them to set up international floodlit friendlies, and since they beat an array of top clubs they considered themselves the best in the world. Such was the excitement around the idea of Honvéd and Puskás appearing at Molineux, under floodlights, the BBC filmed the second half live. This spurred Hanot and his colleagues to do something about it. They eventually coaxed UEFA to set up a tournament for the national champions.

You would wonder what such a sporting, old-school, stickler for rules, regulations and fine detail would think of today's tournament which features more losers than winners. The lack of sporting integrity, with title winners from many countries having to play qualifying games while teams who finish third and fourth in bigger countries march in, would leave him cold. Football or UEFA certainly owe him.

So there you have it, a competitive, forward-thinking Frenchman annoyed at a bragging English manager and we now have a competition neither of them would recognise. He also found time to conceive the idea of the best player in Europe, coming up with the Ballon d'Or.

Fanorak Fact: Arsenal had lights on one stand, in the 1930s. Southampton had floodlights at The Dell in 1950. Wolves though had more powerful, modern lights and liked to show them off.

Object: Paint Brush

Subject: Penalty Kick and William McCrum

If you have the chance to venture to Milford, in County Armagh in Northern Ireland, you will see a statue erected to William McCrum. The red-bricked model village of Milford was built by his father, Robert Garmany McCrum, to house workers in his linen factory. Robert's company, Milford Linen, was world famous. Robert was a daunting figure; strict, serious and god-fearing, he was a successful factory owner who made millions from the cotton trade. William was the very antithesis as a sports-mad scholar, an extrovert who lived life to the full. He was fond of the dramatic arts and loved football. William was at best an average goalkeeper but it was from this vantage point that he changed football, and has gone into history, by inventing the penalty kick.

It's difficult to imagine the game without penalties yet, like most radical changes, football initially rejected the idea. When the Irish Football Association proposed William's idea of the penalty kick, IFAB laughed at and publicly derided the idea. The proposal whipped up a storm, and the newspapers and wider football community sneered at the outlandishness of the idea. At the time, the press described the penalty kick as a 'death sentence' for football. IFAB promised to consider the proposal at a later meeting but were disdainful, dismissively describing it as the 'Irishman's Motion'.

In their eyes, such situations would not occur, not in their wonderful game. Football was a sport played by gentlemen. Even the great C.B. Fry, captain of Corinthian FC – the 'gentleman amateurs' – had his say on the concept of the absurdity of the penalty kick. He suggested, like some P.G. Wodehouse figure, it would be time for a quick cigarette break, saying, 'The penalty kick was a standing insult to sportsmen to have to play under a rule which assumes that players intend to trip, hack and push opponents and to behave like cads of the most unscrupulous kidney.'

Football itself was adamant there would be no way players would cheat to gain an advantage. Proof that even then, those in charge of the game were hopelessly out of touch and unaware of how quickly football was spreading. With its popularity, football had also become more ferocious and intense. More serious injuries were occurring, with reports of violent outbursts among players on the rise.

William's concept of awarding those fouled in the box with a penalty kick was about integrity and the spirit of the game. Before penalties were awarded, defenders would save clear, goalscoring opportunities with a handball, knowing at worst that they had only conceded a free kick which half the team could block by standing in front of the ball. The penalty award felt like a fairer option. It improved the flow of the game, lessened serious injury but also added more drama to proceedings – and William loved drama.

A few situations arose in the intervening term between the Irish Football Association pitching William's idea to IFAB. Several high-profile incidents had been brought to IFAB's attention. There was also a controversial FA Cup tie between Notts County and Stoke City. This game acted as a catalyst for change and the implementation of a penalty award. With Notts County leading 1-0 in the last minute, Stoke were denied a clear goal because County player Jack Hendry deliberately stopped the ball with his hand. Stoke were awarded a free kick, inches from the goal line. The keeper, by the letter of the law, was allowed to stand in front of the ball and blocked what should have been a free tap-in. It was a huge talking point, highlighting how unfair the rules were. The public's reaction to this event gave the penalty kick the green light.

On 2 June 1891, an IFAB meeting was hastily arranged in the Alexandra Hotel in Bath Street, Glasgow. It was chaired by the host and SFA president W.G. Snedden with members of Scottish, English, Welsh and Northern Irish associations. The proposal was passed and the penalty kick was made law. At the same meeting, the centre circle was formally introduced, umpires were removed and replaced with linesmen, and referees were now allowed on to the pitch; until then, they used to officiate from the touchline. A busy night.

William McCrum's idea of a penalty kick was quickly assimilated into the culture of the game. It proved a hit, encouraged more skill and sportsmanship and also added that sense of theatre and tension to the proceedings. It also helped to quell the aggression and violence which had been allowed to permeate into the game. The addition of some form of jeopardy and punishment had helped make the game fairer.

You could practically write the script for William. It was the classic tale of the strict successful father devastated by his son's failure to take over the business. William was someone with diverse interests and a completely different personality to a disappointed Robert. Not made of the right stuff, William was shut out of the family business. He rebelled by travelling, seeing the world, and amassing eye-watering gambling debts. The narrative was driving his life toward a default position of the clichéd, flawed, imperfect conclusion and he didn't disappoint. His cheating wife left him with their child, for another man, to live in the south of France.

In the end it was the Wall Street Crash that finally did it for him; the linen business and any income were gone. He died penniless, in a boarding house in Armagh before Christmas, 1932. What a contribution to the game, though.

Object: Facchetti's Napkin Story
Subject: The Striker-Defender

Giacinto Facchetti was arguably one of the finest defenders Italy has ever produced. Unusually for an Italian defender, he loved to attack, yet still managed to do what was asked of him by his demanding coach Helenio Herrera. Yes, he was a cavalier footballer, an overlapping left-back who loved to get forward and thunder in shots by coming in on his right, but he was also a great team player who did what was asked. Not only was he a great player but carried the shirt well, both for Inter and Italy. One of those players who had it all, even the Hollywood good looks, he was far too handsome for a defender. Facchetti once explained his role in Herrera's team to Jock Stein by drawing it on a napkin.

Facchetti made a name for himself at his hometown club Trevigliese and was signed to Inter as a striker. When Inter manager Herrera saw how dominant he was in the air, and his physique, he moulded him into a striker-defender. He played 476 league games for Inter Milan and scored 59 goals, ten of which came in the 1965/66 season. Facchetti won four Serie A titles and the European Cup twice. He played 94 times for Italy, captaining them 70 times.

His style of play was the inspiration for a young Franz Beckenbauer to attack more and go from being a sweeper to play through the opposition and score more as a result. Beckenbauer was a huge influence on Johan Cruyff, too, so for the modern game Facchetti was a hugely inspirational figure. He proved helpful with advice. Sit down, grab a nice bottle of Italian red or a coffee and listen to this tale.

Many of my generation often wonder why Scotland was so successful at football in the 1960s? Was it the hunger and desire to come out of poverty? The knowledge and coaching of the great managers? Could it be as simple as the hours spent every day kicking a ball and playing football all the time? Scotland is a football nation with more clubs, players, and spectators in terms of its size than most comparable countries. In the 1960s, the halcyon days for newspapers, editors had money and could afford to send journalists, a photographer and coaches on fact-finding football trips to see how clubs were run. The readers loved it.

In 1963, the *Daily Express* arranged for Celtic's Jock Stein and Kilmarnock's Willie Waddell to go out and shadow, chat, watch and learn from the Inter coach Helenio Herrera. They had to learn from his methods as he was then the best coach in the world. The canny Scots were allowed inside his inner sanctum. They would eat with the team and talk football, compare ideas. Herrera was famed for refining and tweaking catenaccio and turning negative football into an art form. But Stein and Waddell wanted to know more, especially about training, diet, team shape and tactics.

One evening, Stein was sitting talking football with the amiable Facchetti, and as the wine flowed (for Giacinto; Jock was teetotal) the football chat continued. Stein had been watching how Herrera had set up and was wondering why Facchetti was attacking, then defending. He wanted to know how he fitted in. Was he playing as a sweeper? He was a left-back, surely? What was this system Herrera played? Facchetti wasn't only going up for set pieces or corners, he was attacking from his defence. At first, a slightly reluctant Facchetti kept it general and didn't get too specific. Eventually he would communicate his role as a striker-defender. He couldn't explain it but picked up a napkin, took Stein's pen and explained Herrera's tactics, and his place and role in them, on the napkin. Stein kept it, he understood, Facchetti smiled and the evening was forgotten about. It was all innocence and curiosity. Football people chatting about the game.

When Stein returned to Glasgow he pushed his left-back Tommy Gemmell forward. He would score 63 times in 418 appearances for Celtic, not bad for a left-back. The napkin would come in handy when Celtic met Inter four years later in the European Cup Final in Lisbon; they beat a side managed by Herrera and featuring Facchetti. Gemmell scored, and would also score in the 1970 final in Milan against Feyenoord (one of only three British footballers to score in two finals, the others being Phil Neal and Gareth Bale).

Scottish football reached wondrous heights then. The evening before Celtic beat Inter 2-1 in 1967, Kilmarnock lost out in the UEFA Cup semi-final. Six days later, Rangers were beaten in the final of the Cup Winners' Cup. That napkin deserves its place in our museum.

Object: Fishing Trawler
Subject: Catenaccio

Catenaccio is a difficult football system to explain – it's even more challenging to identify the origins. It is often incorrectly attributed to Inter Milan's world-renowned coach, Helenio Herrera, and his great adversary at AC Milan, Nereo Rocco, but they only popularised it. It was in fact created by an Austrian named Karl Rappan in the 1930s. As a coach, Rappan was becoming increasingly irritated as his lowly part-time Genevan side, Servette, struggled to compete against quicker, faster, fitter, full-time teams. Rappan devised a system that allowed his side to rest, absorb pressure and then hit on the counter-attack, thus catenaccio was born. His use of the 'door-bolt' won him two titles and a job as the Swiss national coach.

The system itself introduced the use of two wing-backs as defenders; the traditional line-up of 2-3-5 was thrown out. The inside-forward and centre-half joined a midfield three. The full-backs would slot into a centre-half position, and when they had pressure exerted on them, the spare man, who would be 'the bolt', would slide along behind, to cover.

As time passed the more successful catenaccio became, many started to forget about Rappan's version of the system. Anyway, how could something so 'Italian' come from an Austrian working in Switzerland? A country famed for an army knife, watches and cuckoo clocks? Football demands a narrative arc, something more romantic and literal to help make the story stick. Football loves a yarn and Italian is such a poetic and romantic language. A major reason for the system's emergence through Italian football was due to so many Swiss coaches starting to influence their Italian neighbours and as a bigger football nation, Italy slowly engulfed the Swiss.

Rappan's system was developed and advanced by Italian coaches in the 1940s. Manager Gipo Viani introduced the idea of playing a libero, or a sweeper, behind his three centre-backs. With his side Salernitana struggling, Viani noticed, while on his early-morning constitutional, that a fishing trawler miraculously appeared off the shoreline. He stopped to watch the fishermen haul in their catch, but then noticed apart from their main net, they had a reserve net to scoop up the fish the first one didn't catch. When Viani applied the trawler's approach to his defensive line-up it worked immediately, and Salernitana won the Serie B title in 1946/47 to achieve promotion to Serie A. All he had to do was remember that the bolt referred to was a player and not floundering haddock. This more nuanced catenaccio would slowly be adopted by Rocco at Padova, Triestina and then, most notably, when he took over at AC Milan.

Object: Treaty of Rome
Subject: Jean-Marc Bosman

Jean-Marc Bosman's actions may not have felt like it at the time but they proved Herculean. The Belgian took his club RFC Liège, then the Belgian FA and then UEFA to court, to challenge them over transfer rulings, in 1995. Bosman, who was 25 at the time, was unaware it would take so long, figuring a week, maybe two, then he'd get playing again: 'I thought the court action would take just a few weeks. It took five years. The case was thrown around, through many courts before the final ruling by the EU judges in Luxembourg on December 15, 1995.' This would be a huge story and a significant landmark case, one that would impact and change the game forever.

If Bosman received a pound for every footballer's life he changed, he would be an incredibly wealthy man. Football has destroyed him though. While many players are now millionaires, Bosman is nearly destitute thanks to the sport ostracising him. He may have won his case but personally, he lost so much. Bosman told *The Independent* in 2020, some 25 years after the ruling, 'I can't deny that it has been tough. I haven't worked for years. My life now revolves around my two sons.'

By the time the case was finished in 2000, Bosman's playing career was over. Despite attempts to get fit and secure a contract, by the time he was edging towards turning 31, the game had moved on and left Bosman behind. You would assume football would have a duty of care and find a paid position for him after he had quit the game. How great an adviser would he have been? Here was a principled, strong-willed individual who knew what football clubs were doing was wrong and ultimately illegal. Bosman was about freedom and trying to free footballers from archaic contracts. He would have been perfect in an advisory role, giving younger players guidance and helping clubs carry out and adhere to the ruling with his name on it. Football remembers you, especially if you have the strength to challenge it.

His career began so promisingly. Bosman captained his national under-21 team and played for Belgian first division side Standard Liège, then RFC Liège. Nearing the end of his contract, he tried to sign with French club Dunkerque in 1990. Bosman was 25, in his prime, and RFC Liège valued him at around £500,000. If Dunkerque wanted to sign him they would have to pay in full, up front. They couldn't afford the fee and the deal was off. To compound the issue, RFC Liège reduced Bosman's wages by 75 per cent to £500 per month and refused to sell him elsewhere. Undeterred, Bosman challenged the legality of their actions.

Football and the media roundly framed Bosman as a crackpot. He was portrayed as an idiot and mocked for his audacity at daring to go after those who held the power. The player and his lawyers, though, had an ace up their sleeve – his club's and football's flagrant disregard for employer laws, set down by 1957's Treaty of Rome.

When boiled down, the Bosman ruling ended transfer fees when players were out of contract. Before 1995, clubs didn't have to let players leave for free. Players were the club's property. The judgement meant professional footballers in the EU (except in Malta) were able to move freely to another club at the end of their contract. It also ended the rules limiting the number of European players in teams. Footballers were like normal workers, allowed freedom of movement, to work where they wanted.

Despite the upside, players had more power and greater freedom of movement, so some felt the changes meant that with increased wages and agent power the wealthier clubs would become more dominant. Instead of transfer fees, players would move for bigger salaries. It allowed greater freedom for workers (players) but smaller clubs found it difficult to hold on to their talent.

The stress and anguish became too much. Bosman's marriage collapsed and he moved back in with his parents. He later said, 'People think I made millions with the court case, but I didn't. There was no compensation. I couldn't find work. I fell into a depression and started drinking. I lost friends. When I tried getting back into the game, no one wanted me. My name was poison.' Bosman himself required help financially from FIFPro, the players' union. But one of the biggest disappointments for Bosman was that the football authorities, mainly FIFA and UEFA, after everything he had lost, refused to accept the ruling existed. Some years later they ignored the change in the rules until they were forced, by law, to act. Yet it is perhaps the mark of the man that despite everything, he admits, even today, he would do it all again.

Object: Bin

Subject: Brian Clough

This bin is here as an introduction and as an excuse to talk about the bewilderingly complex career of Brian Clough and to remind the FA of the best manager they never had. The bin itself featured as part of his opening gambit as manager to the Leeds United first team: 'Right you fucking lot, as far as I'm concerned you can take all the medals you have won and throw them in that bin over there.' Then, to Norman Hunter, Clough said, 'Hunter, you're a dirty bastard and everyone hates you. I know everyone likes to be loved, and you'd like to be loved too, wouldn't you?'

'Actually I couldn't give a fuck,' replied Hunter.

Then Johnny Giles got it. Clough rounded on everyone. To Eddie Gray he said, 'If you had been a horse, you'd have been put down years ago.' Talk about introductions. Clough's approach was to dominate, break down, then control. But these were experienced pros and history proved Clough's approach, on this occasion, failed spectacularly.

Let's rewind. Clough returned from national service with the RAF and joined his local club, Middlesbrough, in 1955. He was a third choice striker until reserve goalkeeper Peter Taylor sang his praises. Clough got his chance, proving a wonderfully prolific striker with 204 goals in 222 games. He was called up for his country, playing only twice. Clough then signed for Sunderland, scoring 63 times in 74 matches. On Boxing Day of 1962, while playing against Bury, Clough destroyed his cruciate ligament when he collided with their goalkeeper. It was over for the free-scoring striker. Sunderland offered him a job coaching the youth side.

At 30, in 1965, he began his coaching career at Hartlepools United (as they were called at the time), becoming the youngest manager in the Football League. He brought in Taylor, who was managing Burton Albion, as his assistant. They then both left for Derby County in 1967. The Rams were toiling, stuck in the Second Division. Clough had plans, though, and chopped through the club from top to bottom. Backroom staff and employees (allegedly including tea ladies laughing after the team were beaten) and players, were let go; only four of the original team remained. Clough would sign Roy McFarland, Archie Gemmill and John McGovern. Strong-willed and determined, and going against the club owners and board, his side won promotion. In three years Derby were crowned First Division champions. The following season Derby reached the European Cup semi-finals.

When at Derby he won the Texaco Cup in 1972, beating Airdrie in the final, before guiding the Rams to their first league title. Years later, Clough's first trophy win at Nottingham Forest came in the now-defunct Anglo-Scottish Cup. They beat Leyton Orient in the final in 1976/77. He claimed, unlike other clubs, that he took these competitions seriously. The experience gained in the tournament was influential in preparing the side for future domestic and European success.

Clough was unusual at the time because he was a 'tracksuit manager'; he was the boss and the coach. He liked to play and teach and instruct. Whatever he was doing worked. His methods were unorthodox, sometimes insane, but he knew football and the psyche of players.

Clough could handle himself with the press and media too; savvy, sharp and quick with a line. This raised his public profile and made him popular with TV producers who recognised the viewing public enjoyed his opinionated take as a pundit. He would soon be on football shows and the chat show circuit – the viewers loved him but the football establishment, those running the game and the FA didn't appreciate him, and nor did directors or club owners.

This arguably caused rifts at Derby, and after a fall-out with chairman Sam Longson, Clough and Taylor headed, briefly, to Brighton & Hove Albion before Clough went solo with Leeds. The attempt to do the same at Brighton as they did at Derby failed. Clough's approach was to bully players who were unable to reach his standards. It didn't work on the south coast. In July 1974, after publicly calling Leeds United players cheats, he was done before he had really started. The move to Elland Road lasted a mere 44 days and Clough was left again to bide his time and wait for the next adventure.

In January 1975, Clough and Taylor arrived at their biggest challenge yet; Nottingham Forest. In an astonishing 18-year career as Forest manager he took them from sixth from bottom of the Second Division in 1975 to winners of the First Division championship in 1978. He also won the League Cup on four occasions. Then, unbelievably, with a provincial club, Clough won back-to-back European Cups in 1979 and 1980.

Clough's CV – he did fail at Brighton and Leeds and was an incorrigible loudmouth, despite his record at Forest – still wasn't enough for the FA when he was interviewed for the England job. In as much as Clough would have been able to motivate and organise his players and handle the media, the FA said no. In football terms, this meant they felt he was too much of a maverick and a smart arse and didn't want him coming in and taking over. Clough, who was interviewed in 1977 and later 1982, was not offered the job he so coveted, yet remained pragmatic, 'I'm sure the England selectors thought if they took me on and gave me the job, I'd want to run the show. They were shrewd because that's exactly what I would have done.'

Object: Army Assault Course
Subject: Il Ritiro

If I held any sway, the first thing I'd do is bring back the old-style apprentice system to football, and make academy players coming through spend one day a week doing menial, thankless tasks. Forget labour laws and bullying. Treat them like a slave, force them to polish boots, paint the ground and clean toilets, where's the harm? The second would be to ban any player who squeals and screams when tackled. Thirdly, I'd bring back the magic sponge to cure malingerers of ails and breaks and while we're here, I'd stop the madness with players wearing gloves and short-sleeved shirts. The last and the best: I would bring back the Italian training camp, called Il Ritiro (to withdraw).

Footballers need seclusion and discipline to get fit and most importantly, focus 100 per cent on football. Il Ritiro provided that. Originally, Inter Milan's Helenio Herrera was the first to adopt this method for football. The idea came to him when he was coaching at Barcelona; in 1959 he stumbled upon a book about 16th-century mysticism and exercise. The mind needed relaxation and required an environment where players could attain peace, with no outside influence. When players were coached hard, and discipline was everything, they were in lockdown, treated like monks or soldiers, it worked. The intensive period of training and team building improved camaraderie but the players were expected to focus on training and tactics and get their mind and body in the right place. Herrera's stock in trade was the fitness of his sides and their ability to counter-attack and occupy space. This kind of regime was perfect for him.

The original training camp was done for pre-seasons. Il Ritiro was also used in preparation for a huge game or to get back on track after a bad run of form, and that also worked. It has evolved to withdrawing before most games now, in an attempt to galvanise and prepare a day before a game. Coaches, the clubs and society as a whole now deride the concept. They claim it is out of touch, out of date and a step back to a cruel, bygone time.

Most Italian clubs still do it and the players don't like it. Sometimes the coach is made to do it by the club hierarchy. Now, if teams suffer a bad run of results, they are sent on Il Ritiro. It's an attempt to see if the coach can punish the side back into action. Most high-profile calls for Il Ritiro come from chairmen, presidents or owners, not the managers.

The modern coach now understands the best recipe for success and improving results is for players to rest, stay away from the game, spend time with their families and be happy in their heads. Il Ritiro's function has evolved. It is now used by Italian sides in a terrible run of form. After a heavy defeat, coaches take the players on their Ritiro as much as a mercy mission, to keep them out of the spotlight and away from the press and media.

So if Italy ever get near a World Cup Final or a side were preparing for a Champions League Final, you can imagine it is ideal to get away from the clamour, media and distraction and allow players to focus solely on the football and prepare correctly. The closest teams elsewhere get to any sort of bonding is to fly over to Dubai during freezing UK winters and complain about the golf courses. If they want to go hardcore about getting a side fit, revert to the 1970s tried and tested fitness approach of Scottish managers. Make players run up and down sand dunes until they are sick, then make them go again. Give it a few days and they will be petrified and way too traumatised to ever play badly again.

Object: Spider's Web

Subject: Queen's Park

On 9 July 1867, three men gathered in 3 Eglinton Terrace, in the South Side of Glasgow. The minutes from that evening reveal a beautiful and simple motion, 'Tonight at half-past eight o'clock a number of gentlemen met at 3 Eglinton Terrace for the purpose of forming a football club.' They named themselves Queen's Park after the local public area they trained on. The meeting might sound quite matter of fact and far from spectacular but this meeting was crucial. The formation of Queen's Park Football Club was the start of Scottish football (for anyone keen on streets and wondering where Eglinton Terrace in Glasgow is, don't bother; it was taken over as part of Victoria Road and the address today would be close to the Victoria Bar).

The late, great broadcaster and historian Bob Crampsey compared Queen's Park's importance, in terms of significance to the sport of association football, as the formation of the Royal and Ancient Golf Club of St Andrews and Marylebone Cricket Club to golf and cricket respectively. Queen's Park were instrumental in introducing the early rules, and rolling out association football in Glasgow and then Scotland, starting the Scottish Cup and forming the SFA. Not bad for a bunch of amateurs.

Queen's Park organised the first official FIFA-recognised international match when, on 30 November 1872, Scotland met England at West of Scotland Cricket ground, at Hamilton Crescent, off Peel Street, in Partick, Glasgow. I used to work across the road from that cricket ground. Then it was an army barracks, and now it's flats. The playing surface always amazed me. I used to think what a waste, using that as a cricket pitch, it should be a football pitch. It took me off on dreams and I genuinely felt something magical or special around the place. At lunchtimes I used to walk around it, peering in. One day, apropos of nothing, while chatting about football with an older Thistle fan and colleague, I commented on the pitch we were both looking at. He explained the significance – that Scotland played England there in that first international match. I didn't know I was working across from Hamilton Crescent.

Queen's Park provided the 11 players. More than 4,000 watched Scotland play in blue, the colours of Queen's Park before they changed to the black and white hoops. When you consider the team line-ups you can tell this was still football in its infancy. Reports vary as do the formations and team setups; some say Scotland set up with a 2-2-6 and England with a 1-1-8 or a 1-2-7 shape. Sounds more like bus numbers than football formations.

The newspaper reports of this 0-0 draw point to something bigger and, more in keeping with what the side would become renowned for: passing. Scotland (or the Queen's Park side) passed the ball, which was unusual for the time. They effectively frustrated what was a much better team.

Writing in *Nutmeg*, the football periodical, in 2017, Jonathan Wilson said, 'However, perhaps the single biggest event that transformed the sport into the modern game of football was what happened at the West of Scotland Cricket ground in Partick on November 30, 1872. An unfancied Scotland side held England to a 0-0 draw in the first-ever international fixture, but what was important was the way they did it. They passed the ball. Passing, the basis of the modern game, the key aspect of the great central stream of tactical thought, began as an expedient Scottish ploy to frustrate England.'

The following March, Queen's Park formed the SFA with eight other clubs. Football or a close version to what we know today, was played mostly in public schools, with different codes and rules. Following on from Ebenezer Morley and the FA in England in 1863, Queen's Park set about trying to unify, organise and lay down some rules. The team itself continued to train hard and worked at a style of play, one which turned heads of coaches across Europe. A passing game, one requiring a great first touch, ability to control the ball, tactical awareness and a collective team approach.

In this era, football was one of kick and rush, tough tackling and getting the ball to the most skilled winger, who would dribble with the ball. Queen's Park played with collective cohesion and it brought success. The 1880s saw the club attract great names such as eight-time Scottish Cup winner Charles Campbell, who won 13 caps for Scotland. Wattie Arnott was capped 14 times for Scotland; a great all-around sportsman, he was a proficient cricketer and tennis player. Robert Smyth McColl scored for fun at Queen's before turning pro and moving to Newcastle and then Rangers. They also had Andrew Watson, the first black footballer, who captained Scotland in his first game, a 6-1 win over England. No football museum in the world could open its doors and not have something to highlight the importance of the original Queen's Park side.

Practically 100 years after the meeting, Celtic, in 1967, playing a pass and move game handed down and evolved through the decades from great footballing minds, became the first British team to win the European Cup, reaching the pinnacle of the continent using an approach set up by Queen's Park.

For years Queen's Park were known for being the only fully amateur side in Scotland's professional leagues. They made a virtue out of it. The club's Latin motto was 'Ludere Causa Ludendi' – 'To play for the sake of playing'. In 2019, the club's membership took a historic vote and decided to become professional.

Object: Massive Football Boots
Subject: Günter Netzer

In the 1970s, if Johan Cruyff was Steve McQueen then Günter Netzer was Robert Redford. Perhaps, though, with his hair and love of fast cars, James Hunt might be more appropriate. Netzer was a superstar in the Bundesliga; a maverick, attacking midfielder in the Borussia Mönchengladbach side who took on Bayern Munich and wrestled the title from them in 1970 and 1971. He spent ten years starring in the team from 1963 to 1973, playing 349 times and scoring 129 goals.

As well as being a remarkable playmaker, he was astute off the park. He cultivated a clever media image, the antithesis of the safe boy next door Beckenbauer. Netzer was a long-haired playboy, opened a nightclub called 'Lover's Lane' (a business move; nightclubs were for owning, not for drinking in) and bought and drove high-end fast cars, especially Ferraris and Porsches. He was considered too hard-headed and not a team player by the German national side and signed for Real Madrid in 1973, winning two La Liga titles with the Spanish giants.

An effortlessly stylish footballer, he looked the part too with his flowing blond hair. He could change games with a pass, bring in team-mates, and see options on a pitch that few others could. Long, short or diagonal, he had every pass in the toolbox – and a level of precision that made him one of the best playmakers in the world. He was often referred to as 'The Conductor' (his nickname at the club was 'Karajan', after the conductor Herbert von Karajan, though that was probably more attributed to his hair). He was outstanding with free kicks, controlled games, an entertainer who loved a spectacular goal or two. Netzer was up against his own team-mates Berti Vogts and Rainer Bonhof but also saw off his rivals at Bayern – Franz Beckenbauer, Gerd Müller, Paul Breitner and Sepp Maier – to become German player of the year in 1972 and 1973.

When Barcelona signed Johan Cruyff, Real Madrid responded by signing Netzer, making him the first German to play for the club. Like Cruyff, Netzer was the son of a greengrocer, and both left their local clubs (Ajax and Mönchengladbach) for Spain, in the same year, 1973. Like Cruyff, he always knew his own mind. Netzer was a maverick in an era of cold professionalism, one of the reasons why he only earned 30 caps for his country; he was too much of an individual superstar when coaches like Helmut Schön demanded a team collective.

Two moments encapsulated his character and single-mindedness; the first, when West Germany played England in the European Nations' Cup – the European Championship as it is now known. In 1972 the quarter-finals were played over two legs, then four nations headed to the finals. In the first leg at Wembley, coach Helmut Schön had selected six Bayern Munich players. With Beckenbauer and Netzer, not one but two playmakers featured in the starting XI, and the West Germans set up in a 1-3-3-3 formation. They dictated play and the rhythm of the game. When Beckenbauer moved from sweeper up the field, Netzer would fall back and cover. This was Netzer's idea and he was the architect of the victory. He suggested they copy the way Mönchengladbach set up. The coach was happy to let him and Beckenbauer organise and set up the way they wanted. The game is considered a watershed moment in German football.

Hoeness scored the opener. The Germans looked in control but with 12 minutes remaining, England scored an equaliser through Franny Lee. West Germany then found another gear and Netzer scored from the spot when Siggi Held was brought down, then Gerd Müller got his obligatory goal, the final one of the game. It was felt at the time that this was the start of a golden age. Beckenbauer was imperious, Netzer linked up play, and Uli Hoeness was powerful and lightning-quick.

West Germany would go on to win the trophy in Belgium – though if England had won the tie, the competition would have been played at Wembley. Two years later, his nation would win the World Cup, although Netzer was edged out in favour of Wolfgang Overath at the competition.

Until then, the Germans had struggled against England, and it's hard to believe that they were something of a bogey team. No side from the European mainland had previously taken points from England in a competitive game at Wembley. The Germans had not only won 3-1 but played better; their movement and passing was slicker, they were more cohesive as a team and technically superior. Netzer proved he was not just a maverick but one who influenced games.

The second moment was during his last game for Gladbach, in the 1973 German Cup Final. His manager Hennes Weisweiler decided to leave him on the bench. It was reported the coach didn't think he was fit enough. The truth, kept from the public, was that in the build-up to the final against FC Köln, Netzer had informed the club his mother had died and more pertinently, told the manager he was leaving for Real Madrid. Fans and pundits were shocked that Weisweiler had dropped him.

When Netzer found out he wasn't starting, he collected his bag to leave. His team-mates Vogts and Bonhof pleaded with him to stay, to come on and prove everyone wrong. He was persuaded to take his place on the bench but at half-time and later in the second half when the coach called him to get ready to go on, Netzer refused. The game ended 1-1 and went into extra time. The crowd were roaring and squealing for Netzer. As extra time began, Netzer told his coach he was going on – and he did. Remarkably, he substituted himself on. Imagine a player doing that now. Not only did he walk on but three minutes later, he received the ball with his back to goal, turned and ran at Köln, then passed out to Bonhof and continued his run into the box. Bonhof played a perfect pass to Netzer, who rattled a powerful left-footed shot into the top corner. His last game for the club – the stuff of dreams. The commentator called it perfectly on the full-time whistle, 'Günter Netzer – superstar!'

Single-minded, opinionated and strong-willed, he was one of football's rock stars. He was at Frank Sinatra's daughter's wedding, sitting at a table that included Neil Diamond and Sammy Davis Jr. He also had special boots made as he was a size 13 but only 5ft 10in.

Günter Netzer: Superstar. Indeed!

The Unknown Knowns

Football is full of people we should know more about. We may have heard fleetingly about either their astonishing or sometimes tragic lives. This wing is dedicated to their undervalued contribution and an attempt to highlight their story.

Object: KKK Pillow Slip
Subject: FA Racist Snub to Jack Leslie

Jack Leslie should have been the first black footballer to represent England when he was selected in 1925, but sadly he was sent packing once selectors were informed of his ethnicity.

Leslie played for Plymouth Argyle, signing in 1921 from Barking Town. He impressed at Barking, scoring 250 goals. He played for Argyle for 14 years, making 401 appearances and scoring 137 goals. He was a left-sided attacker, inside-left and centre-forward.

In an interview in 1978, Leslie confirmed he remembered the day, quite vividly, when his manager at Plymouth, Bob Jack, invited him to his office for a chat. It would have been memorable because players lived in fear of the dreaded call into the manager's office. 'One day, a Tuesday as I remember it, the manager calls me in,' he said. He was asked to take a seat and nervously sat down, then Jack continued, 'Johnnie, I have got great news for you. You have been picked for England.' But then, sadly, the story quietly and cruelly petered out.

Leslie was left wondering what was happening. Before the press were informed of his official selection, the player was dropped out of the first national team to the reserves, who would still travel. But he was then dropped from the list completely. 'Suddenly, everyone stopped talking about it,' recalled Jack. 'I did hear that the FA had come to have another look at me. Not at me football, but at me face. They asked, and found they'd made a ricket. Found out about me daddy, and that was it. No one ever told me officially, but that had to be the reason.'

Leslie's suspicions could be accurate for at that time, Plymouth were a Third Division side. None of the selectors would have been to a Plymouth game. For this tournament, due to the England side's fortunes being so poor, the FA decided to try a fresh approach in the home internationals and selected the player based on their attacking and goalscoring skill. It sounds as though the decision was based on facts and figures in match reports. They only decided to check him out when rumours circulated he might be black. It was clear that they had been unaware of his ethnicity.

The first black player to play internationally anywhere in the world was Andrew Watson, who appeared three times for Scotland between 1881 and 1882. Anyone who visits the wonderful Scottish Football Museum at Hampden Park will know about him. He is especially popular as in two of his games, the full-back captained Scotland to a 6-1 victory in 1881 against England at the Oval cricket ground in London (Scotland had four goals disallowed – probably due to differences in the rules). In the following game, against Wales, he skippered the side to a 5-1 hammering. His final cap was against England in March 1882, and Scotland won 5-1.

Arthur Wharton was the first black player to play professionally in the English Football League, in 1885. Wales selected Eddie Parris from Bradford Park Avenue in 1931. The first non-white player to represent the England national team was Hong Y Soo – better known as Frank Soo, he was born in Derby and brought up in Liverpool to a Chinese father and English mother. Playing primarily for Stoke, he represented England in nine wartime international friendlies.

You can imagine how courageous a player Jack Leslie was. If you saw the way black players were treated in the 1970s, imagine what it would have been like in the 1920s.

On finishing his career, the Canning Town-born Londoner came back home and settled down. He returned to his trade as a boilermaker. After retiring and bored, Jack's wife nudged him to head over to West Ham and ask if they needed anything done around the club. Ron Greenwood immediately recognised Jack and found him work on the ground staff, in the boot room, among football people, and despite this being viewed, by some, as a demeaning and insulting role, he was adored by the staff and it was a job he loved. He died in 1988, aged 88.

Following the events in the USA and the Black Lives Matter campaign in 2020, Leslie's story was quite rightly brought up, allowing the modern era a chance to reflect on his treatment. A crowd-funder was started and Plymouth supporters raised money for a statue. The target was reached through high-profile support from social media. The Football Association also came on board to sponsor the campaign, with then-chairman Greg Clarke saying, 'Stories like this are incredibly sad. Discrimination in the game, in any form, is unacceptable. We must always remember pioneers like Jack Leslie and be thankful that football is in a very different place today.'

Clark would, in November of the same year, have to stand down as FA chairman after he was heavily criticised for making derogatory comments during an appearance before a Digital, Culture, Media and Sport committee. The 63-year-old looked and sounded desperately out of touch as he made several inappropriate comments, mainly his use of the term 'coloured'.

Object: Scout's Hat
Subject: James Richardson Spensley

James Richardson Spensley is one of those people worthy of a biopic. He's straight out of a boys' own adventure, filled with action and virtuosity. Born in London's Stoke Newington, on 17 May 1867, his family hailed from Swaledale, Yorkshire. On graduating in medicine, he moved to Genoa in 1896 to work for a British mining company. His role there was primarily to aid and help ill English sailors working on coal ships.

Richardson Spensley could speak Greek and Sanskrit and also wrote for the *Daily Mail*. An all-round sportsman, he was a keen boxer. He paid five lire to join Genoa Cricket and Athletic Club – a club formed by British expats. Anything to play some cricket.

In 1897 he opened a football section in the club. Richardson Spensley was also a defender who later became the goalkeeper, the captain and probably even made the tea at half-time. Eventually, his football wing had superseded the athletics club and became Genoa Cricket and Football Club. He persuaded the club's board to start admitting local Italians to improve the team and he would become their first player-manager.

Italian football was in its formative stages thanks to other 'founding fathers' such as Edoardo Bosio, the son of a Swiss Italian brewer in Turin. Bosio had been working in Nottingham, where he noticed the genuine excitement for Notts County and Nottingham Forest, loved their strips, how much football was being watched and the fervour at the games. He and Herbert Kilpin in Turin set up clubs there. These were informal get-togethers for a workout and some fresh air, and it was Richardson Spensley who formalised proceedings, setting in place the rules and competitions.

The first official and competitive game in Italian football would soon take place, when Genoa CFC and Football Club Torinese faced each other on 6 January 1898. The side from Torino won 1-0.

This led to the formation of the Italian Football Federation and by May 1989 the three Torino sides (Bosio and Kilpin's Internazionale di Torino, FC Torinese and Ginnastica Torino) faced Richardson Spensley's Genoa, in a four-club, one-day tournament held in Turin. Richardson Spensley also set up and participated in the first Italian football championship in 1898, which Genoa won. He would win six titles. He was also a philanthropist and an active member of the community, setting up schools for street children.

As he also knew Robert Baden-Powell who set up the Scouts, Richardson Spensley and Mario Mazza founded the first Italian scouting movement in 1910. Richardson Spensley tried to enlist in the forces on multiple occasions and was eventually allowed to join as a lieutenant in the Royal Army Medical Corps.

He would die heroically when, out of compassion, while tending a wounded German soldier in no man's land during the First World War in 1915, he was shot by a German sniper. He was taken as a prisoner of war, tragically dying of his injuries on 10 November 1915 in the officers' prison at Mainz.

Object: Great Northern Railways Locomotive

Subject: Jimmy Hasty

Like many clubs formed in this era, League of Ireland's Dundalk FC, were formed in 1903 as Dundalk G.N.R. – Great Northern Railways (Ireland) and, like Manchester United, were originally a works team. One of the sides most famous players Jimmy Hasty was born in Sailortown, Belfast. He played for Dundalk in the early 1960s and was the epitome of the modern striker; 6ft 1in, fast, skilful, lithe and possessing calm reassurance and marvellous balance. He could hold up the ball, bring in team-mates, pass superbly and take on defenders for fun. Every Dundalk attack was played through him. Along with his balance, he could head the ball superbly and was equally proficient with his left and right foot.

Hasty also stood out for another reason – he only had one arm. He had lost an arm after an accident in a mill on his first day at work, aged 14. He refused to give up, though. When others would have quit, Hasty fed off the adversity and learned to cope. As a promising amateur, he received interest from Nottingham Forest but because of his arm, there were issues over insurance. He played for Islandmagee before moving to Newry Town, then Dundalk.

He caught the eye at Newry when he bagged 38 goals. Three Dundalk directors, headed by Jim Malone, had been watching the player and decided to go for it and make him an offer. They signed him. This created a rift with other Dundalk board members angry at the player being signed without their consent. When they heard he only had one arm, it became so heated that Malone put his money where his mouth was and promised to underwrite every penny if the signing proved an error of judgement. Malone would be proved correct.

When Hasty started to find the back of the net, and he did – he played 170 games for Dundalk, scoring 103 goals – the crowds flocked to see him. At first, it was intrigue and curiosity. Was this true? Did their latest striker only have one arm? The Oriel Park gates had to be locked, such was the fervour to see their latest hero. It was true, the lad did only have one arm, but what a player.

When he got into his stride, any doubt was soon forgotten. He scored on his debut against Cork Celtic in November 1960 and soon was the talk of the town. He was not only a great scorer but also adept at laying off and assisting others. In the first month, Hasty's goals and his assists yielded 24 goals for the team in five league ties. Hasty himself underlined he was no fluke when in December, Dundalk travelled to Milltown to face Shamrock Rovers. A rammed stadium saw the player score twice and set up two in a 4-2 victory.

Over the second two seasons Hasty had been prone to injury, perhaps not being able to fully protect himself, especially when he became so prominent and an easy target for opponents. However, he helped the club win the league title for the first time in 30 years in 1962/63. The following season, injury-free, in 1963/64 he scored 35 goals. Once the faithful got over the novelty, his ability quickly superseded any disability. Supporters stopped looking at what remained of his arm and marvelled at his touch for a big man and his ability to control the ball and bring in team-mates.

Hasty scored in the European Cup against FC Zurich when the Lilywhites narrowly lost to a side who would beat Galatasaray then PSV Eindhoven and reach the semi-finals of the competition that year. They were down 3-0 in the first leg, played in Dublin. But in the return leg, Hasty set up one, scored another and hit the bar. Dundalk, according to reports and some rare footage, were all over Zurich.

The player is still legendary in Dundalk and parts of Belfast. He played for Dundalk from 1960 until 1966 before moving to Drogheda and then eventually back home to Belfast due to work commitments. He worked as a bookmaker. Hasty was murdered outside his Belfast home by the loyalist Ulster Protestant Action group, a group with links to the UVF, on 11 October 1974, as he left to go to work.

Object: Poacher

Subject: Bican the Unknown Scorer

When Ronaldo's collective career goal tally hit 760 it was assumed that took him past Josef Bican's record of 759. It is almost impossible to reach an accurate figure due to the era Bican played and the various divisions he played across. This doesn't stop stat mad voices chipping in with all kinds of numbers. The Czech FA did an in-depth count of his official goals and found he had 821 goals. FIFA also stated he had 805. For our sanity and a bit of fun let's use industry 'Stat-Nav' Rec.Sport.Soccer.Statistics.Foundation (RSSSF) who threw the proverbial spanner in the works. Over 28 years as a player, they have tried to include friendlies, tournaments and any game where there is an official record. They have 948 goals from 621 official games and a further 864 goals in 468 friendlies. The bad news for Ronaldo is that the German Erwin Helmchen, born in 1907, scored 981 goals in official games.

Bican was born in Vienna to Czech parents in the immigrant suburb of Favoriten, an industrial area most famous for brick factories. His father František was a footballer but died early due to complications from a damaged kidney after refusing an operation. Losing his father while so young, he was brought up poor – no shoes on his feet poor. Bican was tall for the time. The astounding goalscoring rate is put down to his powerful sprinting and speed. It is said Bican could run 100m in 10.8 seconds, which was only half a second off the then-world record.

He started at Hertha Vienna and by 18 was signed by Rapid Vienna in 1931. By 1933, aged 20, Bican received international recognition when he was called up to the illustrious *Wunderteam*. He scored in the 1934 World Cup when Austria beat France.

In 1937 he signed for Slavia Prague and applied for Czech citizenship. He wanted out of Vienna as he could see what was happening with the Nazi party and left for the Czech Republic. He played there for 11 years and was Europe's top scorer across five seasons. He was the top league scorer on 12 occasions. In one season he scored 57 goals in 26 games.

He played internationally for three countries: Austria (19 caps), Czechoslovakia (14 caps) and once for Bohemia and Moravia (a partially annexed territory of Nazi Germany).

With Bican's record, career and stats rightfully re-assessed, a few points were highlighted. His lower profile, in comparison to say, Pelé, was blamed on Bican missing a chance to play in the 1938 World Cup in France because of an administration error with his registration for Czechoslovakia. The subsequent two tournaments were cancelled because of the Second World War. It was agreed that he would cost upwards of £300m in today's transfer market.

Sex and Drugs and Sausage Rolls

Footballers can be a bit debauched in the nookie stakes. Young, fit, healthy people, with a flash car, loads of cash with too much time on their hands. What could possibly go wrong? Not keen lovers of reading, apart from the *Racing Post*, few become poets, artists or classical composers.

Object: Floodlights
Subject: Dino Drpić

It would seem that footballers are footballers everywhere you go. Local lad comes through the club's academy, fast cars, money, glamour model wife on their arm. Then the fame, the anger issues, gambling addiction. For this particular no-nonsense 6ft 5in Croatia Zagreb player, if you had to create the perfect tabloid fodder footballer then look no further.

This set of floodlights is here in honour – or shame – of Dino Drpić. The Croatian defender and his then-wife Nives Celzijus had sex in the centre circle of Zagreb's Maksimir Stadium. Drpić asked friends at the stadium to leave the floodlights on so they could make his dream come true. Yes, I suppose we love those special, unforgettable nights, those magical nights under the floodlights.

However, his dream of having sex on the centre spot in effect would be the moment that ruined his career. When his wife took to the TV chat-show circuit to promote her book, she spilt the beans. While appearing on Serbian RTV Pink's *The Ami G Show,* she revealed the story, 'Dino had arranged that people should turn on the stadium lights for us and he finally fulfilled his dream of having sex in the middle of a football pitch. It was very naughty.' His club immediately placed the naughty boy on the transfer list. After the scandal hit, Drpić was transferred to Germany where he and his wife became known as the David and Victoria Beckham of Baden.

Also, in keeping with many footballers, Drpić struggled to cope with fame and money. Despite the fast cars, flash lifestyle and glamour model wife, he didn't have his troubles to seek. His gambling issues have been extensively reported, and at one point he was even given a cash loan by his club to help pay off his debts but still he continued to frequent Zagreb's casinos. These are the kind of actions that fill tabloid newspapers.

Drpić also had anger management issues, with several violent outbursts. These fights are not so bad if it's 'just the lads, letting off steam in training', great-for-team-spirit kind of outbursts. The game changes when you start having fights with the police. After being transfer listed, he was eventually released from the club's books.

I'm not sure having sex on the centre spot is exactly the best or most romantic of moves. Rats, mice and foxes do all sorts on that grass. Then there's the amount of body fluid, spit, blood and sweat from players, so it might not sound as romantic as you'd first think. I'd need the groundsman in, giving it a thorough going-over, a clean and a short trim before any of that malarkey.

I have sympathy for players who are hung out to dry. Was it all a bit of an over-reaction? Maybe the club wanted him out and this was their perfect opportunity. They were grown-ups, they were married, it was a mistake, at least they didn't do anyone any harm but from that point onwards Drpić's career veered off course. I wonder what sort of deal his agent could get for his life story.

As for his now ex-wife, Nives, she published a book called *In Bed with Cristiano* about her romantic dalliances with footballers. She also released a saucy single with the awe-inspiring Lennon and McCartney, Leiber and Stoller, Bacharach and David-style lyrical wonder, 'Goal, goal, goal, score me a goal. I'm naked, you are naked, score me a goal' and 'fill me like Ronaldo'. Which is nice.

Object: VHS Cassette
Subject: Bosnich & Yorkie's Porno

If Mark Bosnich tried to draw a line in the sand, he'd probably snort it. That was then. He has since moved on and sorted his life out. When you consider their vigorous training regimes and vanity and add the boredom factor, there should be a multitude of sex scandals taking place in football. A conveyor belt leading to a revolving door for a sex addiction clinic for the likes of Bosnich and, in this incident, Dwight Yorke. Bosnich and Yorke find themselves in the alternative museum because of their stupidity while attempting to discard the evidence of a homemade porn tape.

In 1998, Manchester United's Yorke and his best pal, Aston Villa's Bosnich, had rigged up Yorke's flat to secretly tape and record their exploits with four women. To spice it up and add some much-needed authenticity, for some reason, the players were dressed as women and Bosnich was spanked. According to Yorke, no nookie took place so technically it was only a nearly orgy. Once they were sober and watched their performance and realised the skill and expertise required to properly edit and produce anything remotely professional, never mind perform under pressure, Yorke tossed the video into the rubbish bin. Yes, the rubbish bin. 'Oh, I wonder what bin goes out today? The household bin? The brown garden bin? No, it's the discarded homemade porn tape bin.'

So you can only imagine how proud the tabloid journalist who unscrupulously raked through Yorke's bin must have felt that day when he stumbled upon a VHS tape, took it home and found a major tabloid porn scoop sting handed to him on a plate.

Bosnich had issues. There were addictions, junk food, over-eating, and coke. Yes, there were the Nazi salutes and Hitler impersonations when Villa played Spurs and there was a failed drug test at Chelsea. The goalkeeper has been through the mill. Many were judgemental and sanctimonious. Imagine if you had the chance to even behave half as badly as Bosnich and come through the other side, relatively unscathed? You'd do the same.

It doesn't take much to anger Sir Alex Ferguson, but Bosnich succeeded. In his book, Ferguson claimed Bosnich was a terrible professional. He also said he ate too much junk food and this made him impossible to train and deal with. Ferguson wrote, 'We played down at Wimbledon and Bosnich was tucking into everything: sandwiches, soups, steaks. He was going through the menu. We arrived back in Manchester, and Mark was on his mobile phone to a Chinese restaurant to order a takeaway. I said, "Is there no end to you?"'

Eating fatty food isn't a great lifestyle choice for a top sportsman but would later fade into insignificance. Yorkie was the teacher's pet, but he was capable of winning games; he had a use, he could score. Ferguson saw Bosnich as a liability and he was dispatched to Chelsea. The Australian was a top goalkeeper and when fit, one of the best in the country. At Chelsea he hit his lowest point. He failed a drug test before a game in November 2002 and received a nine-month ban. He would eventually open up and admit he had several problems. He was hooked on cocaine and had a ten-gram-a-day habit.

Thankfully he is well now and a pundit on Australian TV and recovering. He's quite a candid and entertaining contributor. And he's clean. Good luck, and Sir Alex says you have to stay out of McDonald's.

Object: Tord Grip's Accordion
Subject: Sven-Göran Eriksson

With hindsight, when you look at the cold, hard facts and the prevailing thought process around at the time, it was unbelievably brave of the FA to appoint Sven-Göran Eriksson as England coach in January 2001. These were different, more ambitious and invigorating times. The FA had spent millions headhunting the top business CEOs of the day and had appointed an ambitious boss, the Scotsman Adam Crozier from Royal Mail.

This was the new, sexy FA; a thrusting, ambitious, corporate powerhouse and they were keen to shake it up so they signed their first overseas manager. And by overseas we mean a pesky 'foreigner'. Eriksson was the most un-English person in the world (and he spoke like the chef in *The Muppet Show*). His term as coach was certainly eventful; crashing the 'golden generation' out of three tournaments at three quarter-finals, caught up in a media sting and shagging anything that moved.

When Germany beat England in the last game played at the old Wembley in October 2000, manager Kevin Keegan resigned and the FA ultimately went for a 'non-British' appointment in Eriksson, coach of Italian side Lazio at the time. It may be argued that England's idea of itself, the 'England expects' notion, the 'it's coming home' narrative is overplayed. They certainly laid down the rules for the modern game at a time when Charles Dickens was doing the after-dinner circuit when the FA rules were set out by Ebenezer Morley in 1863.

England has always excelled in the bureaucracy, organisation and running of the game. To this day, they

are strategically placed within UEFA, a member of IFAB –
who make the rules – and are most certainly established as
a major footballing nation. It has been a while though, and
they haven't won a tournament since 1966.

At Eriksson's formal appointment at the then-FA HQ
in Soho Square, there were protests; people showed up to
complain about a foreigner being appointed. And what of
the *Daily Mail*? They were predictably unrepentant as they
slavishly played to their readership, 'We've sold our birth-
right down the fjord to a nation of seven million skiers and
hammer throwers who spend half their life in the dark.'

England were sitting bottom of their 2002 World Cup
qualifying group when they took the radical move – and the
board of the FA chief executive, led by Crozier, unanimously
approached Lazio for Eriksson and offered a five-year contract.

Eriksson quickly turned the team's fortunes around,
underpinned by two memorable results: a 5-1 trouncing of
Germany in Munich, then a late equaliser against Greece,
from a David Beckham free kick, which allowed them to
qualify automatically for the World Cup in Japan and South
Korea in 2002. At the finals, England finished second in
Group F behind Sweden after drawing with the Swedes
and Nigeria and beating Argentina. In the round of 16 they
hammered Denmark 3-0 before being beaten by ten-man
Brazil, going out 2-1 to the eventual winners.

Eriksson took England to the 2004 Euros in Portugal.
In the group stage they were up 1-0 against France,
Beckham missed a penalty to make it two, and Zinedine
Zidane scored twice in injury time. The first was a superb
free kick and the second from a penalty after Steven Gerrard
was careless with a back-pass, Henry was brought down by
David James and Zidane dispatched from the spot. They
beat Switzerland 3-0 and Croatia 4-2 to reach the quarter-

finals, where they faced hosts Portugal. A 1-1 draw saw the game going into extra time (despite a clear goal by Sol Campbell being disallowed), it finished 2-2 and England were beaten 6-5 on penalties.

In January 2006, Sven had been stung by the 'Fake Sheikh' undercover *News of the World* reporter Mazher Mahmood, famed for tricking drunk and gullible celebrities. Mahmood had convinced Eriksson he was a wealthy Arab businessman. Eriksson suggested he buy Aston Villa; the club was up for sale and the owner sick and old. Mahmood's extravagant sting – a night of lobster and £900 of vintage champagne – was enough to allow Eriksson (who was accompanied by his agent, Athole Still) to suggest 'everything was possible' when asked if he would be interested in the Villa job. He was caught on tape saying he would leave the England job if he won the World Cup.

During the sting, over a few days at Dubai's seven-star Burj al-Arab hotel, then on a luxury yacht, Sven suggested he would want a deal like José Mourinho's £5m-a-year arrangement at Chelsea. He suggested he could tap up David Beckham, who was unhappy at Real Madrid and desperate to return home, and 'that he would sell more shirts in a week than they had in ten years'. He suggested if it was a London club he would come tomorrow and it would be up to him to convince him to come to Birmingham. Each bit of gossip was further damaging his career.

Eriksson didn't help himself in terms of the optics with this whole embarrassing episode. His revelations about Wayne Rooney having a ferocious temper and Rio Ferdinand being lazy were tepid, but when he said Michael Owen was unhappy at missing out on a return to Liverpool and was only at Newcastle for the money, and because they paid more than Real Madrid had, there was no turning back. No matter how drunk, vulnerable, or cruel the 'sting' was, this looked wrong.

When the tabloid story broke, the FA announced that Eriksson was leaving the job after the 2006 World Cup, something both parties claimed was always the case. England won their group by beating Paraguay then Trinidad and Tobago, and drawing 2-2 with Sweden, but it was not enough for the English press. Even when a Beckham free kick helped to beat Ecuador, the performance was described as dreary and uninspiring. Then it was Portugal when Rooney was red-carded for stamping on Ricardo Carvalho and the famous Cristiano Ronaldo wink. The tie ended 0-0 and England went out 3-1 on penalties. The press became more vicious toward him, yet the Swede did not lose a qualifying match in either the World Cup or the Euros until a defeat against Northern Ireland in 2005. This would be one of only five losses during his reign.

Eriksson, until 2020 at least, was still working in football having managed across 42 years, with 16 teams and worked in eight countries. He was still managing the Philippines in 2019. Only an absolute football nut or a sadist would continue but he was still ploughing away. In Sven's case, the reason was due to losing £10m to a financial advisor, Samir Khan. He won a lawsuit in 2013 against Khan for losses in failed investments. Khan denied the Swede's allegations that he had taken large loans in his name. He later admitted it was true and apologised but Khan himself was bankrupted.

Sven was a great coach, starting from his success at unfashionable IFK Göteborg in Sweden, winning the league, two cups and the UEFA Cup. Over two spells at Benfica he won three league titles and two domestic cups. Then at Sampdoria, he won a domestic cup. At Lazio, when AC, Inter and Juventus were in power, he won an unprecedented title, four domestic cups, the Cup Winners' Cup and the UEFA Super Cup. Most tellingly, his low loss rate meant by the time he vacated the job in 2006, he had taken England from 17th to fifth in the official FIFA world rankings. The harsh truth about the Swede's appointment is that his tenure was always overshadowed by the press and fans only ever wanting Terry Venables.

We know this is a nookie wing but we like Sven too much to even start talking about the stuff with Ulrika Jonsson, Faria Alam and Nancy Dell'Olio. If we started talking about this we would need to mention the secret former lover of Sven, who isn't too good with the finer points of the words 'secret' and 'former', who spoke to *The Mirror* in 2013, Marisa Cauchi. The millionairess was irked at being edged out of his memoir after she had a four-year relationship with the super Swede. She claims that she and at least five other lovers were also elbowed out of the book. It kind of explains the constantly happy, if somewhat tired look on his face.

The accordion belongs to Sven's loyal assistant, Tord Grip, who loved to whip it out and dazzle with his Swedish squeezebox.

Object: Cream Pastries
Subject: Antonio Cassano's Madrid Diet

Italian player Antonio Cassano was the epitome of the modern footballer; an exceptionally quick, talented, technically gifted, and deep-lying striker, who could play as an attacking midfielder. He also had a short temper and was prone to losing the plot, going crazy at referees, team-mates and coaches, especially Fabio Capello. Cream pastries are here to represent Cassano's time as a Real Madrid player. In Madrid, Cassano was scoring like a sex machine. He was lithe, lightning-quick, and technically efficient. On the pitch, however, that's another story.

While at Madrid, the player lived in a hotel and explained in his autobiography, *Dico Tutto* (*I'll Tell Everything*), 'In Madrid, I had a friend who was a hotel waiter. His job was to bring me three or four pastries after I had sex. He would bring the pastries up the stairs, I would escort the woman to him and we would make an exchange: he would take the girl and I would take the pastries. Sex and then food, a perfect night.' Cassano's argument, and his misplaced theory, was that he played better after sex and cakes.

Cassano claimed he'd slept with more than 600 women by the age of 25. It is not too difficult to see where it started to go wrong when he had a diet like that. That's a lot of pastries. After six months in the Spanish capital, he started to notice he was piling on the beef or the cream. The club in the end started to fine him for every gram he was overweight.

Cassano's childhood was troubled and his father left, so it was his mother who raised him while working two jobs. In Bari's old town it was a life of being one step ahead of the police and living on your wits. This was before its gentrification. Any treats were a blessing. Cassano himself stated quite openly that if he hadn't been a footballer, he would have been a criminal and was close to going off the rails. Miraculously though, he had a skill. He could play football and was appearing for Bari by the time he was 17.

I remember seeing him against Inter back then. He received and controlled a pass with his heel and continued to run, then cut back inside and made Christian Panucci and Laurent Blanc look ordinary before sending the keeper Fabrizio Ferron the wrong way.

Capello, who played a strange mix of father-figure and frustrated headteacher, signed Cassano, aged 19, to Roma in 2001. Roma were champions. He signed for a fee of €30m, making him the world's most expensive teenager. He spent five years at Roma, mostly arguing with his manager, team-mates and referees. The final year was spent trying to organise a better deal. He left, acrimoniously, to sign for Real Madrid for €5m.

As fate would decree, Cassano could not believe his bad luck when Capello was named Real Madrid boss. Madrid were going through one of the worst spells in their history and brought in the strict Italian. Capello's time at Madrid was mired in high-profile fall-outs with David Beckham over his contract renewal, and Brazilian striker Ronaldo's fitness. Crucially, though, it was the fans who were unhappy at his defensive style of play. They wanted a more entertaining, cavalier approach. Cassano knew with Madrid's fans and top stars up in arms with Capello, he could play the averages and constantly push his boss's buttons.

Overweight, unfit and out of form, Cassano was caught doing a training-ground impersonation of his boss. He continued to challenge his authority. Too fat to play, he couldn't be loaned or sold on. Yet Capello had a soft spot for the player. Team-mates from the time said they had rarely seen Capello so lenient with other players.

Cassano's lack of discipline and issues over fitness and his weight would follow him throughout his career. At Milan, returning overweight to pre-season training, the club's CEO had to intervene. He threatened to move him on if he did not lose weight and get fit. There were concerns over his fitness and his stamina, then it was discovered it was a health issue. He had suffered an ischemic stroke. He then needed surgery to correct a heart defect. The player buckled down, got healthy and fit, and, remarkably, returned to play in Serie A. He scored in his first match back, continued his great form and was selected to play for Italy in the 2012 Euros.

Such was Cassano's refusal to act like a team player and his reputation for upsetting team harmony, Capello created a word for this kind of behaviour: *Cassanata*. The Italian sports media, press and pundits now use the term generally, for any player lacking team spirit.

Some of his highlights – in a Coppa Italia Final, he was sent off and gave the referee the devil horns sign. Incoming Roma boss Luigi Delneri, who was tough and didn't like Cassano's indiscipline, dropped him when he joined in 2004. Bruno Conti, the incoming Roma coach, brought Cassano back and made him skipper; his head became so big that his neck struggled to cope. When Luciano Spalletti took over in 2005, Cassano said, 'You're not coaching those useless players you had at Udinese. This isn't your house, it's my house.'

Cassano's final season was spent trying to get away from Roma. Entrenched in a row over his contract, he did the unthinkable and turned on his strike partner, Mr Roma himself, Francesco Totti, over a payment received for appearing on TV. He had a public row with Capello at Real

Madrid when he was made to warm up on the touchline for most of the second half and wasn't used as a sub. In the dressing room after the game, he told his boss, 'You are a piece of s***, you're more fake than Monopoly money.'

He would also play for Inter Milan, Parma, Sampdoria and Hellas Verona but retired from the game in September 2017, aged 35. Cassano's career and personality will always be discussed, for good and bad, few players can claim to have had their name evolve into a euphemism.

Object: Orange Speedos
Subject: Dutch Pool Party

It is 1974 and the World Cup is reaching a glorious climax in Munich, with the final only a few days away. The Dutch are mesmerizing the football world with Total Football (their version of it; the system existed before but they only tweaked it, and journalists cleverly re-branded it). Grown men, commentators and journalists are extolling the virtues of these fit, handsome, sexy men. The world has fallen in love with the Dutch side and long hair, love beads and their liberal attitude to life. They play with freedom and a pulsating rhythm but this controlling style of play needs discipline and stamina, so they must be amazing in bed, right?

I'm not sure what the Dutch for 'shit hits the fan' is. If it has anything to do with the way they think, it's probably something to do with checking the tulip manure on the wheels of your bicycle and being rattled on the head by a windmill. What exactly is claimed to have happened that night is best described in this lurid headline, 'Cruyff, Sekt, Nackte Mädchen unde ein kühles Bad'. Or, 'Cruyff, Champagne, Naked Girls and a Cool Bath'.

The German tabloid *Bild* had gone for the Dutch side and as you can imagine, much was made of their sinfulness. The Germans had got to them. Mind games. They had brought the egotistical big heads down a peg or two.

The idea the West German side won the World Cup by putting the Dutch off their stride is a misnomer. It didn't look like that after one minute when Cruyff was brought down in the box and Johan Neeskens scored before a West German player even had touched the ball. If editors of *Bild* intended to put the Dutch off, after the opening to the final, it looked like it had backfired.

Bild had bunged waiters to allow photographers in to see girls frolicking in a naked pool party. *Bild* was the biggest-selling tabloid in West Germany. The headlines read like the Dutch base at Hiltrup-Munster would be Fellini's *Satyricon*, but in truth was probably more like a *Carry On* movie or *Benny Hill*. This was less a sensational-sexclusive-super-soaraway-sizzler and more a damp squib.

Cruyff denied being involved and, allegedly, spent most of the evening before the World Cup Final on the phone to his wife convincing her he wasn't part of it. The images were vague and the story more so. To this day no one knows exactly what happened. What can only be confirmed and revisited is what was reported in the press versus what we know as hard facts.

If the idea was to unsettle the Dutch, it worked; they had to deal with their wives and partners and explain that nothing happened. The players denied the story and said it was lies. Dutch manager Rinus Michels said it was an attempt by the Germans to undermine his team and cause worry and concern to their wives and families.

The closest we have to something resembling the truth is this list of facts: after beating Brazil in the semi-final, the Dutch players celebrated at the team hotel. The session lasted late into the evening, and some players and girls ended up naked together in the pool. The hotel staff tipped off *Bild*.

Having read, researched and pored over in forensic detail as many versions of the Dutch pool party as possible I can reveal around 95 per cent of what is written is wrong. The inaccuracies would see the case break down in a court of law. The defence points to this random account which states, 'The night before the 1974 World Cup Final between the

Netherlands and West Germany, tabloid newspaper *Bild* bribed security guards of the hotel where the Dutch players were staying and sent in several scantily-clad girls to the pool area.' Okay, let's look at this. Fact one – the incident occurred after the semi-final victory over Brazil on Wednesday evening, so four days out. Also, the girls involved were waitresses and staff from the hotel, who were invited for some drinks and joined after their shift. This would tie in with the fact the pool was indoors. Let's continue. 'As the women mingled, out popped the paparazzi to the pool area and a scandal was born.' Fact two – the same as fact one, the pool was indoors. The Dutch players consequently spent hours on the phone with their wives desperately trying to explain the situation. They would lose the final, 2-1.

The event happened on Wednesday, but such is the nature of this kind of journalism, the story was kept back by the German tabloid until the weekend for maximum disruption and effect, and newspaper sales.

Fact three – Cruyff being up all night on the phone to his wife. No. He was spotted during the day at the hotel reception on the phone convincing her that it was a lie. On the day in question, she was travelling from Barcelona to Amsterdam before heading to the final in Munich on Sunday. The whole event, if unfortunate, sounds like skinny dipping in the pool and after it has been forced through the tabloid grinder comes out as 'drink and drug-fuelled orgy'.

To throw a giant curveball into the story, Auke Kok, the esteemed Dutch journalist, published a book in 2004 called *1974: We Were the Best*. In that, Kok states that the swimming pool party did occur and that the players were behaving like rock stars. An assistant coach had to be sent home because he went all Keith Moon, throwing wine bottles at the hotel bar wall, empty ones mind you.

No matter the accuracy of the story, the players would not have known this at the time but the pool party, then the defeat to West Germany was, with hindsight, the beginning of the end of Total Football.

Sublime and Ridiculous

Sometimes football can be too surreal and bizarre to comprehend. This wing tries its best to help make sense of the sublime and the ridiculous.

Object: Pig's Head
Subject: Luís Figo

The Pig's Head sounds more like the name of a rural pub, but this particular porcine noggin was launched at Real Madrid's Luís Figo, the famed Portuguese midfielder.

Such was the ire and anger toward the former Barcelona legend that when he returned to play against his old side, the reception was horrendous. In the intervening months since he signed for Madrid, Barça fans had time to reflect on the decision taken by the handsome but treacherous Judas.

Those present at the game couldn't believe the level of hatred and anger directed at their one-time hero. They joined in, though. It would be remiss not to. The noise and whistling toward the 'traitor' must have been astonishing and would have been amplified within the cauldron of the Camp Nou. Even on TV there was a wall of sound, the deaf were healed, the sheer white noise virtually broke sangria glasses and sent chandeliers clattering up and down the land.

The unfolding cacophony of whistles and boos erupted whenever Figo kicked the ball and escalated – if it were possible – when he ventured toward the touchline. During the second half, when Figo approached to take a corner in front of the section housing the Barcelona Ultras, the *Boixos Nois,* the bedlam reached fever pitch and a frightening crescendo. The madness wasn't confined to the Ultras. The normally clipped and polite stadium announcer, the now late Manel Vich, even before the match, when reading the team line-ups, after he read Figo's name deliberately left a gap for the 100,000 fans present to boo. Cue a noise that could only be compared to fighter jets flying overhead.

To call it a hostile atmosphere would be to attribute the most useless of euphemisms. Fans were using anything they could get their hands on; the usual items such as lighters, a whisky bottle (empty), and a suckling pig's head. It was so volatile that police in riot gear were cowering from the crowd. Camera close-ups showed the player's troubled expression at corners, yet such was Figo's professionalism he still had a great game.

The reason for such a dreadful reaction was because the Barça fans had loved and idolised him. It's how football fans show their emotion. While he played for Barcelona, the fans adored Figo and there was a real bond with him. He had played in a side that won two league titles and the European Cup Winners' Cup in 1996/97 with players like Ronaldo, Rivaldo and Patrick Kluivert. Most importantly, Catalans felt that with Figo playing for them they were finally showing the world the calibre of player they could attract. Not only one of the best players in the world but also one who was universally respected. Here was a player who remained dignified and statesman-like on and off the park. He had even supported Catalonia's independence. So when he left them for their arch-rivals in the summer of 2000 they were devastated. In five seasons at Barcelona Figo played 249 games, scoring 45 goals.

This is football and nothing is ever as simple as it appears. When we look in detail, this was all about power games. This was the start of the Galacticos era at Madrid, of superstar signings and promises made to thousands who would be voting in their next president. That summer would see both clubs stage presidential elections.

The hopeful candidate for Madrid, Florentino Pérez, was promising the fans Figo in return for their vote. Barcelona's presidential candidate had run on a ticket telling the fans that Figo was going nowhere. He was. Meanwhile, Josep Lluís

Núñez, the incumbent and out-of-touch president, was telling everyone that Figo was bluffing; Núñez would remain strong and wouldn't have a gun held to his head by Real Madrid or Figo. The Catalans weren't without fault. Núñez had been approached by the player but refused to take it seriously. Figo explained later, 'I was at Euro 2000 and things were going fine. However, the possibility of one of the candidates to the Real presidency – it was Pérez – signing me emerged, and I spoke to president Núñez about that offer.'

Those running as presidential candidates for Barça, especially favourite Joan Gaspart, were unequivocal that Figo was staying. Meanwhile, at Madrid, Pérez was telling the 80,000 Madrid electorate that if he didn't lure Figo to the Bernabéu, he would pay their season ticket money for the following season.

Figo had become a political pawn for both. The player had stated he wanted to remain at Barcelona but signed a pre-contract with Real Madrid to force Barcelona's hand and improve his position in contract negotiations. He assumed the contract would not be triggered. As far as Figo was concerned, two crucial issues had to come into play to force the move through. The first was that Pérez was voted in. No one expected Pérez to beat the favourite, Lorenzo Sanz. He did. Secondly, Real Madrid had to break the then record world transfer fee and pay €62m to meet the release clause. They did. Figo's plan spectacularly backfired and, as he had signed a pre-contract agreement, he would, whether he liked it or not, be going to the Bernabéu.

Pérez won, Gaspart deposed Núñez, and Figo was on his way. Allegedly, the pre-contract had a clause in it that if Pérez won and Figo declined and stayed at Barça, he had to pay a penalty of £18.75m. The player had no option other than to start reading the small print and stop signing contracts everywhere (he once received a two-year ban from Italian football when he controversially signed for Juventus and Parma at the same time). Oh, and don't take corners for Madrid in the Camp Nou.

Object: Toilet Roll
Subject: Neeskens v Núñez

Even I will accept that a lonely loo roll is a strange exhibit in such an esteemed museum, but this paper represents something that saw a player's career at one of the biggest clubs in Europe come to an end. While Barcelona's president, José Luis Núñez, was answering a call of nature he noticed he was out of toilet paper. He asked the player in the adjoining cubicle (whom Núñez knew was one of his star players, Johan Neeskens) to pass a roll under the stall. Neeskens chose to ignore his pleas, leaving him high but not so dry. How did Núñez react? Like any calm, level-headed, dispassionate president, he transferred Neeskens at the earliest possible moment. He was kicked out of the club and sent packing to New York Cosmos.

Núñez appears like a kindly figure yet like most who reach this level, they are made of sterner stuff and hold on to a grudge like studio boss Jack Woltz in *The Godfather* to Johnny Fontane. Núñez was a Spanish construction giant who transformed Barcelona, rebuilding both the infrastructure (the stadium was improved, capacity raised to 120,000, a museum and a smaller stadium were also built, and in 1979, at Johan Cruyff's insistence, La Masia youth academy was revamped). He was the longest-serving president, holding office from 1978 to 2000.

The incident took place in the toilets of Hércules CF, in the Rico Perez stadium in Alicante. Nothing worse, when you need a decent wipe and your stall neighbour stalls on your pleas. If I was Neeskens, I would do the same. I was brought up not to speak to strange men communicating from a toilet stall, club president or not. Had Neeskens been 34 with his pension pot looming, you could understand a lucrative move to the then big-spending Cosmos. Even if the player had served his purpose and was no longer of any use, kicking him out for not passing a toilet roll under a stall for most people would be regarded as an over-reaction. After all, Neeskens was aged 28 and had helped Barcelona win the European Cup Winners' Cup.

At the time, his choice of the Cosmos was unusual as he could have walked into any major European club at this point. The North American Soccer League wasn't a great level, and for many it was seen as a waste of talent with the Dutch midfielder having at least another four years in him, easily.

Neeskens had left Ajax to join Barcelona and team up with Cruyff and Rinus Michels. If Total Football was a style evolved and popularised by Michels and his Dutch side at the 1974 World Cup, and Cruyff was the architect, then Neeskens was the heartbeat, the silk and the steel. He was a tireless runner, great technically, astute and able to play across the park – he started as a full-back at Ajax, then moved into a central midfield area where he supported his partner in crime, Núñez's nemesis Cruyff. He is regarded as one of the finest footballers the Netherlands has ever produced. His work rate – born of his position as a box-to-box midfielder and dedication to the cause – made him a huge favourite wherever he played.

As for Núñez, it was ironic for the son of a customs officer that he would later be done for bribing tax inspectors. Despite all his work for Barcelona, he will always be remembered for being sent to jail for six years after a corruption investigation. His sentence was later reduced to 26 months.

What most likely happened is that Neeskens had decided he wanted away and knew how to play it by upsetting Núñez.

The players were streetwise and knew how to annoy people; meanwhile, his best pal Cruyff was singing the praises of the money and the glamour (though not the surfaces – Cruyff hated Astroturf, and despite signing a pre-contract with the Cosmos and promising to join them, he chose instead to sign for LA Aztecs, who were managed by Rinus Michels and played on lush grass). Their agent Cor Coster had already established great contacts with many US clubs, particularly the Ertegun brothers, from Atlantic Records (the label of Led Zeppelin, Dusty Springfield and more), who owned the Cosmos franchise. It would have been party central in New York. It is most likely he knew the toilet roll incident, combined with his association with Cruyff and his agent, made him an immediate adversary of the president. Anyone with any links to Cruyff probably had their card marked.

Neeskens returned to Barça as a coach with Frank Rijkaard in 2006 and would help them win the Champions League; both were sacked when Pep Guardiola took over in 2008. But toilet roll? Football people, eh?

Object: Shipwreck
Subject: Raith Rovers Shipwrecked

In 1923, the Raith Rovers side, of Kirkcaldy (not Raith; if you say 'dancing on the streets of Raith' you will have your head kicked in) were shipwrecked. They are not the only football team subject to figurative imagery and described as lost at sea, having gone off course or even become rudderless under ropey management, but they are one of the first football teams to be, quite literally, shipwrecked.

Raith, who the previous year had enjoyed a trouble-free and successful tour of Denmark, decided they would set sail for a tour in warmer climes. They would play in the Canary Islands. How forward-thinking were they – taking the lads off on tour to unwind and train in a hot spot.

The 13 players, management and staff set sail on a ship called the SS *Highland Loch*, from Tilbury Docks in Essex. The boat itself was stopping off in Spain on its way to Buenos Aires and full of a cargo of chilled beef. Oh, the glamour. The team were excited as they were heading for Vigo to witness a bullfight.

The ship was struggling off the coast of Galicia in north-west Spain, negotiating Cape Finisterre when they got into difficulty (in Roman times, they thought this was the end of the world and, if you've seen it when it gets choppy, you'd understand why the name in Latin, *fines terrae*, means 'end of the earth'). The call to abandon ship was made early in the morning and the players, at first, thought it was a prank. Why wouldn't it be? Players on holiday. Banter. They were sinking? Yes, pull the other one. But when they woke and realised it was real, they were later congratulated for their bravery and calmness, making sure women and children were off first. The Raith goalkeeper had been an able seaman in the navy and helped everyone with their life jackets.

They made it on to lifeboats and were towed ashore to Vilagarcía by local fishermen. Despite their boat being badly damaged, it was re-floated on a high tide and rescuers managed to guide the wreck back to Vigo harbour, allowing the players to collect their belongings and the rest of the staff to pick up the team's hamper full of strips and equipment.

They managed to catch a P&O liner which was embarking from Vigo for Lisbon and then the Canaries and made the rest of the tour. They were made of hardier stuff back then. Nonchalantly climbing off the ship down a rope ladder in pyjamas on to a life raft, through a storm. Can you imagine today's top stars doing that? They would be trampling over women and children and need an Instagram Live feed to film their dramatic helicopter rescue. When on the P&O liner the captain invited the team to the top table as his guests after hearing about their chivalrous actions in evacuating the ship. The cinematic and traumatic journey didn't seem to affect the team, who won their four games. But most importantly, they are in here to show players were a different breed then, and class acts.

Object: White Handkerchief
Subject: Pañolada

On most occasions, the waving of a white handkerchief or flag in conflict is internationally recognised as a protective sign of truce. It indicates that those approaching are unarmed and prepared to negotiate. As part of the Geneva Convention, those waving the flag aren't allowed to shoot or be shot at. That is why, when watching Real Madrid or Barcelona, fans start to wave white handkerchiefs, you may look at each other and ask what is happening here? Are they happy? Are they upset? Someone help.

On rare occasions, the handkerchief is also used to show appreciation for a wonderful performance. This only adds to the confusion of the neutral. The gesture is mostly used in protest, as a show of disgust, when a team is going through a bad run of form and a sign of displeasure and frustration toward the team, coach and board.

In Spain, they call the mass angry waving of a white handkerchief the pañolada. Such is the power of the pañolada as a statement that fans making the gesture can have a manager sacked within hours of the final whistle. In one game in 2017, Barça fans decided to use the waving of the white handkerchief to protest against poor refereeing decisions. They had become sick of what they felt were several clear decisions that had gone against them, claiming that referees weren't even subtle about it. The fans felt it was a deliberate act of contempt against them and claimed the La Liga referees' organisation, the LFP, were complicit.

In a statement, they also managed to call the LFP president Javier Tebas a Francoist and a self-confessed Real Madrid supporter. Barça fans decided to wave their handkerchiefs in protest in the 12th minute as they, the fans, are often referred to as the 12th man.

The most recent high-profile white handkerchief moment in the Santiago Bernabéu came in March 2019 when Real Madrid were unceremoniously beaten 4-1 by Ajax, as the Dutch side won 5-3 on aggregate in the Champions League. The fans weren't slow in reaching for the white handkerchiefs to let the team know they were livid. Madrid's Argentine coach Santiago Solari was next for the pañolada treatment. The Champions League was all they had to play for after back-to-back defeats against Barcelona in the Copa del Rey and La Liga left them 12 points adrift. It was the first time since 2009/10 that Real had been beaten and knocked out in the last 16 stage of Europe's elite competition. The Spanish press also weighed in, adding to the humiliation. But the white handkerchief action was headline news across Europe.

The idea that a handkerchief can change the way a football side is run is quite a concept. A tip, though – be like everyone else across the globe does and flip the bird or give the two fingers and boo, then there's no dubiety. If you have to whip out a handkerchief, use it to blow your nose, or dry your eyes.

Object: Wind Machine
Subject: Arbroath's Wind

In a pre-season friendly at Arbroath's Gayfield Park, Aberdeen's Jim Leighton took a goal kick and the ball failed to reach the outside of the penalty area; instead, it got caught and spun in the wind, blew back over his head and out of the stadium into a nearby carnival. Well, it was July. Welcome to summertime in Arbroath.

This wind-assisted kick has gone into folklore. Dons legend Willie Miller revealed that the ball came to him in the arc of the 18-yard box and he was left to deal with it. Whether Willie manfully beat nature and cleared his lines by rattling the ball up the park, or if the ball whirled up and away due to his clearance, no one can recall. Maybe his clearance whooshed out over Jim's goal and landed in the nearby showground?

You get the point. It's an extremely windy location. Gayfield Park is a beautiful and quaint stadium, and its susceptibility to wind could be down to its geography. It's a short throw-in from the beach and is the closest stadium in Europe to the sea. When the tide comes in, the pitch is effectively watered. On certain days, when it gets blowy, it is also susceptible to the odd tidal wave.

Arbroath FC were formed in 1878 and played locally at Hospitalfield and Woodville Park before purchasing a rubbish tip at the seafront and building Gayfield, which opened in 1880. Arbroath loved the ground's tight and compact shape and the fact opposing teams, in a packed ground, couldn't swing a cat. In one Scottish Cup tie, Arbroath beat Rangers. Rangers launched a protest claiming the park was too small, saying they 'had been beaten on a back green'. The game was replayed and Rangers won.

For most, the town of Arbroath, in Angus, on the North Sea, is famed for its Smokies but for football fans, there's an affinity with the picturesque ground that is Gayfield. Even when the sun shines, the wind can still blow you off your feet. Fans of the Red Lichties don't have a suntan. They always look more weather-beaten. Those brave holidaymakers who venture to Arbroath return with a bowed posture, reminiscent of a half shut knife, from walking into gales. Many out-of-towners are known to become perplexed by the power and ferocity of the wind. Tourists sunbathing in Arbroath come home looking like Worzel Gummidge.

Arbroath directors, fond of a penny, are still trying to get the tight Aberdonians to let some light into their wallets and part with the cash to pay for that lost ball. You can imagine BBC Scotland's *Sportscene* presenter and commentator Archie Macpherson trying to handle a piece to camera, a killer gale toying with him and his crew as the North Sea wreaked havoc with his cameraman, Archie's notes and his comb-over flapping like a polythene bag on a farm's barbed wire fence. Archie would still manfully struggle through to bring us a random Scottish Cup tie from Gayfield. Though maybe for this sort of game the producer might have sent another commentator, like the late Alistair Alexander, who had better and more robust hair.

These days the North Sea is more like the deceased artist formerly known as Prince's backing band; part of the new power generation. The North Sea has a rich history from the Vikings to the Hanseatic League to both world wars. Economically it is important for shipping, fishing, oil and gas and of late, massive wind turbine farms. The sea is packed full to brimming of wind farms that create energy by harnessing the power of the wind created in the sea.

The wind aside, on 8 August 1982, a certain George Best showed up to play for Arbroath Vics at Gayfield. George had the town talking, no show without punch – he brought along former Miss World, the Swedish model Mary Stavin. Arbroath Vics were celebrating their centenary against Arbroath. Best was paid £1,500 and after the game, there was a Q&A session at the social club, and George proved a natural storyteller and drank nothing but tea all night. George's agent Bill McMurdo was friends with someone at the club. What an amazing time.

Fanorak Fact: Arbroath hold the world record for the biggest victory in a senior game, winning 36-0 against Aberdeen Bon Accord in 1885. And, from the same game, Arbroath's John Petrie holds the world record for the number of goals scored by one player in a competitive match, netting 13. Remarkably, on the same day, 12 September 1885, Dundee Harp beat Aberdeen Rovers 35-0.

Object: Red Card
Subject: Mankini Streaker

We know referees are idiots. Sometimes we watch them at work, and think how bad they are at their job. If an electrician incorrectly rewired your house or a joiner fitted a kitchen arse for elbow, they'd be hunted. Yet referees are paid a fortune to run about, showing off in front of a crowd, blowing a whistle and brandishing cards. It's a great life, surely.

The top refs travel to Europe's great cities, on budget airlines, stay in their best budget hotels and lord it up when doing European games. Along with their inherent self-belief and haughty arrogance, they bring something else; a baffling level of idiocy, one in which their incompetence is matched with a lack of common sense. They turn into those 'only carrying out orders' officious types.

One incident worth examining occurred in March 2011 in a match in the Blue Square Bet South between Dorchester Town and Havant & Waterlooville. Referee David Spain red-carded Dorchester player-manager Ashley Vickers – after he apprehended and stopped a streaker.

You can hear the *Benny Hill* theme music playing as the 'streaker', dressed in a mankini and wearing a black wig to mimic Sacha Baron Cohen's comedy creation Borat, runs across the pitch. The streaker was athletic and muscular and even went as far as to wear socks and football boots.

You're hardly likely to streak if you're an overweight, unfit, football casual. You have to love yourself and want to share your brilliance, and body, with everyone. He was zooming about the park for quite a time, so the game was stopped as the woefully underprepared security staff couldn't get a grip of him.

When Vickers said knickers to this and did a neck-high tackle in the 70th minute, the crowd's reaction was mixed; some were cheering and whooping at the streaker, others squealing at Vickers for being a killjoy. The referee, though, remained unimpressed amid the chaos and when he gave Vickers a red, the noise became one of hysterical confusion and disbelief.

Alan Young, 21, streaked for a bet. He said later, 'I loved it. Probably a little too much. I didn't expect the tackle; he should play rugby. The stewards were fine. They even gave me my wig back.' Some 458 spectators watched the surreal event as 'Borat' ran amok.

Vickers wasn't too happy and added, 'I'm dumbfounded and speechless at being sent off.' Despite being both speechless and dumbfounded, he managed to continue to speak, 'It beggars belief. The stewards got nowhere near him, I thought I was doing them a favour.' Again being unable to speak, the words continued to flow, as Vickers told the *Dorset Echo*, 'My only thought was to get hold of him so we could get on with the game. I managed to grab him and bring him to the ground, and the funny thing was the stewards actually thanked me for it. But the ref decided to send me off.'

The game was still in the balance at 1-1 after the red card but Dorchester had lost it with the match official. Going into the last ten minutes, two more Dorchester players were red-carded and they lost 3-1. We can only assume referee Spain was enjoying the show too much. For those interested in the laws and rules of the game, the Vickers red card was for violent conduct.

Object: Tractor

Subject: Cruyff's Transfer to Barcelona

Many assumed, in 1973, after Johan Cruyff had won a third consecutive European Cup, he had outgrown Ajax. Yet the player had agreed to his future by signing a long-term deal. Then the Ajax players had a vote to pick a captain – the options were Piet Keizer or Cruyff. When the players chose Keizer, who was one of Cruyff's closest friends, the superstar saw it as a brutal betrayal and a dressing-room coup. Cruyff's decision to leave not only his employees but his lifelong club, who he had supported as a child, shocked not only Ajax but Dutch and European football. Cruyff immediately knew where he was going. The decision was made. He spoke to his agent and he and his family were bound for an ailing Barcelona side. Within weeks he would be signing for the Catalan giants.

The Ajax board were determined to hold out and sell him to Real Madrid for top dollar, but Cruyff refused, stating he would not play for Franco's side. Cruyff was adept at picking and choosing his arguments depending on how he wanted the scene to play out. He bad-mouthed Real Madrid, yet as a 15-year-old he had something of an epiphany while watching them play. Cruyff was a ball boy when Benfica played Real Madrid in Amsterdam in the 1962 European Cup Final and while viewing the players closely from the sidelines at pitch level was mesmerised by Madrid's Alfredo Di Stéfano. Suddenly, football made sense to Cruyff; the movement, the technique, anticipation and acceleration, the Argentine's role in the side. He was everywhere, controlled the play, constantly moving, and had wonderful vision. Cruyff may have more to thank Madrid for than he would care to admit.

Ironically, the Franco regime from decades before had impacted upon Cruyff's transfer. The country had been allowed to descend into such a perilous financial state that Spain couldn't afford to approve the transfer and allow it to go through. A fee of six million Dutch guilders, around $2m at the time, was the most expensive in the world. In 1973, Spain was still trying to move on from the vestiges of fascism.

In 1936, the Spanish military and right-wing conservative groups were being funded by both Hitler and Mussolini and overruled the prevailing left-wing government. They wanted uniformity and identity adhered to in Spain, but the country descended into civil war for four years. Franco controlled the government in Madrid and despite support from around the world from the International Brigade, the Catalan and Basque regions were hit hard.

The transfer was so huge, the equivalent of $12m today, that the Spanish government wouldn't allow it to proceed – too much money for one footballer. Barcelona managed to have Cruyff imported into Catalonia by registering his transfer as a piece of agricultural equipment. The transaction of the fee of six million guilders – three million to Ajax and three million to Cruyff – was paid via a loan from Banca Catalana. Due to the unusually high price, the fee couldn't be processed, so some creative thinking was required and in the end it was ingenious.

In Sid Lowe's 2014 book, *Fear and Loathing in La Liga: Barcelona v Real Madrid*, he explains that Cruyff said, 'If I remember the story properly, they had to buy me as some sort of 100 tractors.' Lowe further clarified, stating that it was *biene somoviente* – livestock too. Let's not allow the facts to get in the way of a great story. Tractors it is; Cruyff not only had that X-Factor but the X-Tractor.

The Flawed, the Crazy
and the Cheats

There's an element in the make-up of footballers everywhere which takes them to a bloodthirsty, cut-throat place, a mix of divine artistry and flawed morality where they will do anything to win.

Object: Dentist's Chair
Subject: Gazza's Flawed Genius

The dentist's chair is here to remind us of the flamboyant brilliance of Paul Gascoigne. Few goals sum up and distil the player's career better than the one he scored against Scotland at Euro '96. A minute earlier, England's goalkeeper David Seaman had saved a penalty from Scotland's Gary McAllister. Gazza sensationally broke up the park and scored an unbelievable goal.

But why the rehearsed celebration? Leading into Euro '96, the press were obsessed with Gazza's drinking and his misbehaviour was becoming a major tabloid story. On a pre-tournament trip to Hong Kong, Gascoigne visited a nightclub and did 'the dentist's chair'; this involved those taking part being strapped into a chair, while a barman poured Drambuie and tequila down the willing participant's throat. When the press got hold of photos there was an outcry and calls for Gascoigne's expulsion from the squad.

Concerns were made about the player's drinking and claims were circulating that he was an alcoholic. This was a time of excess and 'he liked a drink'; he wasn't an alcoholic, was he? Tabloids hounded and harangued and goaded Gascoigne while at the same time calling for him to get help. England's manager Terry Venables had a way with his side, adopting a 'team that drinks together sticks together' approach. I'm not sure of the cost of a chartered flight and hotel accommodation for such a trip but the bar bill must have been something else.

Gazza may have been sporting a questionable new hairstyle but his goal was perfection. The game was still finely balanced as Scotland applied pressure, winning a penalty which Seaman saved. From the resulting corner, Scotland, conceded a free-kick. Seaman launched it, Teddy Sheringham brought it down, and fed in Darren Anderton. Gascoigne, galloping through the middle, is found by Anderton. Gazza allows the pass to bounce before deftly lobbing the ball with his left foot, over Colin Hendry, then perfectly volleying his shot past Andy Goram with his right.

It was a goal you'd dream of scoring. Then he acted out the celebration. He lay flat out for his team-mates to celebrate and re-enact the dentist's chair. After his display, the tabloids changed their tune. Suddenly Gazza wasn't a troubled, kebab-eating, overweight alcoholic. He was, at least at that moment, a genius.

Everyone knows how his life has unfolded and as we speak in 2021, he is winning and has some calm but no one can ever take that goal and that moment from him.

The press proved correct, he would become a troubled soul. Now priorities, hopes and expectations are re-evaluated. He is still with us, for now, and that's the most important thing.

Object: Syringe

Subject: Robin Friday

The term 'cult hero' is bandied around liberally, yet few footballers fit the title more accurately than Robin Friday. Football is often anecdotally referred to as the new rock 'n' roll. It sounds like Friday was in the wrong business and maybe he should have taken to the stage in a rock band, not to the pitch as a footballer.

Friday's demise and troubled life are so off the rails that football itself has opted out of even mentioning his name. He is known only as a cult figure at his former clubs Cardiff and Reading and is remembered in a book by Paulo Hewitt and former Oasis bass player Paul McGuigan, called *The Greatest Footballer You Never Saw: The Robin Friday Story.* He also features in a song by the Welsh indie group Super Furry Animals.

Friday's fate seemed preordained. He was in trouble for most of his youth, eventually ending up in and out of borstal at Feltham, in Hounslow. The stories have a strange, opaque nature to them. His tales are mythical, he existed in an era when stories were passed on, and did not play higher than the Third Division so there are few recordings, only one grainy short clip and loads of still photos, of him playing. These were the days before games in the lower divisions were filmed. Other than Reading and Cardiff fans, most people would not know who he was.

Robin Friday was the ultimate 1970s 'troubled' cult footballer. On the park, a major part of his game, despite his skill, was his reputation for intimidating opponents. Between this and retaliating when he was targeted, he had a dreadful disciplinary record. Off the park he was a heavy smoker and drinker, womaniser and drug user. Footballers from this era could run it off in training, sweat it out, then start again. To those who could only dream of being a professional footballer and come close to being anywhere near that level, it was terrible to see a player who made it, with such talent, self-destruct. Looking back now, we see life differently. You think of players who are troubled and think how skilled the coaches who managed to get a tune out of them were. These managers were like psychologists who knew how to handle characters such as Friday, George Best, Frank Worthington, Tony Currie and Don Givens.

Most of his exploits are difficult to verify, but for the record there was the one in which he defecated into Mark Lawrence's bag and another where he spiked the punch at his own wedding with LSD. He was reportedly banned ten times from the local pub, The Spread Eagle, across from Elm Park, Reading's previous stadium.

At 15, he would take speed and methadone when attending gigs in London. He eventually found work on a building site and played semi-professionally for Hayes. While on the site, he fell off some scaffolding and was seriously injured after landing on a metal spike. However, he somehow managed to recover and was spotted by Reading and signed for £750.

One of Friday's goals has gone into folklore. Against Tranmere, he controlled a pass on his chest then let rip with the outside of his right foot, perfectly connecting with the ball which swerved, curved, then dipped into the top corner. Proof that this did happen came from the famous Welsh referee Clive Thomas. He is best known for controversially disallowing a goal in a World Cup game between Brazil and Sweden, when he had blown the whistle for full time after a corner was taken, but no one heard him and Brazil scored.

Thomas witnessed this particular goal by Friday, and having witnessed goals by the greats of the game claimed it was the best he'd ever seen.

Friday only spent two seasons at Reading, scoring 46 goals in 121 games, he helped the side gain promotion to the Third Division in 1976. He was sold to Cardiff but retired from the game in 1977, aged 25. He returned to live with his parents and became a decorator. He had lost the passion for the game, but without the routine and focus of training and playing, his life came apart. He would be found dead after suffering a heart attack after overdosing on heroin, aged 38, on 22 December 1990. While most football fans are amazed at his hedonism, there's no celebration of it, more a poignancy and appreciation of a colourful 1970s character who will now always live forever, in this alternative football museum both for his football ability and his many imperfections.

Object: Rachid Harkouk
Subject: Loose Cannon

When discussing Rachid Harkouk, Martin O'Neill said he had the hardest shot he had ever seen in football. Harkouk had many of the crucial elements in his character that combined to fully equip him for the role of a cult figure. Fans loved him. They thought he was nuts, completely and utterly mad on the pitch. He was different. He played his own game. The type of player Motty would politely describe as explosive, mercurial, or my favourite euphemism, 'a loose cannon'.

On one occasion while playing for Crystal Palace, 'Rash the Bash' lost it and set about throttling George Best. He had watched Best break his team-mate's leg. Best launched a tackle like a karate kick at Ian Evans's leg, leaving it in such a state that it was left lying the wrong way. Incensed, Harkouk attacked Best, grabbing him by the throat, and had to be restrained by team-mates. He might be able to accept it was part of the ferocity of the way the game was played then but what he couldn't forgive was the lack of remorse on Best's face.

Harkouk was another of those gems Palace were able to pluck from obscurity and those hardened, skilled players from the killing fields of Sunday league football. Players who thrived on pitches that were frozen one week and like the Somme the next. Following two seasons at Chertsey Town and Feltham, Terry Venables signed him to Palace, then playing in the Third Division.

Venables allowed him to unleash his personality and power, always encouraging him to fire shots from anywhere. Instead of stifling Harkouk's unconventional style, Venables actively encouraged the player to keep doing his thing. The fans took to Harkouk. He was nicknamed 'Spider' because of his ability to weave around the opposition while being all arms and legs. He scored goals from impossible angles and smashed in long-range piledrivers. People were starting to notice this Palace side, with players including Vince Hilaire and Kenny Sansom.

Harkouk left Palace in 1978 and had two uneventful seasons at Queens Park Rangers before signing for Notts County in 1980, and a year later he helped them gain promotion to the First Division. He remained there until one of the biggest moments in his career, one for the football dreamers, a wonderful change of fortune. In 1986, his form for Notts County saw him earn a call-up to represent Algeria in the World Cup (his father was Algerian, his mother English). He played four times in total for Algeria, twice in warm-up games, and twice in the competition itself. It was here, in the Mexico World Cup in 1986, in the second game against Spain, that he was tackled by Andoni Goikoetxea and his career was over.

The Butcher of Bilbao, who dined out on breaking Diego Maradona's ankle in 1983, ended Harkouk's career prematurely. The player characteristically plays down the tackle, blaming it on the length and thickness of the grass on the pitches in Mexico. The fans loved Harkouk, but of course, full legendary status generally comes with more than being a bit explosive and having an astonishingly powerful shot; it comes with a price.

Since having to retire from the game aged 30, Harkouk has not had his troubles to seek. Despite a career which fans at Palace and Notts County still rave about, his actions outside of football have overshadowed his playing career. The signs were there while at Palace, when police caught him and team-mate Barry Silkman in possession of £250,000 in forged notes. They received a nine-month suspended jail sentence. Both stated they received the money when they played a game against a prison team.

After he left the game, his troubles continued and in 2012, he was sentenced to 28 months after pleading guilty to supplying amphetamine. He isn't perfect but is trying to move on. Like most players from this era, who were never highly paid, he has admitted to struggling but remains involved with Notts County's former players' association. However, Harkouk did something most fans can only dream of and scored amazing goals, got the teams he played for promoted, and actually represented his national side at the World Cup.

Object: Colosseum Postcard
Subject: Lazio's Luciano Re Cecconi

It would be fair to say the Lazio side of the 1970s, featuring Luciano Re Cecconi, put Wimbledon's Crazy Gang to shame. In terms of their pranks, wind-ups and practical jokes, they went to another stratosphere. Of the exhibits featured in this book, the death of Re Cecconi is one of the saddest and most tragic. He has become a legendary figure at Lazio but for the wrong reasons after he was accidentally shot dead when a prank ended tragically.

Re Cecconi and his friend entered a jewellery shop, their faces buried in their jackets, hands up their jumpers as if packing a firearm and yelled to the owner, who they knew, to put his hands up. The owner, whose shop had been broken into a few weeks previously, retaliated by pulling out a shotgun.

This side were notorious for their practical jokes. Re Cecconi was known to love pranks and playing along. On the pitch he was the pumping heartbeat of the team but lost his life in such ridiculous circumstances. Re Cecconi was the *mediano* (a box-to-box midfielder) in the 1974 Scudetto-winning Lazio team. He had the energy, skill and vision that could quickly flip defence into attack. This type of team had strong personalities and needed a coach who could marshal and galvanise them, bringing order and focus to the chaos. Enter one Tomaso Maestrelli, who led Lazio to their first Serie A title in 1974.

Maestrelli joined the club when they were in the second tier. He took explosive characters such as Giuseppe 'Pino' Wilson and the mercurial striker Giorgio Chinaglia, who openly admitted he would vote for the neo-fascist Movimento Sociale Italiano in the upcoming elections, and channelled their energy into a team. Chinaglia had a boutique in Rome which had been ransacked so he carried a .44 Magnum. This was the mindset then.

The coach and Re Cecconi had a great relationship. Maestrelli had worked with the midfielder when he impressed as a youth at Serie C level and was signed by Foggia. Maestrelli was the coach who had the greatest impact, and this continued when they teamed up again at Lazio.

Lazio had Chinaglia scoring, the Darlington-born Guiseppe Wilson stopping at centre-half and Re Cecconi's boundless energy and creativity in midfield. Many would have had the larger-than-life, gun-toting Chinaglia as the most likely member of the team to be shot, but that fate fell to the man they would call *l'Angelo Biondo* – the Blond Angel, due to his bright blond hair.

In December 1976, Maestrelli died, succumbing to stomach cancer aged 54. The dark winter continued six weeks later when practical joker Re Cecconi and team-mate Pietro Ghedin decided to visit that jewellery shop. Re Cecconi was dead at the age of 28 and would go down in history as an immortal Lazio hero. His team-mate Chinaglia would go on to play for New York Cosmos, with Franz Beckenbauer and Pelé. It's strange how life works out.

Object: Maradona's Tank

Subject: Maradona, Napoli, Hand of God and Will

Diego Maradona's health was rapidly deteriorating during the writing of this book. He had recently been rushed to hospital having undergone surgery for a brain bleed but it appeared he was through the worst, still weak but seemingly out of danger. However, a few weeks later, on 25 November 2020, his death was announced. He was only 60 yet he seemed to have lived six lives. Maradona will forever be remembered as one of the finest, if not *the* finest to grace the beautiful game.

Our exhibit covers his best years as a player, between 1984 and 1990, his move to Napoli in 1984 and the unprecedented success he brought to the side. He also managed to win the World Cup with Argentina in 1986. People often refuse to accept that Maradona won that trophy single-handedly. Without searching Google, can you name three other players from that side? He also took Argentina to the final in 1990.

It was an unbelievable turnaround. Suddenly, Napoli were winning titles. This was an unheralded and magical time for the club. In May 1987 he delivered Napoli's first Scudetto and in 1990 they won their second and to date, their last. During this period they also won the UEFA Cup, the Coppa Italia and the Italian Super Cup. They grabbed the power off the rich clubs from the north of the country – whose fans would mock the Neapolitans, compare their stench to dogs and sing about cholera and earthquakes.

In truth, Napoli and Maradona were made for each other. As Ed Vulliamy wrote in *The Guardian* in 2019, 'Maradona and Naples shared a common heartbeat and soul.

To understand Maradona in those days was to understand Naples, and vice versa: the same unearthly magic, the same brilliant light, the same maleficent shadows.'

Maradona's £5m move from Barcelona to Napoli broke the world transfer record, coming a couple of years after signing for Barcelona for what was also a world-leading fee of £3m. Some 75,000 fans filled the stands and thousands more lined the streets to welcome their hero's arrival by chopper at the Stadio San Paolo. Well, it was the mid-1980s. He guided them to the title and boy, did Napoli party – four days of full-on celebrations with hundreds of thousands in the streets. Maradona had delivered.

To Mexico City and the Hand of God goal at the 1986 World Cup quarter-final when Argentina took on England in the Azteca Stadium. With the tie goalless in the second half, Maradona received the ball deep and was allowed to run without a tackle laid on him. He accelerated, played to Jorge Valdano and instinctively continued his run hoping for a return. The ball flipped up from England's Steve Hodge's attempted clearance and looped back towards Maradona who out-jumped goalkeeper Peter Shilton to slap the ball into the net.

Time has passed but then there was still tension, animosity and heat in the air from the Falklands conflict. Maradona was demonised. Having initially denied the handball, he then conceded there may have been some divine intervention. In his book *The History of the World Cup*, Brian Glanville was less sympathetic, 'Brazen and shameless, Maradona was all mock innocence, talking about the "Hand of God".' Glanville continued, sounding like he was speaking for the nation, 'For England, rather, it was the hand of the devil.' It sounds a tad dramatic but at the time this was how the press and media portrayed Argentina and Maradona's dastardly act.

Then, four minutes after scoring the handball goal, the cheeky devil showed his other side, one of sublime skill. Despite being on the greatest football stage, there was something natural, wonderful and practically childlike about the goal. He dribbled and danced around English players like the precocious kid in the playground. This was football in its purest form. Maradona's second effort was voted goal of the century.

At the World Cup in 1990, Maradona faced Italy in the semi-final, in Napoli's Stadio San Paolo stadium. He was charged with taking the crucial penalty in a shoot-out against the hosts. Before the game, he had asked Napoli fans to support Argentina against their nation: 'Napoli non è Italia,' Maradona told them. 'Napoli wasn't Italy.' Most did not but the Ultras in Curve B believed their leader and did what he asked. Diego scored the penalty that put out the hosts. Sadly for him, Italia '90 ended in defeat to West Germany and a positive drugs test leading to a 15-month ban.

Luigi Caffarelli, his Napoli team-mate, said of Maradona, 'He was the architect of our success on the pitch and in the dressing room.' In many of his obituaries and tributes from former players and colleagues, it transpired that Maradona was a great team-mate. He was a team player and didn't behave as you would imagine, like a superstar. He read the game superbly. When he wasn't on the ball he would be strategic and had great tactical intelligence. He would also coach and advise and point and move into a position that would help set up the team's shape. It turned out that he was supportive, loyal and didn't judge his team-mates, despite being light years ahead of them in skill and ability. He would prefer to help and guide than criticise and demean. The Argentine had been in dressing rooms as an international footballer from the age of 16, so knew the importance of the team dynamic.

His death brought tributes from the biggest names in the game. Thousands took to the streets. Maradona was more than a footballer; he was a flawed, imperfect global icon but to those in Buenos Aires and Naples he was a god. Napoli renamed their ground the Diego Armando Maradona Stadium. The president of Argentina, Alberto Fernández, declared there would be three days of national mourning for Maradona. Sadly, months after his death, claims and counterclaims over his estate have been as dramatic and chaotic as his turbulent life.

The original object in place for this exhibit was a Damien Hirst-designed, diamond-encrusted hand of god. But that was changed when Maradona's belongings were revealed. He did not leave a will. He threatened not to leave any inheritance and give his money to charity. Lawyers now expect a complex probate trial. The inheritance will be divided among his eight children to six partners, but that won't be the biggest problem, as legal experts are preparing for a complicated case due to hangers-on and opportunists. The main prize will be his image rights, real estate, investments and jewellery. Then there are the luxury cars when he worked for UAE sides Al-Wasl and Fujairah FC. When he was honorary president of Dynamo Brest in Belarus, he received a Hunta Overcomer amphibious tank.

In May 2021, news broke that seven people who had looked after and treated Maradona before his death had been charged with involuntary manslaughter. This came after a report from a medical board was submitted to prosecutors claiming Maradona 'was left in agony for more than 12 hours, did not receive adequate medical attention, and could still be alive if he had been properly hospitalised'.

Fanorak Fact: Maradona made his debut as Argentina manager on 19 November 2008 against Scotland at Hampden Park, the same venue where he scored his first goal for Argentina, in 1979.

Object: Basketball
Subject: Thierry Henry Handball

This hand represents one of the most blatant handballs ever to take place on a football pitch. It's certainly as bad, probably more blatant, in terms of its intent than Maradona's 'Hand of God' goal. French striker Thierry Henry didn't just handle the ball, he did a full repertoire of the Harlem Globetrotters, and you could hear him whistle their theme tune 'Sweet Georgia Brown'.

The handball occurred during the second leg of a World Cup play-off game and took place in Paris, on 18 November 2009. France beat the Republic of Ireland 2-1 on aggregate to earn a place in the following year's finals in South Africa.

The Irish were incredibly unlucky. Not only did they go out in such an unfair manner but they had also finished second in their group to Italy, the reigning world champions. The Republic were coached by the wily Italian Giovanni Trapattoni (born on St Patrick's Day, 17 March 1939) and in their group had remained unbeaten. As you'd expect with an Italian at the helm, there were six draws and four wins, and games were won sparingly with few goals scored.

For a place in South Africa, Ireland had to face France in a play-off. FIFA had decided it would be appropriate to change the seeding draws so that Portugal and France wouldn't meet (they wouldn't want one of their big teams eliminated at this point, would they?)

The Republic were huge underdogs against a side with Henry, Nicolas Anelka, Karim Benzema, Patrice Evra and William Gallas. Yet Ireland were no mugs. They had a great spine of a side with Robbie Keane, Damien Duff, Richard

Dunne and Shay Given, experienced players who were capable of giving any side a fair fight. One of their key strengths though was that under Trapattoni their organisation, discipline and team shape made them difficult to beat. The side had remained consistent. France coach Raymond Domenech, on the other hand, was thought of as one of the crumbliest coaches in Europe, a bit of a flake. At Croke Park in the first leg only an Anelka goal separated the two sides. The French were unconvincing and despite shading the first game, the tie was anything but over.

Paris was a sea of green for the second leg and the city was bouncing. During the game, the French remained unconvincing but the Irish were in control and growing and feeling their way through the 90 minutes. Duff played a one-two down the left and cut back a perfect low pass to an unmarked Keane to score in the 33rd minute. His 41st goal for his country set le chat among les pigeons and levelled the tie at 1-1 on aggregate. The Irish played with high intensity and the French couldn't handle them; everything Domenech's side attempted was either foiled or wouldn't click.

The Republic were on top, totally controlling the game, and the French knew it. The game entered extra time and, if it was a boxing match, Ireland would have been ahead on points. The French played like they were gearing toward a penalty shoot-out.

In the 103rd minute of the second leg, the French were awarded a free kick inside the Irish half in a central position. Florent Malouda fired a speculative hoof into a crowded penalty area. Given was static on his line and with his defenders standing off, the ball bounced in the six-yard box, falling to Henry where it came off his forearm not once but twice; at one point it looked as if it rolled down his left arm. He managed to play on and cut it across in one quick move for Gallas to score. After the obvious handball, Henry, a silky, graceful player and normally a class act on and off the field, ran off to celebrate, each stride another step into insurmountable reputational damage. Football was shocked. What hope did the game have if a player like Henry was capable of such blatant gamesmanship? He had robbed Ireland of a shot at glory in the World Cup. At least Maradona had the decency to earn some redemption by then scoring one of the finest goals ever scored.

It doesn't matter who they are, professional footballers will do anything to sneak an advantage. The French would go to South Africa. Dunne said that after the game Henry sat with him and told him he handled the ball. When his conscience set in a few days later, and with those sponsoring him probably having had a word in his ear, Henry issued what sounded like a watertight legal statement disguised as an apology, 'The fairest solution would be to replay the game, but it is not in my control. Naturally, I feel embarrassed at the way that we won, and I feel extremely sorry for the Irish, who definitely deserve to be in South Africa.' Henry continued, 'I said at the time and I will say again that yes, I handled the ball. I am not a cheat and I never have been. It was an instinctive reaction to a ball that was coming extremely fast in a crowded penalty area.'

Imagine though, just imagine, if he didn't celebrate the goal and instead got the ball, placed it down for Given to take a free kick and told the referee he handled it. He would have been lauded across the world, made head of FIFA and receive bungs and loads of freebies.

After progressing to South Africa, France instead went on to have a nightmare and finished last in their group with players going on strike, not to mention the vuvuzela-induced migraines. Karma?

The Football Association of Ireland's chief executive, John Delaney, confirmed that his organisation accepted a payment of €5m (around £3.67m) from FIFA for missing out on qualification, so it wouldn't sue the world game's governing body. FIFA president Sepp Blatter was fuming at such claims, saying the money was a loan to help finish building a stadium. The FAI would only confirm it was a favourable deal which had also included a detailed confidentiality agreement.

Object: Toy Jaws Shark
Subject: Suárez's Bite

Many footballers have a bit of edge and dig to their game. Luis Suárez quite literally had plenty of bite. The Uruguayan has those sort of teeth that would hurt too – big chomping gnashers. European football has always welcomed football superstars from South America, from Maradona to Messi, to Neymar to Suárez. All united by their extraordinary skill and will to win at any cost. They bring unbelievable levels of skill and are great entertainers, yet they also bring a level of ruthlessness and gamesmanship that we, the European football fan, at times find difficult to comprehend.

It is difficult to comprehend the mentality of a professional athlete biting someone. This is in no way to condone his actions, but perhaps if we shed some light on his background, we may better understand the drive and what it means to come from nothing. If you saw where Suárez grew up and knew of his life you could begin to understand the temperament and ferocious drive that would take him to the top. He was one of seven boys and his family struggled financially.

Suárez grew up playing football on the dirt patches of Montevideo, barefoot. This was not the 1920s; this was the 1990s. When his parents separated and with no money, he took a casual job as a road sweeper. That said, it's still unforgivable to bite a chunk out of anyone but equally he's playing a sport with millionaires and has this in his nature; it's part of his upbringing and desire to survive and to win at any cost.

Uruguay faced Ghana in the 2010 World Cup quarter-finals. Ghana took the lead before half-time from a 40-yard shot from Sulley Muntari before Diego Forlán equalised with a superb free kick. As neutrals willed on Ghana in a great game, John Paintsil whipped in a free kick which was headed goalwards by Dominic Adiyiah, then Suárez used both hands to save what would have been a certain goal. Suárez was sent off and in tears, but when the subsequent stoppage-time penalty was missed, Suárez was spotted celebrating in the tunnel. Ghana were beaten on penalties after extra time. Suárez 'had that in his game'.

Okay, but what of his biting crimes and misdemeanours? In chronological order, let's get our teeth into some of the bites, at least those he was caught for. When playing for Ajax in 2010 against PSV, he had a nibble on the shoulder of Otman Bakkal and received a seven-game suspension.

In 2013, while playing for Liverpool against Chelsea, he felt a bit peckish and had a chew on Branislav Ivanović. There was something ridiculous and bizarre about this one. He wasn't even subtle about it, not that biting an opponent is ever subtle. Immediately after biting, Suárez held his knee as if he had been wronged and feigned a limp. He received a ten-match ban.

His biggest offence was the third bite, in front of a massive worldwide viewing audience during a 2014 World Cup group stage fixture in Brazil, while playing Italy. The Uruguayan didn't hold back this time, biting with his big teeth into Italy's Giorgio Chiellini. He wasn't punished during the match but was later banned for nine games and sent home from the tournament. In a brief comedic moment, knowing he was caught, Suárez started to hold his mouth as if Chiellini had inflicted pain on him by being too firm and caused an injury to his precious teeth.

Suárez moved from Liverpool to Barcelona that summer, but his later departure from the Camp Nou shocked the football world. He left in a last-minute transfer window deal for Atlético Madrid from Barcelona in the summer of 2020 for £5.5m. Suárez had spent a successful six-year period with the *Blaugrana*. Several reasons were given as to why he was jettisoned, especially his closeness to Messi. Then there was the rumour the club told Suárez he was considered too old, at 33, despite scoring at least 20 goals a season while there. The most likely reason would be the wage cut due to Barcelona's perilous financial situation. They are in debt to the tune of £1.1bn due to both Covid-19 and their wage bill. Messi was irate when Barça let his friend go. Perhaps he knew, football being football, that Suárez would come back to bite them. He did. He was central to Atlético's La Liga title win in 2020/21, pushing out Real Madrid and knocking Barcelona down to third position with his 21 goals.

Humble Origins of the Game's Giants and Unusual Clubs

Some of the biggest European clubs started as attempts to arrange a leisurely game. The continent also has its fair share of quirky, strange and unusual club sides with tales to tell, many of which were also caught up in the European Super League debacle.

Object: Newspaper Clipping
Subject: FC Barcelona

This object is a cutting of an advert placed in a magazine, *Los Deportes*, by sports fanatic and Swiss-born Hans Max Gamper-Haessig, better known in Catalonia as Joan Gamper. The advert was placed in the few sporting clubs and gyms in Barcelona. He was looking for people interested in starting a football team. Twelve responded: two from Switzerland, two from England, a German and the rest from Catalonia. They would, in effect, be responsible for forming Futbol Club Barcelona.

The object for our alternative museum could easily have been a wall to represent the club. Barcelona from 1899 until 1900 were based at the former cycle track grounds at Bonanova and then, briefly, from 1900 to 1901 at the Hotel Casanovas grounds (currently the site of Hospital de Sant Pau). They were based in the Carretera d'Horta grounds from 1901 to 1905, then in the Carrer de Muntaner grounds from 1905 to 1909. The nickname 'The Cules' was attributed to the supporters who followed the side in the Camp de la Indústria between 1909 and 1922. 'Cules' in Catalan means 'buttocks' or 'butt'. The name derived from this era when the side played in a dilapidated ground which held 6,000; Barça games were so popular that locals would sit on the wall and passers-by could only see a wall of buttocks.

A much-shared image exists of Barcelona playing in what looks like a partially completed stadium built into a quarry. Crowds are perched high around the ground, looking on. It regularly does the rounds on social media and is erroneously mistaken as the Camp Nou. This image was taken in a match between Barcelona and Sparta Prague on 10 April 1921 (Camp Nou didn't open until 1957) and is of the Estadi Català (Camp de Foixarda). Architect Jaume Mestres proposed to build a stadium on a disused quarry in Montjuic. The intention was to build it for the 1924 Olympics but the Games were instead awarded to Paris and the ground fell into disrepair when funding ran out. Barcelona moved again to Camp de Les Corts in 1922 until 1957. Such was their popularity that the club kept outgrowing each venue, and they eventually moved to a bigger stadium in the west of the city, the Camp Nou, in 1957.

When Gamper formed Barcelona in 1899, he hoped that sport would bring people together. He started a sports organisation that was open to everyone no matter their social standing. It would be inclusive, open and democratic. He believed sport could galvanise people and recognised the importance of fan ownership of clubs. The club would be owned by the people and have a strong Catalan identity. He would become president for the first time in 1908 when he stepped in to save the club from bankruptcy. He did this by moving to Camp de la Indústria in the spring of 1909. With the stadium's capacity of 8,000, Barcelona were able to generate more income.

Barça were the first side to win the newly formed Spanish league, La Liga, in its inaugural season, 1929. As of 2021 the Catalan giants have subsequently won 26 La Liga titles, the Copa del Rey 31 times, the UEFA Champions League five times, the European Cup Winners' Cup four times, the Inter-Cities Fairs Cup three times and the FIFA World Club Championship three times. In 2008/09, Barcelona won La Liga, the Copa del Rey and the Champions League, becoming the first Spanish side to win the treble, which they did again in 2014/15. The club has not been relegated and Barcelona are one of the most supported teams in the world. Their social media following is one of the highest in the sports world.

Barça's modern era was defined with the arrival of Johan Cruyff, first as a player and later as a coach. Barça won their first title in 14 years before he headed off to the 1974 World Cup.

The first crop from La Masia came to fruition with Cruyff's return as a manager. Cruyff coached Pep Guardiola, who was eventually being earmarked as someone to follow that pathway; he would have marvellous success as a manager. During Guardiola's reign one game perfectly crystallised everything the club had been aiming for in the previous three or four decades. Barcelona beat Manchester United 3-1 in the 2011 Champions League Final at Wembley in one of those era-defining performances.

United boss Sir Alex Ferguson was magnanimous in defeat, 'Nobody's given us a hiding like that but they deserve it, they play the right way and they enjoy their football. They do mesmerise you with their passing and we never really did control Messi. But many people have said that. In my time as manager, it's the best team I've faced.'

This win was the third Champions League clinched by Barcelona in six years and Guardiola's tenth trophy in his three years in charge at the Camp Nou.

Barcelona fans own the club. They have more than 170,000 members, known as *socios,* who elect the president. It's also a hugely popular club worldwide because of social media and past and present players like Andres Iniesta, Xavi, Lionel Messi, Luis Suárez and Neymar.

The city of Barcelona may have been around since Neolithic times and been founded by Romans, and we know those pesky Romans loved to build a wall. Everywhere they ventured they couldn't wait to get the hod, spirit level, bricks and cement out. There's one around Barcelona, sections of which can be seen in the old town. Then, Barcelona was called Barcino, which sounds more like a 1970s disco or a Brazilian defender.

La Masia nurtured serial Ballon d'Or winner Messi, plus regular nominees Iniesta and Xavi. The building was closed in 2011 when Barça moved to a state-of-the-art residential centre at Ciutat Esportiva Joan Gamper, which fittingly brings our story full circle.

Object: Beatles Keyring
Subject: St Pauli

The Hamburg-based club FC St Pauli, have, over the years, become the hip, liberal and acceptable face, quite literally the flag-wearers, of modern supporters. Most discerning fans know of the team and respect the message. But what makes their Ultras so revered?

I know about St Pauli because they are based in Hamburg's Reeperbahn. Most Beatles fans know the city moulded and shaped the ramshackle early Fab Four (or five, when Stu Sutcliffe was there) into a tight and efficient, hard-working beat combo. We could use the lazy analogy that the Beatles were a raw footballer sent on loan to toughen up and get game time in the Indra and Star-Club, honing their sound, stagecraft, and confidence. Though any random testing would have returned with blood tests drowning in Phenmetrazine (Prellies).

Much as it was then, the red light district is still controlled by gangs and organised crime. St Pauli fans living there are subject to the area's gentrification and know they are losing their identity. The football world's love for St Pauli is more down to their left-wing activism and post-punk DIY approach to getting their message out there. They are as renowned for their philosophy as they are for playing football, possibly even more so. The messages are clear: no football for fascists; no human is illegal; football has no gender.

They are politically and culturally ahead of the curve as is their taste in music. This part of Hamburg isn't into poodle-permed 1980s soft rock. The locals are mad for techno and dub. Taking a strong anti-fascist stance is nothing new in music, from The Dead Kennedys to The Specials, but in football it takes quite a level of insistence and even courage to face down fascism.

However, being the underground poster boys of political correctness isn't always easy when points count. As we are allowed to meander, let's continue with the music analogy and imagine they were a record label. They would be Sub Pop and if they are, they need a Nirvana, whose punk rock ethic and stance were firmly against racism, fascism, homophobia and sexism and they left a global imprint that would be politically to the left.

Football teams are judged on the pitch. Since their relegation in 2011/12 they have remained in Bundesliga II. This has meant, of late, a *Hamburger Stadtderby* – a derby between St Pauli and Hamburg, not to mention fixtures against neighbours Hansa Rostock and tasty matches with Nürnberg and Fortuna Düsseldorf.

Commentator Tim Caple, who covers German football extensively for BT Sport, ESPN and Eurosport, agrees, especially with the level of competition of Bundesliga II, 'It's competitive because it's well balanced and every year it is simply impossible to predict. Again, case in point, who thought Hamburg would miss out again? Next season [2021/22] Schalke will arrive with lofty expectations. Ninety minutes with St Pauli and Ezgerbige Aue will remind them how tough it will be to get back first time.'

Reputations mean nothing. The second tier of German football is tough and the sides used to playing there remain fearless. Caple continued, 'In this league, there are no super-elite with bottomless pits of money and those who arrive in the division with a name and reputation find it means zero, as Hamburg have found. They may have the most expensive squad in the division but the gap between top and bottom is €23m.'

St Pauli need a 30-goal-a-season superstar to emerge from their youth academy. Football is about winning. They are the German team you'd want to support, if only they could start to win and get promoted back to the top tier. The club isn't perfect but ultimately they have an ethos of caring about football and society. Outside of Germany, they are viewed as a cult club with left-wing politics. Many football clubs were set up originally to help the poor and disenfranchised in their community; Celtic, Everton, Manchester City to name a few. St Pauli, like those clubs, have won many hearts globally but need to start winning locally.

Object: Screwdriver
Subject: AC Milan

Italian football loves a nickname. This screwdriver is here to represent AC Milan, more commonly known as the *Rossoneri*, the red and black, but originally nicknamed *Casciavit* (the screwdrivers) due to the blue-collar background of their fans. The club, like many in Spain and Italy, have English origins. They were formed in 1899 by expats Alfred Edwards and Herbert Kilpin as a football and cricket club.

AC Milan were originally known as Milano but changed to the anglicised version of the name until Mussolini came on the scene and forced them to change it back, as he and the fascists tried to latch on to Milan. For most football fans of my generation, Milan were one of the great European clubs, evolving into a footballing superpower and attracting top players. Not so much with a build it and they will come, but a pay them and they will come attitude.

Pivotal to the turnaround in the club's fortunes was Silvio Berlusconi, who bought Milan, when they were struggling, in 1986. The club's modern-era decline had started when they were demoted to Serie B in 1980 after the Totonero illegal betting scandal covered earlier in the book. Milan had won their tenth Scudetto title, and with it the right to wear their gold star. They would come back up straight away but had accrued debts, were without the talismanic Franco Baresi due to injury and were unable to attract top talent – and were soon relegated again.

Around then we knew about Milan because of Joe Jordan, Mark Hateley, Ray Wilkins and Luther Blissett but times were changing. Welcome to the stage Silvio Berlusconi. He had the ubiquitous billionaire owner issues such as abuse of power, sex with underage prostitutes, and tax fraud (which he was too old to serve a sentence for) but boy did he bring success. Milan won eight titles, the European Cup twice and Champions League three times, adding to the clubs two European Cup titles in the 1960s.

Berlusconi brought the strategy of a modern conglomerate and rebranded Milan. Until then, clubs were owned by the same families for generations; they were insular, small-minded, and whatever your opinion of him as a politician or a party organiser, he shook Italian football up. AC Milan would become a crucial part of his business empire. He understood the concept of price is what you pay, value is what you get, and spectacularly applied that to football.

His TV stations would set the benchmark for the rest of European football. He kept it simple with football discussion and debate shows, highlights packages, and rolling football news. These services and shows were often used as an editorial device to attack the rest of Italian, and indeed European football. Parma coach Arrigo Sacchi was brought in and derided for being a former shoe salesman and worse still, someone who was so bad as a player he wasn't worthy of the role of Milan boss. Sacchi reminded the press, 'I never realised in order to become a jockey you have to have been a horse first.'

Berlusconi liked the way Sacchi played with a full press, and how his players attacked the ball and would entertain. The side already had Baresi, Roberto Donadoni and a young Paolo Maldini but in came Ruud Gullit and Marco van Basten. Later, Carlo Ancelotti joined from Roma and Frank Rijkaard would join his Dutch mates in a team that would become one of the most exciting in world football. They won the Scudetto and then won back-to-back European Cups.

The owner was not shy about using one of his many TV shows or newspapers to publicly criticise his managers. Throughout his explosive and eventful 25-year reign, Berlusconi changed managers 15 times. In effect he set in place a blueprint that would be used throughout football. Real Madrid would do the same a few years later with their Galacticos, the European Cup evolved into a superpower tournament called the Champions League, and the modern, highly branded English Premier League would follow the same pattern. He also brought in modern-thinking advances in sports science that would help players play for longer, and state-of-the-art training facilities.

In April 2017, Berlusconi sold Milan to a Chinese consortium for €740m and re-entered the political arena. While he was prime minister he used the same rhetoric and tone used in football. He couldn't stay away from the game, however, and bought Serie C side Monza, and also re-entered the political arena as an MEP.

Object: Cash Cow
Subject: Hoffenheim

If Hoffenheim was transplanted into the UK, it would have cricket playing on the green, children flying kites, picnics, joy, and the Salvation Army band playing in the park's bandstand. Hoffenheim isn't a throbbing metropolis. It is not a bustling, throbbing city. Hoffenheim is a village, located about one hour from Stuttgart. It has a population of just a few thousand. It is set on the outskirts of Sinsheim, a remote rural town of some 25,000. It is so far off the beaten track that the GPS just surrenders and clicks on to a John Coltrane stream of consciousness freeform groove while telling you to go any way you chose.

Clubs like Hoffenheim and RB Leipzig are not popular in Germany. Fans there don't like teams owned by rich individuals. They are considered plastic clubs; the German fans dislike commercialisation and believe football is the people's game. Clubs who have bankrolled their way to success because they don't use the 50+1 model like the others are loathed. The 50+1 model simply refers to ownership; the fans own 50 per cent of the club plus one share. This means it's their club and keeps out anyone trying to take over. It has helped foster a different feel to German clubs, allowing even the giants to seem more proactive, traditional and community-based.

Hoffenheim is 96 per cent owned by Dietmar Hopp. The local entrepreneur and billionaire is one of the richest men in Germany, worth around £13bn, and co-founded the software company SAP. He quit in the mid-2000s to do charity work for his foundation and to focus on his football club, something he started investing in from 1990. Hopp's vast wealth allowed a small village club in the eighth tier to gain promotion to the third tier between 1990 and 2001. By 2005, Hopp knew that Hoffenheim required serious investment if they wanted to reach the Bundesliga. He brought in influential German coach and head of sport and development at Red Bull, Ralf Rangnick, and went in big on players. They made it to the Bundesliga in 2008 and moved from the 5,000-capacity Dieter-Hopp-Stadion to the Wirsol Rhein-Neckar-Arena, which holds 31,150 and cost Hopp £80m. He has structured the club well, bought wisely with players such as Demba Ba and Roberto Firmino and until 2019, employed one of the youngest managers in world football, Julian Nagelsmann.

Nagelsmann was just 28 when Hopp appointed him as head coach in February 2016. The side were 17th in the Bundesliga and destined for relegation but he secured their safety. Nagelsmann took over at RB Leipzig in 2019 and worked his magic, taking them to the top of the Bundesliga. In May 2021, it was announced that he would be the next boss of Bayern Munich.

While at Hoffenheim, Nagelsmann introduced innovative ideas such as the use of technology, drones over the training ground and focus on touch, passing, accuracy and direction with a Footbonaut (a machine first brought in by Jürgen Klopp while he was at Dortmund, to test players on their control, reaction, precision and skill). Who would have thought that playing football involves controlling the ball and making the correct pass? Hoffenheim also brought in a giant video screen to pause and analyse during training. Nagelsmann famously said that '30 per cent of coaching is tactics and 70 per cent social competence'. His secret? Man management, a great analytical mind and embracing technology.

It certainly worked and he took Hoffenheim into the Champions League. For most countries around the world looking in, their story is held up as a football fairy tale. Their journey from an amateur side is seen as an example of how a football club should be run, with a robust plan (and a billionaire backer) to realise your dreams. Yet for Hoffenheim, the journey has been a controversial one. The German supporters are the most vociferous in Europe, especially the Ultras. They think Hopp has bought sporting success and Hoffenheim are an artificial club preventing a 'real' club from having success. There have been countless protests from opposition fans about commercialisation and anyone trying to 'buy football' aimed at Hopp.

From a neutral perspective, the Bundesliga's 50+1 concept has kept the quality of football high. The fans are always up for it because stadiums are full due to an affordable pricing structure for tickets. The Borussia Dortmund CEO Hans-Joachim Watzke, speaking to the league's website, bundesliga. com in 2017, summed it up perfectly, 'The German spectator traditionally has close ties with his club. And if they get the feeling that they are no longer regarded as a fan but instead as a customer, we'll have a problem.'

Object: Ashtray
Subject: NAC Breda

The Dutch gave us Rembrandt, tulips and Total Football. They also gave us Nooit opgeven altijd doorgan, Aangenaam door vermaak en nuttig door ontspanning, Combinatie Breda, more commonly known as Dutch Eerste Divisie (second division) side NAC Breda. It's one of the longest names for a football club in the world. NAC Breda are also known as the Pearl of the South.

Perhaps we should look at the full name of NAC Breda and see if the translation helps simplify things. It translates as, 'Never give up, always keep going pleasant through entertainment and useful through relaxation combination Breda.' The Dutch aren't without irony when it comes to short, sharp, brief and laconic language. How did that meeting go to decide the name? Who was there? What were they thinking? Was there something herbal brewing in the teapot?

Breda is in the southern Netherlands, in the province of North Brabant, and was occupied by Germany until 1944. They were liberated by Polish troops, led by the decorated general Stanisław Maczek, who led the Polish First Armoured Division. The town celebrates Liberation Day each year, in October 2019, and to mark the 75th anniversary NAC Breda temporarily renamed their stadium after Maczek.

Despite playing in the Dutch second division, NAC Breda are one of the best-supported clubs outside of Ajax, Feyenoord and PSV. In 1975 the board moved their home matches to Saturday evenings. The evening games, Avondje NAC (An Evening NAC) made more of an event of the matchday experience and was pivotal to galvanising their fierce support.

The already boisterous and passionate support attracted younger fans. You had two groups, the Vak G, more hooligan based casuals, and closer in the stadium to the away support. Then there's the B-Side, your slightly more sensible younger supporters but no less fanatic. Collectively they created an intimidating atmosphere. While playing Feyenoord in 1979, a linesman was hit by an ashtray. When the referee postponed the game, riots broke out. This became known as the 'Ashtray Incident'. They haven't won the Dutch title since 1921. The current league, the Eredivisie, wasn't formed until 1956. Their last win came thanks to Antoon 'Rat' Verlegh, their legendary one-club man who gave 40 years' service to the club. Such was his commitment and dedication to NAC Breda that the stadium was named after him and one of the club's nicknames is *De Ratten* ('The Rats').

Verlegh was involved with the club from the day they were founded until his death in 1960. He was a player, trainer, secretary, vice-chairman and then honorary chairman. For more than 19 years with NAC Breda, Verlegh played 295 league games and scored 125 times. It sounds like Nooit opgeven altijd doorgan, Aangenaam door vermaak en nuttig door ontspanning, Combinatie Breda were lucky to have Verlegh; however, by naming their stadium after him he will always be remembered by fans, not just of NAC Breda but by those visiting from other clubs. What a wonderfully fitting accolade.

Fanorak Fact: The much-decorated Polish tank commander Stanisław Maczek died in Edinburgh, in 1994, aged 102.

Object: Irish flag
Subject: Real Madrid

Why are Real Madrid, *Los Merengues*, so fond of the white strip? Some say it was the influence of the world-famous amateur side, Corinthian. The London outfit was formed to create a club environment like Scotland's Queen's Park, to harvest a team spirit and collective, to improve the English national team, and beat Scotland. It worked. They pooled the best public schools and universities for their talent. On some occasions, the entire England squad could be made up of Corinthian players. They toured the world playing friendlies and exhibition games.

Many suggestions are put forward for Madrid's iconic all-white strip. One suggests that as they were the oldest club in the capital, they didn't have to add any other colours to distinguish them from opponents. And they have kept the same strip ever since.

As Barcelona had already done, Real Madrid opted to take part in this interesting sport from the British Isles called football. Graduates from Oxford and Cambridge had brought the game to Spain and had a side in Madrid called La Sociedad (The Society). They organised Sunday morning games but after many disagreements and a split, some left to form their own team. Chief among the dissenters were Julián Palacios and two brothers, Juan and Carlos Padrós. Palacios would become the first president. In 1901, their club was named Madrid Football Club and in 1902, a board was elected with Juan Padrós in charge, and the club was officially founded.

Land close to the bullring in Madrid was the original location for the fledgling club and the location of their first games. Among the backroom staff and integral to the club's formation was Spain-based Englishman Arthur Johnson, an Irishman who, although born in Dublin, strangely chose to describe himself as 'English' when in Spain. He brought the method, and Madrid found that his system, shape and approach 'to playing football in the correct way' worked. He was, according to the official Real Madrid history, the only one who knew what he was doing. He set down some basic rules about staying in position, not running around everywhere, and more importantly passing. Sounds simple. He played at centre-forward and scored the club's first goal. By default, he would later become the first coach of Real Madrid.

Such was the enthusiastic response to the club formation that Madrid set up a tournament in homage to King Alfonso XIII. The initiative became the Copa de España, now the Copa del Rey. Madrid proved efficient at the game, winning the competition four consecutive times between 1905 and 1908.

The club didn't become Real Madrid until 1920 when King Alfonso XIII decided he would call them Real – meaning Royal. Anything for free tickets and a comfy seat, eh? Real Madrid's most illustrious era occurred after Santiago Bernabéu took over as president, in the post-war period. Bernabéu had been at the club as a junior since 1909, played for Madrid between 1912 and 1927, then served as president from 1943 until he died in 1978.

He set about rebuilding the club, including a brand-new stadium and training facilities. He also signed the top players of the day such as Alfredo Di Stéfano, Ferenc Puskás and Francisco Gento, arguably creating one of the best football sides ever. This team found unprecedented success, winning four Spanish titles and the first five European Cups.

Bernabéu was instrumental in the formation of the first European Cup in 1955/56 (along with *L'Equipe* editor Gabriel Hanot); 16 sides took part, some by invitation. Over the subsequent two decades they won 14 league titles, five Copa del Reys and had another European Cup victory.

They had an illustrious spell at the turn of the millennium when president Florentino Pérez built a side packed with the world's biggest stars. Pérez promised he would sign only one player a year but it would be the top player, the best in the world. The Galacticos (Spanish for superstars) included Luís Figo, Zinedine Zidane, Ronaldo and David Beckham.

Madrid, like Barcelona, are undoubtedly one of the biggest football sides in the world and earned €750.9m in 2018/19, thanks mainly to their dominance in the UEFA Champions League. It would be interesting to know what the founding fathers Julián Palacios and the Padrós brothers would make of Facebook, Twitter and Instagram. They would be too cool for all that (just don't mention the European Super League).

Object: Flares

Subject: Livorno's Ultra

Football clubs have always been political. The word *politics* comes from the Greek language, 'affairs of the cities', so it is only natural that the social and political attitudes of a specific area would be connected to football. Certain clubs are naturally more political because of their base and the people who live there. The city of Livorno is generally regarded as hard-working, genial, socialist and made up of immigrant families.

In the 15th century, Livorno, a port town in Tuscany, passed progressive laws allowing merchants from across the continent into their port. Even then it was a distinctive multicultural city full of Jews, Turks, Moors, Armenians and Persians. So they had the sense to allow immigrants in when they opened up their borders. That is still reflected in their all-encompassing and welcoming attitude and the politics of the club.

Associazione Sportiva Livorno Calcio, FC Livorno, or just Livorno to us, was founded in 1915 and became a founder member of Serie A. The club has more than ten different Ultra groups, chief among them the *Brigate Autonome Livornese 99* (Autonomous Livorno Brigade).

Cristiano Lucarelli, Serie A's top scorer in 2004/05 and a local boy, the classic working-class hero and socialist, even wore the number 99 on his back in honour of the aforementioned Ultras. He famously said, 'Some musicians buy themselves a Ferrari or yacht with a billion lire; I bought myself a Livorno shirt.' He isn't faking it; he has the tattoo to prove his love for Livorno, and a ring tone that plays 'The Red

Flag'. When ultras were arrested and charged after rioting at an away game, Lucarelli paid for a bus to bring them back home. Lucarelli captures the very essence of what the city is all about: football and politics.

When most clubs were formed around the end of the 19th and start of the 20th centuries, at least initially, it was as part of the community. Many were originally in working-class areas, close to factories or shipyards. Yet in many countries, football clubs were exclusively for the middle classes and poorer people were not welcome. These were rowing, tennis or cricket clubs that evolved into football but in some countries across Europe, they wanted it kept like that.

Many of the more working-class outsiders formed football clubs for exercise and enjoyment because they had been excluded from joining existing ones. Some of the more vociferous clubs with left-wing sets of support – Marseille, St Pauli, AEK Athens and Celtic – are against right-wing politics, and are anti-fascist and anti-racist.

We can even widen the debate and go to Argentina and Boca Juniors, who are a port club – Boca means mouth – based in Buenos Aires docks. European migrants, mainly football-mad Italians and Spanish arrived there. They are up against River Plate, the rich club, the 'millionaires' seen as the aristocratic establishment side.

The first Italian Communist Party was even founded in the 1920s in Livorno. Ultras by their nature are committed, fiercely loyal, and fanatical with flares, flags and banners but the most effective Ultra groups also have a political association. Livorno has flirted between Serie A and Serie B. They are most famous for their colourful Ultras on the Curva Nord who pay homage to Che Guevara and Fidel Castro.

Mussolini tried to use football to unify nationalism and fascism. But not everyone joined in. Despite the odd violent outburst, for the most part they have moved away from the ferocious side to a more organised part of their club. The growth across European football of these fan groups can also mean that with the advent of social media they can be more charitable, a force for good, and proactive. And that is a wonderful thing. Livorno continue to be the epitome of leftist ideology.

Object: *The Iliad*
Subject: Ajax

Any football club named after a Greek hero is all right in my book. Ajax, the mythological hero, appeared in *The Iliad* and fought in the Trojan war, taking on Troy's champion Hector in an inconclusive duel. Ajax killed himself, therefore dying unconquered.

AFC Ajax was founded in Amsterdam on 18 March 1900 by Floris Stempel, Carol Reeser and Han Dade after a previous short-lived first version as Football Club Ajax in 1894. They are world-famous with a history of innovation and imaginative creativity. They have won more than 50 major domestic trophies and four European Cups, the Cup Winners' Cup and the UEFA Cup – one of only four European clubs who have claimed those three honours.

Like most successful clubs, Ajax are defined by those who help shape them. The early club's first coach was an Irishman, Jack Kirwan. It has become something of a theme in the alternative European museum, but Ajax were also highly influenced by an Englishman, Jack Reynolds.

Throughout three separate spells at the club from 1915 to 1947 he instilled his football philosophy and was responsible for Ajax's first golden era in the 1930s. Under his reign, Ajax established themselves as the best team in the Netherlands by winning eight league titles and four Dutch Cups.

There was a lull until another Englishman, Vic Buckingham, was appointed as coach between 1959 and 1961 and again for 1964/65. He led the team to another league title. In addition, he brought back the same ethos and spirit which brought success for Reynolds. While at Ajax, Buckingham supervised and mentored a young Johan Cruyff as he came through the youth set-up and gave him his professional debut. When Buckingham moved on from Ajax to Barcelona, he was the first tangible connection and link between Amsterdam and the Catalan side.

We then, arguably, have the most significant part of their history, the arrival of coach Rinus Michels, instilling his philosophy of Total Football with Cruyff conducting the team on the pitch. Cruyff's mentor Michels, who he worked with at Ajax, Barcelona, LA Aztecs and the 1974 World Cup, was credited in developing Total Football. Michels had modified and fine-tuned an established template set in place by the Austrian Wunderteam of the 1930s, Argentina's River Plate of the 1940s and Hungary's Magical Magyars of the 1950s. A game based on use of space, and a fluid tactical system where players could switch positions. Cruyff would develop and evolve it into tiki-taka at Barcelona, a system Pep Guardiola would tweak and use when coaching Barça, Bayern Munich and Manchester City.

Under Michels, Ajax won four Eredivisie titles and three Dutch Cups before he moved to Barcelona following the first of the club's three consecutive European Cups from 1971 to 1973. Ajax remain one of the few clubs with the cup permanently housed in their trophy room. UEFA allow any team who have won it five times, or three times in a row, to keep it.

With Cruyff as a player, then as coach from 1985 before moving to manage Barcelona in 1988, Ajax brought through a generation of talent, including Frank Rijkaard and Marco van Basten. Between 1977 and 1987 they won six Eredivisie titles and four Dutch Cups.

Louis van Gaal replaced Leo Beenhakker in September 1991, yet the fans didn't want him. The Dutch newspaper *De*

Telegraaf even launched a campaign for the return of Cruyff. Van Gaal's teams would feature Edwin van der Sar, the De Boer brothers, Patrick Kluivert, Edgar Davids, Clarence Seedorf, Marc Overmars and Finnish captain Jari Litmanen. He also had the experienced Rijkaard returning from his successful five-year spell at AC Milan. Between 1991 and 1999 he moulded and delivered a side that won four Eredivisie titles, three Dutch Cups, the Champions League in 1995, and the UEFA Cup in 1992.

For most football fans, Ajax are synonymous with Cruyff. I was transfixed by Cruyff and that iconic Ajax strip was so cool. The club was part of his DNA. He came through the ranks, signed on his tenth birthday, starred in every age group and supported Ajax. Rinus Michels, Ajax, Cruyff and Total Football. Cruyff could do no wrong. Well, that isn't quite true; he wasn't smart with money, losing everything to an ill-fated pig farming scam.

Michels was managing Los Angeles Aztecs and took him out there in a lucrative deal. The love of the game or maybe a chance to generate some final income saw him move to Washington Diplomats then back briefly, to Levante, then Ajax for a second spell. In a remarkable 18-month period he won two league titles and the Dutch Cup. Cruyff's agent Cor Coster came up with a profitable gate receipts arrangement. Anything over the average home gate would be halved between the player and the club. With the board aghast at how much was transferring into Cruyff's pension pot, president Tom Harmsen decided against offering the 36-year-old a deal and let him go. Cruyff would head to rivals Feyenoord and help turn the Rotterdam giants around, unbelievably delivering a double and being voted Dutch player of the year. But that's for another book.

An abridged history of Ajax would include the initial Jack Reynolds era, the Michels rebuild with Cruyff, Rep, Neeskens and Haan then the side coached by Cruyff, then Louis van Gaal. Of late, under Erik ten Hag, they have returned with a team from their academy; many have been sold on for huge profit. Matthijs de Ligt signed for Juventus in 2019 for €75million, Frenkie de Jong went to Barcelona for €75m and Donny van de Beek joined Manchester United for €39m plus a possible €5m in add-ons.

Object: Sugar Lumps
Subject: Perugia, Horses and Gaddafi

If I pitched a movie about Perugia and was asked to explain the main protagonist, the club's madcap president, I'd say, 'The owner is a self-made man, who started life as a bus driver in Rome. He then decided to set up a cleaning company, which becomes successful and allows him to indulge in thoroughbred horses. He breeds them, wins the Prix de l'Arc de Triomphe, then sells the horse, using the money to buy a football club, Perugia. There he becomes president and signs Gaddafi's son.' By now you would have called security and had me escorted from the building.

My fondness for Perugia is down to a couple of issues. One is something you notice as a football-mad kid and remains with you; Perugia's kit was similar to that of Middlesbrough. The other was their 'colourful' president Luciano Gaucci, who was forever in the news. By a weird quirk of fate, I started working on this chapter about Gaucci and found out he had died a day before, at the age of 81, in February 2020. I felt guilty at first but then realised his eccentricity and enthusiasm was worthy of inclusion in our museum.

Some of his actions were questionable but football loves colourful, ebullient characters. Many of his schemes were classic, high-profile, attention-grabbing moves to garner some media response. One of my favourites involved the sacking of South Korea's Ahn Jung-hwan. Why? Well, he had scored a golden goal to knock Italy out of the 2002 World Cup. His contract was terminated. Gaucci told *La Gazzetta dello Sport*, 'That gentleman will never set foot in Perugia again.' In truth, the player was a loan signing and the football people at the club had decided before he scored his golden goal that he was going at the end of the season but the best showmen don't allow the truth to get in the way of a headline.

Then we had the story that was so ridiculous it became a parody of itself – when Gaucci signed Al-Saadi Gaddafi, son of Libyan dictator, Colonel Gaddafi. He remained at the club for two seasons from 2003 to 2005. The player played three times for Perugia, mainly down to suspension after doping violations and using Nandrolone instead of milk in his cappuccino. The deal was encouraged by his friend Silvio Berlusconi to 'help repair relations' with Libya.

There was also the fight with a fellow Italian football chairman in the directors' box. Gaucci fined himself £30,000 for bringing the game into disrepute and then gave the money to charity. He sacked Perugia's youth team coach, Nikola Filipovic, for not playing his son. Filipovic explained how it unfolded, 'He asked why his boy Riccardo wasn't in the side and I said, "I'm sorry, Mr Gaucci, your son still needs to mature." He said, "No, Filipovic, I'm sorry. It's you who needs to mature." Then he sacked me.' He also sacked a manager who brought his dog to a press conference, and once promised but failed to sign an ageing Maradona.

Like most characters, Gaucci's exit was equally dramatic. The horses may have helped amass his fortune but they would eventually bring him and his club down. Gaucci had struck a deal with Emanuel Senzaqua, another horse lover, over one of his thoroughbreds (thus the sugar lumps) which would bring his club to its knees. Senzaqua was also a referee in Serie C who was, by chance, officiating a Perugia game a few days later. The game with Siracusa ended 1-1 but threw up many questionable decisions. The Sicilian side were upset with the officiating. Their fans made it clear something was amiss with the referee's decisions. The Italian FA looked into it, and the accusation was that Gaucci had used the horse deal in return for the referee's favour. Senzaqua's explanations proved inconsistent. Perugia were denied promotion; the team's hard work would be to no avail. When the news broke that their promotion had been revoked, the beautiful medieval town was beset by full-scale rioting from the fans.

In 2005, Perugia were bankrupted and Italian authorities started investigating both of Gaucci's sons. Gaucci fled to the Dominican Republic, owing the Italian tax authorities €40m. He stayed there for four years before returning. He received a three-year suspended sentence, returning to and dying in Santa Domingo in 2020.

Object: Blood Bags
Subject: Union Berlin Giving Blood

In 2020/21, FC Union Berlin were perched in the top four of the Bundesliga. It wasn't always like this and it didn't last, although they finished a creditable seventh. They have been on a wonderful journey since their days in the Regionalliga, the German fourth division, which isn't even a professional league, to finally reach the Bundesliga in 2019. The club is based in Köpenick, in what was once East Berlin, and has found itself in many a precarious position. However, they have, due to the support of their fans, literally given blood, sweat and tears to survive. Union were the unofficial voice of dissent against the East German regime.

When German football is discussed, it is always assumed Berliners don't have the same passion for football as the huge support of clubs like Bayern Munich in Bavaria, and sides from North Rhine-Westphalia such as Borussia Dortmund, Schalke, Cologne, Bayer Leverkusen and Borussia Mönchengladbach. However, Berlin has more football teams, than any other German city.

To most outsiders, Berlin is where you find artists and rock stars. It was better known for random sightings of Iggy Pop and David Bowie or intellectual discussion on the merits of Dadaism and Cubism than for being a footballing hotbed. While there is no doubt that Berlin is a punk rock techno city, it's a football city too.

The most famous side in terms of numbers, success and profile would be Hertha Berlin. The various football teams in Berlin represent and reflect the cultural diversity of the city – there's Serbian, Bosnian, Turkish and a Jewish club, plus there's the most successful side, historically, the Stasi club, Dynamo Berlin. They are no longer like that but they did once belong to the Stasi, the army and police, the ministry of state for security.

The notorious Stasi boss Erich Mielke oversaw police, spies, informants and generally controlled a way for Dynamo to find success. The head of East Germany's secret police ruled with fear for more than 30 years and had more than 92,000 spies and 170,000 informants, actively reporting friends and neighbours. Though not all Dynamo fans were supporters of the GDR.

I do know several facts about Union Berlin; for instance, the theatrical punk singer Nina Hagen sang the club's anthem 'Eisern Union'. I also know that their fans helped build and modernise the stadium (their Stadion an der Alten Försterei is in the woods and surrounded by forest, with a capacity of 22,012 – 18,395 standing and 3,617 seats). They also love singing Christmas carols. Each Christmas they have a tradition where fans come together to sing carols and drink glühwein (mulled wine) and sing carols for 90 minutes. When the tradition started in 2003, 89 showed up; now 18,000 go down to the stadium in the woods to sing.

Primarily they are in the museum because, in 2004, the club faced bankruptcy and needed money quickly. They stumbled from one financial disaster to the next. The figure required to save the club was €1.5m. Someone came up with the amazing idea of a campaign entitled 'Bleed for Union'. In Germany, if you give blood, you receive a payment. Fans were encouraged to donate blood and give the money made from the transfusion to the club, allowing it to survive.

In 2008, Union had to update and modernise their ground to gain entry into the German third division. With no money, they turned to the fans again. More than 2,000 worked in shifts and managed to help rebuild the stadium in under 300 days. Volunteers worked 140,000 man hours. That's why I like them.

Object: Prawn Sandwich

Subject: Manchester United, Gritty Northern Drama

Manchester United's history has been dramatic. It is one of unpretentious beginnings, reaching great heights, rebuilding after the war in the Busby era, success, then tragedy and disaster. Then there was a second rebuild, reaching a European pinnacle, followed by famine, then relegation, the Ferguson era, Premier League dominance and European glory, but since 2013 they have struggled to find the correct coach to grapple success from Manchester City, Chelsea and Liverpool.

Like most massive football clubs, their modest origins belie how much of a global brand Manchester United have become. Equally they have a different kind of supporter now. In 2000, captain Roy Keane famously criticised the lack of atmosphere from the crowd at a Champions League game against Dynamo Kyiv at Old Trafford. He blamed it on the 'prawn sandwich brigade'. Keane hit out at sections of the club's support, 'Sometimes you wonder do they understand the game of football? We're 1-0 up, then there are one or two stray passes and they're getting on players' backs. It's just not on. At the end of the day, they need to get behind the team. Away from home, our fans are fantastic, I'd call them the hardcore fans. But at home, they have a few drinks and probably the prawn sandwiches, and they don't realise what's going on out on the pitch.' Keane's comments make for hard reading but most fans know exactly what he means. The comment and this prawn sandwich serve to remind us of the journey of this football side from a works team, Newton Heath, to the Manchester United of today.

They were originally formed in 1878 but were known as Newton Heath LYR, formed by the carriage and wagon department in Newton Heath, the depot of the Lancashire and Yorkshire Railway. They played in green and gold and faced other railway sides in friendly matches. They played games at North Road and changed in a pub called The Three Crowns on Oldham Road, half a mile from the pitch. It took a while before they played their first competitive game, a 7-2 defeat in the Lancashire Cup in 1883/84. Such modest beginnings yet those involved would be starting up a club that would become one of the most famous in world football.

In 1892, Newton Heath dropped the LYR when they were elected into the First Division of the Football League. In 1893, they moved home and struggled for a few years at Bank Street in Clayton. By 1902 they had accrued debts and were hit with a winding-up order. The club captain, Harry Stafford, arranged for five local businessmen to invest £500 each. One of those, a wealthy benefactor and local brewer called John Davies, came on board. He provided some organisation, business nous, and an early eye for marketing and branding as well as money to buy players. Several incidents also led to a change in name. Their noisy neighbours Ardwick changed their name to Manchester City. Davies immediately felt that Newton Heath had to capitalise and also portray the image of a big-city club. Originally they tried Manchester Central, then Manchester Celtic, but those were rejected before settling on Manchester United in April 1902.

Davies also changed their strips to red shirts, white shorts and black socks. They played in white shirts with a red V (easily mistaken for the famous Airdrieonians 'diamonds' shirt), with black shorts and white socks. Then they would move on to the iconic red shirts. When Ernest Mangnall became coach in 1903, the team went on to finish as Second

Division runners-up in 1906, securing promotion to the First Division. In 1908 they won their first league title. In 1909 they won the Charity Shield and the FA Cup. They won the title for a second time, then their manager left – for Manchester City.

During the 1909/10 season, Davies bought premises at Old Trafford and moved the club there. He paid £60,000 for the land and architect Archibald Leitch was given a budget of around £30,000 to build the stadium. United played their first match on 19 February 1910. Playing in red, at Old Trafford, they would go from strength to strength. They were the Reds but would later become the Red Devils (a term borrowed from Salford Rugby Club who impressed the French so much on a tour there, the press called them *Les Diables Rouges*).

The world, and football, was hit by the tragedy of the Second World War; United saw their ground bombed, then rebuilt. Enter Matt Busby. He demanded complete control and in what was a huge change in football, he would handle transfers, tactics, training – he was the boss. Busby drove the side to several runners-up finishes in the league, and an FA Cup victory in 1948, but it took until 1952 before he sealed United's first title win in 41 years.

He continued to bring through his stars, who he coached and mentored, developing a young side with flair, panache and confidence who caught the public's imagination. The media nicknamed them 'the Busby Babes' (in the mid-1950s the average age of the side was 22). They won the league in 1956 and 1957. They started to impress in the fledgling European Cup and were the first English side to play in the competition. The Football League were unhappy about the competition and had objected, having blocked an invite to Chelsea the previous season. It was Busby who fought the

FA to allow his side to play the competition, sensing it had potential. United beat Anderlecht 10-0 before losing out in the semi-final to Real Madrid.

In the following year's competition, while returning from a quarter-final victory against Red Star Belgrade, their plane stopped to refuel in Munich. The plane crashed while taking off, killing 23 people including eight players: Geoff Bent, Roger Byrne, Eddie Colman, Duncan Edwards, Mark Jones, David Pegg, Tommy Taylor and Billy Whelan. From the coaching staff, Tom Curry and Bert Whalley along with club secretary Walter Crickmer were also lost. Many were left fighting for their lives as a result of the crash on 6 February 1958. The disaster has been woven into the fabric of the club, is respected and remembered, and became something that United would draw strength from.

Busby, who had received the last rites after the tragedy, survived and throughout the 1960s began another rebuild, this time led by Denis Law, Paddy Crerand, Bobby Charlton and the upcoming generation of youth players, including George Best. They won the FA Cup in 1963, and the title in 1965 and 1967. In 1968 they won the European Cup at Wembley against Benfica.

The next cycle saw Busby resign in 1969 and the club sink in the 1970s. Wilf McGuinness, the loyal reserve team coach, reluctantly took over but was replaced in 1971 by Frank O'Farrell. He was replaced 18 months later by Tommy Docherty, who succeeded in preventing relegation in 1972 but United did drop down in 1974. The club was in transition and struggling after the departures of Law, Best and Charlton. Docherty won promotion and then in 1976 his team lost in the FA Cup Final to Southampton, although they were back again the following year to beat Liverpool 2-1 in the final. Docherty was dismissed and replaced by Dave Sexton, who signed big players such as Joe Jordan, Gordon McQueen, Ray Wilkins and Gary Bailey, but United failed to win anything. Ron Atkinson replaced Sexton in 1981 and also spent big, bringing in Bryan Robson and Remi Moses from West Bromwich Albion and Frank Stapleton from Arsenal. They won the FA Cup twice, and the Charity Shield. In 1985/86 they started like a rocket with 13 wins and two draws from their first 15 games, only to finish fourth. By the following November, United were in freefall and it looked like relegation was on the cards, so Atkinson was replaced by Alex Ferguson.

Ferguson stopped the rot and the team survived with an 11th-place finish. It's hard to believe now but a year after that they ended up second, only to fall back down to 11th again in 1988/89. It's often said that an FA Cup win in 1990, after a replay with Crystal Palace, kept Ferguson in a job. From then they won the European Cup Winners' Cup and then the Super Cup, followed by the League Cup in 1992 after beating Nottingham Forest 1-0, but it took until 1993 for United to win their first league title since 1967 – in the first season of the new Premier League. The following year they completed the famed Double of the Premier League and FA Cup.

In the 1998/99 season United won the Treble of the Premier League, FA Cup and a dramatic Champions League, when they scored two goals to win in injury time. They won the league again in 2000, 2001 and 2003 and won the FA Cup in 2004 for a record 11th time. They were champions once more in 2007 and a year later defended their crown and beat Chelsea on penalties in the Champions League Final. Their third successive championship followed, but then Portuguese superstar Cristiano Ronaldo left for Real Madrid. Sir Alex Ferguson, knighted after that 1999 success, reached a remarkable 13 championships in 2013 and then announced he was retiring.

David Moyes tried and after ten months was gone. Ryan Giggs replaced him as interim then Louis van Gaal had a go; he won the FA Cup and was sacked. José Mourinho signed a three-year deal in May 2016 and won the Charity Shield, the League Cup and the Europa League but couldn't turn the clubs fortunes around in the Premier League – the competition in which United are always judged. Mourinho was sacked after two and a half years then former striker Ole Gunnar Solskjaer took over, won 14 from 19 and was given a three-year deal.

Manchester United are a colourful side but drama is seldom far away. Sometimes it's that gritty northern drama that gives them their magic. Prawn sandwiches indeed.

Epilogue:

Final Object: Those who missed the cut

The Bolton pie and Wilberforce Montgomery nearly made the cut. The pie is a versatile object. It can be sustenance, the perfect stomach-liner for a day at the football on the sauce, or as a great insult generator as in 'who ate all the pies' (irony alert here, you're the one being abusive to an athlete while clogging up your internal organs) and of course as a missile. While playing in a match for Bolton Wanders against Wigan Athletic, Wilberforce Montgomery was left concussed after being hit on the head by a pie. Montgomery was left pie-eyed.

Former Arsenal player Alex Song has 27 siblings; 17 sisters and ten brothers. He hated when the team headed out to karaoke and people would do their party piece and say one singer one song, and he'd think, lucky you, there's another 26 of us.

Power cards for undersoil heating would have been an interesting exhibit for a Scottish Cup tie in January 1979. The game between Falkirk and Inverness Thistle was postponed 29 times. The reason? Well, the devil is in the detail. Scotland in January? Hangovers, oh and the weather. The tie was earmarked for 6 January and took place 47 days later. Falkirk won but were then beaten by Dundee in the next round just three days later.

Those online anagram generators came close to featuring too. Not many people know that the former Spurs star David Ginola has a fear of anagram generators. His name keeps coming out as Vagina Dildo.

9781785317699

9781785317705

9781785317736

9781785317781

9781785317835

9781785318849

9781785318528

9781785316722

9781785318627